West Germany: A European and Global Power

Edited by
Wilfrid L. Kohl
Giorgio Basevi

The Johns Hopkins University
Bologna Center

LexingtonBooks
D.C. Heath and Company
Lexington, Massachusetts
Toronto

Library of Congress Cataloging in Publication Data

Main entry under title:
  West Germany, a European and global power.

  Based on papers presented at a conference held at the Bologna Center of
Johns Hopkins University, Oct. 5-7, 1978.

  1. Germany, West—Foreign economic relations—Congresses. 2. European
Economic Community—Germany, West—Congresses. 3. Germany, West—
Foreign relations—Congresses. I. Kohl, Wilfrid L. II. Basevi, Giorgio, 1938-
HF1545.W45   337.43   79-2391
ISBN 0-669-03162-3

Published simultaneously in Canada.

Printed in the United States of America.

International Standard Book Number: 0-669-03162-3

Library of Congress Catalog Card Number: 79-2391

Contents

Preface and Acknowledgments

This book is the first in a new series of studies published under the auspices of the Research Institute of The Johns Hopkins Bologna Center. The results of another Bologna Center research project will be published shortly, edited by Larry Gray and Simon Serfaty, entitled *The Italian Communist Party* (Greenwood Press, 1980). It is anticipated that a special seminar and lecture series organized at the Center during 1979-1980 on energy-policy issues in Europe and America will also lead to a book-length study. Other research at the Center is reported in its Occasional Papers series.

For the grant that supported the Bologna conference in October 1978, we are grateful to the Fritz Thyssen Stiftung in Cologne. In the planning stage of the conference we benefited from discussions with Beate Kohler, Wolfgang Hager, and Ekkerhart Krippendorff. Their helpful advice is greatly appreciated. Several staff members of the Bologna Center worked on the conference and the preparation of the chapters for publication. We would especially like to acknowledge the help of Pina Serra, Gertrude Pellegrini, and Janice Delbert. The English translations of the papers by Wilhelm Hankel and Ernst-Otto Czempiel were done by Edith Ronay Grathwol, and the translation of Hermann Priebe's paper was prepared by Robert Grathwol. Their assistance is also gratefully acknowledged.

Introduction

The idea for this book, and for the conference on which it is based, occurred to us in mid-1977 at a time when the German role in the European Community (EC) was becoming a major European problem. It was also a problem critically important in the current economic and political crises of the Western world. Yet our professional backgrounds and tools—those of an economist and a political scientist—were in themselves inadequate to provide satisfactory analysis and a comprehensive synthesis. For Germany's role in Europe can only be analyzed and evaluated using an interdisciplinary approach encompassing economic and political aspects, interests, and aims, and their sociological backgrounds.

In particular, the economist among us was finding the purely economic explanations of Germany's economic behavior during the last two decades to be insufficient. The apparent contradiction between a liberal trade and industrial policy and a protective agricultural policy; the tendency to maintain large trade surpluses throughout periods of booms and recessions alike; the reluctance to allow the Deutsche mark to play a larger reserve role and to take the lead in rallying other European countries toward a more active stand in international monetary relations—these were some of the most puzzling aspects of German foreign-economic policy that seemed difficult to explain on purely economic grounds.

Similarly, the political scientist among us, who had never been happy with the phrase frequently applied to the Federal Republic—"an economic giant and a political dwarf"—suspected that Germany's clear economic preponderance in Europe was now being translated into greater political influence. If so, in what directions? Is the Federal Republic likely to strengthen or weaken its commitment to the European Community? Does Bonn prefer to deal multilaterally or unilaterally with the United States and other countries on global-economic and other issues? Is Germany developing a more assertive, nationalistic foreign policy in the aftermath of the Ostpolitik, enlarging its freedom of maneuver? Since the answers to many of these questions involve German policy on international economic issues, that is, Germany's economic foreign policy, clearly a political-economy analysis is necessary.

Our conference was convened at the Bologna Center of Johns Hopkins University, October 5-7, 1978. More than forty participants—scholars, bankers, international civil servants, and members of parliament—came from the Federal Republic of Germany, Italy, France, the United Kingdom, Denmark, and the United States. After the results of the conference (only parts of which are presented here), and with the further developments of the last two years, we are convinced that Germany remains a problem country in the European Community because of its economic weight. A deeper understanding that Germany's economic and political positions carry responsibilities both within and without Europe is required of all members of the Community.

One recent initiative in which the importance of Germany's role is clear—the European monetary system (EMS)—was launched after we had planned the conference program. Although treated only in passing by some of the contributors, it is seen by all of them as a test case of the willingness and capacity of German policymakers to play a more active and responsible role in the European Community and in the international monetary system. Other developments, only partly anticipated or discussed in this book, underscore the critical necessity of a deeper understanding of Germany's position and potential for leadership among its partners: German-American disputes about the locomotive theory, the decline of the American dollar, the renewal of the oil crisis and the need for a coordinated approach to energy policy, the neutron bomb and other issues in the North Atlantic Treaty Organization (NATO), and the apparent opening of a new debate inside Germany on the role of arms control in détente.

We have divided this book into three parts. The first part includes economic and political aspects of Germany's role outside the European Community, assessing the importance of that Community to that role. The second part treats German policies within and toward the Community. The third part presents an almost unedited transcript of what the six main speakers said at the roundtable discussion at the conclusion of the conference.

Part I opens with a chapter by Wolfgang Hager which discusses Germany's extraordinary trade performance, based on its unbroken record of trade surpluses since 1952. This has, of course, been the basis of the Federal Republic's export-led growth and achievement of postwar prosperity. The reasons for Germany's trade performance are explored, including subtly mercantilistic attitudes of businessmen and the cooperation of the trade unions. An undervalued Deutsche mark has also spurred German surpluses, as has an influx of foreign workers. The result is that the German economy depends on a fair-weather world of stable and intensive interdependence, which worked well until western countries were struck by recession in the 1970s.

As Hager notes, the Federal Republic experienced its first export-led slump in 1975. Yet, contrary to the behavior of other major western economies, Germany in effect refused to share the financing of oil deficits and persisted in having trade surpluses. This lack of cooperation in macroeconomic policy is criticized by Hager, who sees it as unconstructive participation in world economic management. Suggesting that some structural changes are necessary if the German economy is to continue to prosper, he proposes that private consumption be increased by absorbing some of the export surplus in the domestic market.

Traditionally, Germany has emphasized, and perhaps overidealized, a liberal world-trading system. Hager suggests that this may be going too far and could endanger the cohesion of the most important free-trade area for Germany, the European Community and its associated countries. Similarly, Hager suggests that Bonn's policy on North-South relations may reflect an unwise obsession with the notion of preserving a nonexistent market system.

Analyzing further some of the same themes treated by Hager, Wilhelm Hankel assesses how Germany has come to the end of its road to export-led growth. His chapter also contains a criticism of government, trade unions, and the opposition policies for recovering the path to growth. The essence of the chapter, however, consists of Hankel's own proposals for abandoning the road of export-led growth, or "export substitution."

In criticizing his government's policy, Hankel interprets the EMS scheme as an attempt to stabilize and revitalize German export competitiveness by putting an end to the continuous revaluation of the Deutsche mark, thus providing, on this score, an interpretation of the German government's aims in proposing the European Monetary System, which is rejected later by Kloten in his chapter. Hankel's program has two parts. The international part argues for renewed efforts to coordinate policies for balance-of-payments adjustment within the Organization for Economic Cooperation and Development (OECD), the control of the Eurocurrency markets, and the implementation of an effective European regional and structural policy. The national part of his program is based on preferential tax treatments in favor of small and medium-sized enterprises, for the creation of new jobs and the improvement of the general market-competitive atmosphere in Germany.

In her witty and incisive chapter on Germany and the world monetary system, Susan Strange is critical of what she considers "a profound absence of any sense of responsibility for the global system" on the part of the German monetary authorities before the Copenhagen and Bremen meetings of 1978. By the same token, however, she considers the new policy inaugurated at these meetings and the launching of the EMS as historic occasions where Germany could become "the leader of the opposition" (albeit a loyal one) to U.S. hegemony in international monetary relations. This role is only one of five that she identifies as theoretically possible for a country acting in the international monetary system; the others are those of leader in the system, obedient ally, bigemonist partner, and "lone ranger." Although Germany has in the past most often played the role of obedient ally to the leader in the system (the United States), Strange argues that it is time for Germany to assume the more challenging role of leader of the opposition.

Strange presents some precise directions for developing a constructive opposition strategy that could be followed by Germany. The most critical one appears again (as in Kloten's chapter) to be that of allowing the Deutsche mark to become a reserve currency. In any case, she considers that the EMS, unless supported by a well-designed program of relative insulation from the repercussions of continuing U.S. dollar weakness, will fail, as did the schemes for European monetary unification that have come before it. Strange's analysis is partly extended, but also questioned, by Schonfield in the commentary.

The chapter by Hans-Herbert Weber, an official of the German Ministry of Finance, is a typical example of official German views on the prospects for coordinating stabilization policies among industrial countries. In a very frank way, Weber explains Germany's performance and policies and suggests how its partners should behave. Weber ends on a particularly determinate tone. Although asserting that German authorities have no objection to running external deficits, and that they even earnestly wish to reverse their country's persistent trade-account surplus, he indicates that it is hard to imagine how the German economy could be restructured away from export-led growth. This point is strongly criticized by Spaventa in the commentary. Moreover, taken as a whole, Weber's ideas contrast sharply with those of Hager and Hankel presented in this book.

The last two chapters in part I deal with more strictly political aspects of West German foreign policy and the place of the European Community within it. In the more specific chapter, Reinhardt Rummel examines Bonn's attitude toward and role in European foreign-policy consultations begun alongside the Community in the early 1970s, known as the European Political Cooperation (EPC). Terming it "a multilateral tool for a political dwarf," Rummel shows that the EPC helped to forge a Western base and consensus for Ostpolitik and has enabled the Federal Republic to undertake a more active diplomacy in the West after Ostpolitik, especially in areas where Bonn might be sensitive or otherwise reluctant to take the lead alone. He cites the role of the EPC in U.S.-European relations after 1973, in Middle East policy and the Euro-Arab dialogue, in African policy, and as a coordinating mechanism at the United Nations. In offering another level of action for German foreign policy, the EPC has helped Germany assume a more active foreign-policy role. Thus, Bonn might be willing to expand the range of subjects dealt with in the EPC to include certain global and regional security matters. However, Rummel is also aware that the real results of the EPC are still limited and in many respects confined to policy declarations that involve few direct costs. The EPC is likely to continue to be only one of several multilateral frameworks useful to Germany in pursuing its interests, many of which transcend the Community. With regard to the West German foreign-policy process, Rummel notes that participation in the EPC has strengthened the role of the Foreign Office in the making of European policy in Bonn.

In his wide-ranging chapter, Ernst-Otto Czempiel argues that the Federal Republic's postwar foreign-policy objectives—West European and Atlantic cooperation—have not changed, but that Bonn's international behavior sometimes looks different now because Germany occupies a more important place in Europe and the world. As Germany has grown in economic and military importance, so has its freedom to maneuver. Like other major Western countries, Germany frequently acts unilaterally. But this does not mean that it pursues nationalistic goals; rather, that Bonn increasingly makes its own decisions within alliance frameworks. If there are no such frameworks, Germany may take unilateral actions, as in Ostpolitik. The subtle distinction between nationalism as a goal and unilateralism as a process lies at the heart of Czempiel's analysis.

Regarding the European Community, Czempiel notes that German policy exhibits ambiguities: "The Federal Republic does not take advantage of its economic power to create a position of hegemony, nor does it use it to further European integration." Although the EMS may be an exception, generally Bonn has not been active in expanding multilateral procedures at the European level, despite its more pro-European rhetoric. There are no domestic forces within Germany at present that favor intensifying the integration process.

On the other hand, there is no question about German attachment to the European Community, on which much of its trade policy depends. The Community serves also to ease and encourage German unilateralism in global policy in areas (for example, monetary and energy policy) where the Community is not competent to act as a unit. The United States frequently encourages German unilateralism by the way the American government negotiates with European countries. Czempiel is critical of Bonn for not seeking more multilateral initiatives, since unilateralism as a process could eventually endanger the very existence of the European Community. On the other hand, he accepts German unilateralism as the only possible policy in most areas under present conditions, simply by way of "muddling through" like everybody else.

Turning to part II, which deals with German policies inside the European Community, Alfred Steinherr examines German industrial and labor policy and the European Community. He convincingly shows that the German economy on the whole did not gain subtantially from the formation of the European Community. Gains mostly have been accrued by capital owners in the industrial sector and, of course, in the agricultural sector. In any case, at least for industry, similar if not larger gains might have been obtained through a worldwide liberal trade policy. Thus, Germany's joining the European Community has been motivated mostly by political reasons. Even from the point of view of labor mobility, the immigration from low-wage countries was not just a result of the formation of the European Community, as immigrants came largely from countries outside the Community. Moreover, from the structural point of view, this policy of labor immigration is criticized by Steinherr as having delayed necessary reallocations of resources and having generally prevented a more efficient pattern of industrial specialization for Germany. As for Germany's contribution to the Community in this field, Steinherr sees its main features in the liberal attitude that Germany has shown and impressed upon its partners and the EC bureaucracy, particularly in the field of industrial policy, demonstrated, for example, by Germany's contribution to a better formulation of the Spinelli-Memorandum (which in 1973 drew the lines for a program of industrial policy) and by German criticism of the Davignon proposals, in which the European Community Commission presented its views on how to help industries particularly affected by the 1975-1977 recession.

German agricultural policy and the European Community is analyzed by Hermann Priebe. Although agriculture is a small sector of the German economy—3 percent of the gross national product (GNP)—it carries much political weight. Thus, Germany has had considerable influence in the formulation of the Common Agricultural Policy (CAP). It has constantly pushed for the transfer of agricultural protection to the European level. Industry and industrial exports matter, of course, much more to Germany. However, the CAP has been seen as valuable because of a tradition of agricultural protection in Germany, and as a quid pro quo for the wider market provided by the Community for German industrial products. Much of Priebe's chapter is devoted to a sharp critique of the CAP, which, in his view, is irrational, costly, and wasteful when one considers the subsidies and investments that have led to an overexpansion of agricultural capacity and the intensification of agricultural surpluses. Priebe makes several proposals to reform the CAP through an incomes policy and a structural policy. He urges returning the farm sector within the Community to the forces of the free market. The need for reform is made more urgent by Community enlargement, because differences between national agricultural systems will then be so great.

According to Beate Kohler, Chancellor Helmut Schmidt committed the German government to the enlargement of the European Community before the bureaucracy or the Parliament had a chance to examine or debate the issues. However, the chancellor's action now commands a broad consensus among the parties and interest groups that favor enlargement for political reasons; namely, to strengthen democracy and therefore promote political stability in southern Europe. Such stability is seen as vital to German and European security. These political motivations outweigh any economic difficulties that might be posed by integrating the economies of Spain, Portugal, and Greece into the Community.

On the economic side, German industrialists look for further export and investment opportunities in the three new member countries, and even German farmers may benefit from a larger market. However, there is some concern that present EC competition and free-market rules not be watered down, and that new forces for protectionism or state planning be controlled.

Enlargement will affect the Federal Republic's foreign policy with the new members. And it will also complicate the European political cooperation, which is likely to become more focused on southern European issues. But this may be in keeping with Germany's deep interest in promoting security and stability in this part of the world.

Norbert Kloten deals in the last chapter with German monetary and financial policy and the European Community. He starts by presenting a concise but clear overview of official German attitudes throughout the attempts toward European monetary unification of the last two decades. In particular, the well-known position of Germany in favor of the economist approach and against the monetarist approach to European monetary unification during the discussions that led to the drafting and initial implementation of the Werner plan is recalled and documented. Although theoretically the Werner plan had taken the economist approach by recognizing that the maintenance of fixed exchange rates among the EC currencies (an arrangement called the "snake") could only result from a close coordination of economic and financial policies, in practice, that attempt was not successful insofar as participants actually tried to implement the snake exchange-rate mechanism before their economic and financial policies were closely coordinated (the monetarist approach). Kloten tends to interpret the new steps taken at Bremen in July 1978 as a turnabout in official German policy toward European monetary unification. In fact, most of the emphasis in the EMS is on the mechanics of exchange-rate management and the role of the European currency unit (ECU), to the detriment of the need to coordinate economic and financial policies.

Interestingly enough, although not surprisingly, the reader can trace in Kloten's careful wordings the signs of an unwillingness on the part of German monetary authorities to follow the lead of the government in this turnabout. Interesting also are Kloten's comments on how this has really been less of a policy turnabout for Chancellor Helmut Schmidt, who appears to have been always cooler with regard to flexible exchange rates than his earlier collaborators. Kloten, although writing early and before the actual launching of the EMS, does not appear enthusiastic about it. Yet, on the whole, he is optimistic; perhaps too much, at least with regard to his expectation that the "indicator of divergence" mechanism envisaged in the new EMS will effectively correct the asymmetries that plagued the previous "snake" parity-grid mechanism, and thereby limit the freedom of maneuver of a divergent country, possibly Germany itself.

The chapters in this book have not answered all the questions they have raised. But they do shed some light on the central question: What is the economic and political importance of the European Community today for West Germany? Or, phrased another way, the question might read: Has Europe become too small for Germany?

The Federal Republic embarked on the construction of the European Community in the 1950s in the hope of achieving an eventual economic and political union of western Europe within which Germany might regain an internationally acceptable and stable role. However, European integration has not progressed as rapidly or as far as its original proponents had hoped. Meanwhile, Germany has changed possibly more than its European partners and represents now the strongest economy in Europe. This has affected Germany's approach to the European Community, which Bonn views increasingly as a means rather than an end.

West Germany's regained confidence and new predominant economic strength make it a global power in terms of its trade position and its place in the international monetary system. Clearly, Germany's international role now extends beyond the European Community. Today Germany seems to regard EC institutions, its market, and indeed the entire fabric of European economic and political cooperation as a base to be used to support a more active German role in the world at large. This is a significant new development. But is it a positive or negative development for the future of the European Community? The answer at the moment is ambiguous.

On the one hand, approximately half of German trade is with EC partners, so the Community continues to provide substantial economic benefits to Germany. Germany supports the Common Agricultural Policy, despite some dissatisfaction with it. And for whatever series of motives, Bonn has launched a new European initiative, that is, the European Monetary System. Politically, Germany has supported Community enlargement, primarily to buttress democracy and stability in southern Europe. And Bonn participates in the European Political Cooperation, which it would like to deepen, finding it a useful support for German diplomacy.

However, there are certain danger signs, which could work against European integration in the future. The preponderance of Germany's economy, with its continuing heavy dependence on exports and propensity for balance-of-payments surpluses, make this country a source of instability in the European and world economy, especially in a period of economic downturn, which is the prospect for the years immediately ahead. Bonn's reluctance to restructure its economy, or to coordinate its stabilization policies, coupled with its unwillingness to allow the Deutsche mark to take on the role of an international reserve currency, could undermine European cooperation. Similarly, as Hager points out, the German obsession with free trade and the market could endanger the Community's cohesion if carried to extremes.

Politically, it is not surprising that Germany acts sometimes on its own in its economic foreign policy, for the European Community is really only a decision-making unit in terms of commercial policy. Other areas, such as monetary and energy policy, only concern the Community as a consultation framework. However, Bonn's reluctance to take the lead in supporting further European integration (the EMS aside), coupled with a new penchant for unilateralism, could, as Ernst Otto Czempiel admonishes, harm the Community over the long run. For, without new momentum, there is some doubt as to how long the Community will last when new destabilizing forces are taken into account. Such forces are unfortunately looming large again at the time of writing this introduction, with the deepening of the second oil crisis, the flight from the dollar, and the threat of an unorderly return to gold. It is to be hoped that the EMS will provide such new forward momentum, and that Germany will take within it a larger share of that leadership role in international monetary affairs that the United States seems no longer willing or able to play.

Part I
Germany's Role Outside the European Community

1 Germany as an Extraordinary Trader

Wolfgang Hager

Germany is not an ordinary country. That fact has shown itself in many guises in the past. Today it shows itself most visibly in a trading performance for which there is only one parallel: Japan. The most spectacular symbol of this economic performance is a record of unbroken trade surpluses since 1952, whose annual level now seems to have stabilized at more than 40 billion DM. From these surpluses, some of the other elements of German strength are directly or indirectly derived: foreign exchange reserves of some 100 billion DM; and a major role as banker in multilateral credit institutions, whether Community-based, OECD-based (Turkey), or related to the International Monetary Fund (IMF)-World Bank family. Indirectly, the surplus has facilitated export-led growth, and more importantly, steady growth without balance of payments constraints.

Two factors, above all else, explain the extraordinary success of both Germany and Japan in the postwar trading world: an attitude toward the international environment characterized by a deep, historically-derived, sense of insecurity; and a capacity of social (self) control which allows that sense of insecurity to shape a pattern of economic behavior that tends toward overcompensation.

In economics as in military security, however, there is an optimum that lies below the maximum security effort. Balance, or the lack of it, is the yardstick by which to distinguish the optimum from the unsustainable maximum. While in military matters anything higher than the optimum produces arms races and hostile coalitions, in economics the result tends to be a reduction of interdependence leading to a new balance of economic exchange at a lower level of welfare. But Germany, like virtually no other country, is highly specialized to live in a world of stable and intensive interdependence. It is at the core of several systems designed to maintain a stable environment in which this interdependence can florish: the European Community, the rest of OECD-Europe, the Atlantic and trilateral communities, and the nascent East-West European zone of cooperation. Only its relationship with the Third World is left largely unstructured, subsumed under a general and abstract systemic concern.

One of the curious and potentially dangerous paradoxes of German trade policy lies in this strong though abstract concern for the world trading system as a whole on the one hand, and a parochial, self-centered interpretation of its own position within this system (again rather like Japan).

3

For postwar Germany, international free trade has a significance that goes well beyond that of a pragmatic device for raising welfare. Trade is felt to be existential in several respects. International trade is important for the preservation of a liberal domestic economy which in turn (in keeping with classic conservative thinking) is seen as a precondition for the preservation of democracy. The efforts of the state (through antitrust policies and such) to impose genuine conditions of competition (*ordnungspolitik*) will always prove insufficient. International trade will serve to keep industrialists honest, and hence, according to the reasoning just mentioned, serve as a prop to a free democratic society in general.

But the greatest significance of trade lies in its role as a substitute for the possession of continental or imperial markets and sources of raw materials. The notion of *Lebensraum* is dead and discredited. The fear of economic isolation and of national dynamism being frustrated by externally imposed limits continues to exist—much diluted to be sure—and is sublimated into a concern for freedom in international trade.[1] The psychological point to be stressed in this context is the remarkable sense of insecurity in German elites which leads to the conviction that we must try harder.

A third less profound, but perhaps no less important, link between international free trade and national security derives from the impact of the global trade regime on the quality of the bilateral economic relationship between Germany and the community on the one hand, and the United States on the other. German elites have internalized the notion that the military alliance needs to be complemented and reinforced through economic interdependence in what is still sometimes referred to as the Atlantic Community. A move toward protectionism in the world as a whole would no doubt be reflected in the economic relations with the protecting superpower and hence undermine the most crucial security relationship.

Apart from the instances where trade and the trade regime touch on fundamental national concerns related directly or indirectly to security, even the welfare concept of trade is more intense and, for want of a better term, existential, than that of all other nations, except Japan. A widely held view of trade adjustment sees the advanced nations on a ladder whose bottom rungs consist of labor-intensive, low-technology industry, and whose top rungs are the high-technology and skill-intensive future industries. Whereas most nations reluctantly go up this ladder, Germany (and Japan) accept it as a spur to, and guarantee of, national dynamism. The ladder is also seen to be crucial to the containment of distributional tensions within the society, and hence for political stability in general. The notion here is that higher wages *and* secure employment opportunities can only be guaranteed by adding high-value activities whose broad-based technological requirements put them beyond the competition of less developed competitors.

The importance of the industrial ladder as a major form of self-realization for a dynamic nation gone resolutely civilian can also be seen with respect to the attention given by policymakers to its upper rungs: the frontiers of high technology. As a military latecomer, in modern procurement terms, Germany does not have a leading position in aerospace and associated control electronics. Prudent financial management has prevented the state from subsidizing a crash program in most areas of high technology, which might have remedied this situation. The self-perception of Germany's economic policy elite is therefore of a nation whose grasp of the top rungs of the ladder is tenuous. The major exception, both in terms of subsidies and success, has been the nuclear industry, including the full fuel cycle. The implied curtailment of this branch of industrial development and exports through the U.S.-German controversy over the Brazil deal, and the equally proliferation-related U.S. objection to the development of the breeder reactor, did more than threaten a particular industry: it threatened what is perceived to be one of the major, almost the only, future industry, and hence the whole concept of industrial progression as such.

In reality, of course, Germany's industrial strength will continue to rest on the very high and continuously advancing standards of *production* technology across the board, even if the product is conventional.

The vaguely social-darwinistic view of trade-conditioned industrial evolution—a faint echo of similar but perhaps less civilian views in the past—helps to explain the instinctive rejection of comfortable, though perhaps decadent, protectionist solutions to short-term adjustment problems. It also explains the growing contempt or at least lack of sympathy with nations that put tea breaks before productivity and that flirt with the notion of a siege economy.

Although a better than average performance in the military sphere (unless backed by overwhelming power) is highly dangerous, in economic theory at least, it helps to advance the welfare of the total: the law of comparative advantage and the diffusion of capital and know-how allow other nations to share in the success of any one of them. Economic theory, however, also shows a tendency toward balance, at least in the medium run. In fact, the central quality of Germany's trade relations in the postwar period has been a persistent imbalance. A decade ago, Japan, as a dynamic special case, was instrumental in turning the United States away from its long-held liberal convictions: henceforth trade between the two countries was strictly managed. Germany, in a more privileged position within the Community, has escaped being discriminated against by its long-suffering trade partners. Yet clearly, we are dealing here with a potential time bomb within the Community and Western European system.

Germany as a Surplus Country

No other phenomenon marks Germany as an extraordinary trader as much as its persistent trade surpluses. These surpluses first appeared during the

Korean boom. Since then, against all textbook wisdom, there has not been a single year with a trade deficit, and only two years with a current account deficit. The size of the trade surplus doubled every five to seven years: it averaged 4 billion DM in the early fifties, and rose to around eight billion annually by the late fifties and early sixties. Between 1963 and 1966 it ran at more than 10 billion, to settle at a steady 21 to 26 billion each year till 1972. In 1973, 40 billion DM became the lower limit, with a surplus of 57 billion DM in the oil crisis year of 1974.

Imbalances of this magnitude raise more than technical issues. Looked at statically, they raise distributional issues: trade balances say something about the international distribution of employment opportunities in the industrial sector, which for purposes of social stability and real growth is the most crucial one. Current account balances say something about the distribution of national autonomy in setting economic policy targets: only surplus countries can decide on the trade-off between growth and inflation without the added complication of the balance of payments constraint. Indeed, countries such as Japan and Germany, which are structurally in balance of payments surplus, exert, out of necessity, an equally structural deflationary bias on the rest of the world economy. As important, especially in the Community context, are the political implications of surpluses in the field of finance: the surplus country becomes the banker of the deficit countries, and the formal equality of the international economic regime is compromised.

When asked to explain the surpluses, Germans will first cite microeconomic reasons: the superior quality and delivery of German goods; the export-mindedness of German businessmen, and the corresponding weaknesses of their competitors. Every industrialist can cite anecdotes of business behavior, especially by French and British competitors, which prove a lackadaisical attitude toward exports. When pressed, however, that same businessman will admit that he regularly sells at or below cost in foreign markets—if the exchange rate or conjunctural conditions temporarily require it—using a strong domestic base to recoup his losses. This very deep-seated, microeconomic mercantlism, of course, makes nonsense of the short-term adjustment effects ascribed to, say, exchange rate changes. Adjustment to long-range changes, however, is quite effective. A mercantilistic attitude that somehow considers exports more virtuous and important than domestic sales is shared by the trade unions. In most instances, when the competitiveness of a particular firm or an industrial sector is threatened, unions will moderate their demands. This allows profits to be reconstituted, which in turn allows investments to raise productivity, hence reestablishing competitive advantage. Indeed, if anything really sets Germany apart from its neighbors, it is the combination of sophistication and control in the trade union movement. Because it is German, this sophistication turns a blind eye, however, to the consumption (as opposed to job) implications of twenty-five years of German surpluses. German workers have produced more than 300 billion DM worth of goods—more for consumption by foreigners than they received in return.

Unlike the mercantilism of countries such as France, German mercantilism is almost unconscious. The aim is not to produce surpluses as such, but to maintain competitiveness. The attitude is defensive: the overachievement of market security, facilitated by exceptional social control and self-control, leads to the surpluses.

Apart from this general orientation, there has been a series of special circumstances that have favored surpluses. During most of the early and middle fifties, it was official policy to produce surpluses long enough to reconstitute international reserves: the "tower of gold" became the national symbol of this part of the postwar reconstruction task. As table 1-1 shows, trade surpluses continued after this period, but the current account was more or less in balance in the early sixties. Indeed, the consumer boom of

Table 1-1
German Trade and Current Account Balances: 1952-1978
(in billion DM)

Year	Trade	Current
1952	2.1	2.5
1954	3.9	3.7
1956	5.6	4.5
1958	7.3	6.0
1960	8.4	4.8
1961	9.6	3.2
1962	6.5	−1.6
1963	9.2	0.9
1964	9.6	0.5
1965	5.2	−6.2
1966	11.8	0.5
1967	21.0	10.0
1968	22.7	11.8
1969	20.3	7.5
1970	20.8	3.2
1971	23.5	3.1
1972	26.7	2.5
1973	40.6	11.5
1974	57.4	25.3
1975	43.3	9.1
1976	41.8	9.7
1977	44.9	8.6
1978	40.7	16.1

Source: Statistisches Bundesamt, *Lange Reihen zur Wirtschaftsentwicklung, 1978*, p. 183 (rounded figures).

1965 sucked in an extra 10 billion DM worth of imports, leading to the first and only substantial deficit in "normal" postwar history. This deficit, and the period of balanced current accounts preceding it, have left a curiously persistent and increasingly outdated perception in the minds of German elites: the notion that Germany requires trade surpluses to make up for its deficits in the service and transfer accounts. By the second half of the sixties, however, a new and powerful motor of surpluses was becoming effective: the undervaluation of the Deutsche mark. The distortions caused in the world economy by the Bretton Woods bias toward exchange rate stability and belated adjustment, coupled with the effects of the loss of value in the dollar through domestic and external overspending have been analyzed ad nauseam. The political (as opposed to the institutional) conditions favoring what must rank as the most massive experiment in international dirigisme ever undertaken belong in the realm of foreign policy: the United States secured German acquiescence (that is, its willingness to hold nonconvertible dollars) through a direct linkage with the presence of American troops in Germany.

However, the arrangement also served German mercantilist interests. The strength of these interests became visible—for a brief moment—in the bruising battle between the government and industry over the 1969 revaluation of the Deutsche mark. By then, however, the trade surplus had already become structural.

A massive influx of foreign workers had delayed the reduction of industrial activity normal in a mature economy and served to restrain wage demands which would have reduced the competitive edge. Of course, transfers by foreign workers and greatly increased tourism kept the current account surplus modest. Nevertheless, the doubling of the normal annual surplus on trade account from 10 to 20 billion DM from 1967 onward speaks a clear enough language. Moreover, during the period of artifically low exchange rates, increasing portions of German industry had become used to exporting. The investments both in productive equipment and in the foreign sales and service infrastructure continued to produce exports. In the years following the 1969 revaluation, theDeutsche mark was revalued again and again. But, beginning in 1969, these exchange rate changes have always been too little and too late to cause a fundamental reform of industrial structures that would be in keeping with a normal current account balance. Table 2-4 in Hankel's chapter and his comments on the figures make this point clearly enough.

Since 1973, with the trade balance doubling again to an annual rate of more than 40 billion DM, the seemingly built-in forces of nonadjustment have taken on a disquieting automaticity. The most spectacular example was the surplus of 57 billion DM in 1974, when Germany's commodity import bill increased by 16 billion DM. Even Japan had the grace to run a substantial trade deficit during that year. The causes enumerated here clearly are insufficient to explain a phenomenon of this magnitude; nor can some of the additional factors mentioned by Hankel in his chapter, such as the constant terms-of-trade gain induced by the appreciation of the Deutsche mark. We now seem to be in a period of nonadjustment caused primarily by conjunctural forces interacting perversely with exchange rate adjustment.

As the worldwide hyperboom of 1973-74 gathered momentum, Germany, together with the United States and Japan, was the first country to introduce a countercyclical policy. It was the legitimate aim of national policy to counteract the tremendous inflationary pressures at large in the world economy. As in the past, however, attention was wholly devoted to the domestic side of total effective demand, in spite of the fact that by now a quarter of the German GNP was accounted for by exports. The savage, deflationary monetary policy introduced by the Bundesbank caused private consumption to rise by a modest 2.3 percent and 0.3 percent in 1973 and 1974, while exports rose by more than 11.0 percent in both years![2]

In 1975, as Germany's trading partners hit balance of payments and inflation constraints, Germany experienced its first export-led slump. Exports fell by 6 percent while its GNP fell by 2 percent. Of course, the cause and effect regulationship is not as simple as implied in these figures. Japan and the United States had, together with Germany, deflated early and cornered most of the new oil markets, leaving the brunt of the oil deficits to be borne by the weaker countries.[3] These, in turn, were driven to the desperate gambit of correcting their balances by conventional deflationary policies, although the size of the *collective* deficit was constant.

There is, however, an essential difference among the three countries that, by virtue of their superior social control, could gain a head start in the race for new export markets. Japan and the United States recognized the surpluses as a problem and knew that by overshooting their balance of payments target they were endangering the world economy. Germany, on the contrary, resisted the thesis originally advanced by the OECD and the IMF that the unavoidable *collective* oil deficit (some 40 billion dollars in 1974, some hundred billion dollars in 1980) should be shared equally between all countries, that is, jointly financed. In the mid-seventies, Germany could run a balanced trade account with the oil producers, a matter that even sophisticated Germans, myopically disregarding the total world payments system, consider proper and natural. Strenuous efforts will be made to correct the deficit on current account forecast for 1980 as speedily as possible. At least in the earlier period, there was a widespread conviction that other countries could run as healthy a balance as Germany, if only they pursued sensible domestic economic policies. The decision to finance the 1980 deficit by direct recourse to OPEC funds shows some accommodation to the global need for "sharing the misery", although the motives were largely domestic.

While the current account is not the only economic magnitude by which to judge whether Germany's position is in balance compared to its neighbors—total and per capita GNP is another—it does subsume a great deal of the immediate problems of inequality. Seen from abroad, the problem is one of systematic underconsumption. Since 1967, year after year, the difference between the export and import of goods and services has been between 2 and 4 percent of the GNP. The share of private consumption in the GNP has declined somewhat from around 56.7 percent in the GNP in the early sixties, to around 53-54 percent in the seventies.[4] On the other hand, consumption by the public sector has increased from around 14 to 16 percent in the sixties to around 20 percent in the seventies. Gross investments have decreased from around 27 percent in the early sixties to slightly more than 20 percent of the GNP in the mid-seventies. Read optimistically—from the standpoint of balance—these figures would seem to confirm, partially at least, a picture of declining dynamism: state consumption being increased at the expense of investment.

External balance could be achieved if the decline of the share of private consumption were to be reserved by consuming the annual foreign surplus. For some reason that is quite incomprehensible to foreigners, Germans generally think that it is impossible for domestic demand to substitute for the excess 3 percent of foreign demand, although substitutions of this magnitude are routinely required of the deficit countries such as Italy and Great Britain, albeit in the opposite direction. This notion is connected with the firmly held belief that German exports are highly specialized capital goods for which there simply is no adequate alternative market within the country. A look at the trade statistics or a walk around any department store in Europe will quickly prove that German exports include, apart from substantial semifinished goods, the most ordinary consumer goods, from bottle openers to textiles, from gardening equipment to toys. A quarter of the total trade surplus is accounted for by agricultural exports which tripled in the seventies because of the highly artificial undervaluation of the green Mark.[5] In 1977, only 60 percent of total exports were finished goods.[6] Groups 71 and 72 of the Standard International Trade Classification (machinery and equipment other than transport) account for slightly more than 30 percent of German exports,[7] but even some of this presumably could be diverted to investment which would satisfy a marginally higher share of domestic demand in total demand.

As will be shown in the following section, much of the global imbalance of German trade is in effect accounted for by a regional imbalance in Europe, both East and West. The immediate significance for the partners, to make this point once again, is twofold. For one thing, to the extent that their bilateral trade account with Germany is in deficit or export opportunities in third markets are diminished, they are pushed into a near-permanent deflationary posture. Second, the trade account expresses rather better than the current account the maldistribution of *industrial* employment opportunities. These are at the core of political stability, as well as being crucial to real growth. The built-in forces making for a departure from liberal trading rules within an unbalanced community are reinforced by a second level of potential and actual conflict—over the joint trade policy of the Community toward the outside world.

The West European Free Trade Area

If questioned about the economic significance of the Community for the country, most Germans will point to the fact that slightly less than half of the German exports are bought by the other eight member states. This figure does not serve only to underline the importance of the Community, however, but by implication at least the equal importance of the rest of world trade.

In the perception of elites, this world trade is generally thought of as General Agreement on Tariffs and Trade (GATT) trade, and the preservation of a free world trading system is a paramount aim of foreign economic policy. This overestimation and idealization of the world trading system leads to a view of the Community not so much as an asset, but as a potentially weak supporter of the world system. It is to the global system that preservation-of-order concerns are directed, while the sancitity of the Treaty of Rome is taken for granted. It is the thesis of this chapter that the defense of a mythical world trading system may, in the medium run, undermine the cohesion of the real free trade system in Western Europe, reinforcing the centrifugal tendencies stemming from the internal imbalance of that system.

The greater European free trade area consists of, beside the European Economic Community (EEC) proper, the five major remaining European Free Trade Association (EFTA) countries with which the Community maintains, since 1978, an essentially zero-tariff trading regime (except in agriculture). When the second enlargement of the Community is completed, it will include three more countries that are already more strongly integrated into Community trade than Great Britain is at present. The Community share of their trade corresponds to the 50 percent norm of the core members. Western Europe as a whole accounts for two thirds of the trade of most countries of the region.

In fact, even for Germans oriented toward the world market, the export share of the rest of Europe stands at 14 percent, only slightly less than that of all other industrial countries combined (16 percent), such as the United States, Canada, Japan, Australia, and so on. The true importance of the "other Europe" becomes apparent when we see that of the total German surplus in visible trade of some 34 billion DM in 1977, 26 billion were accounted for by non-Community Europe.

The bilateral trade surpluses with the eight countries came to only 9 billion, although Germany's trading strength doubtlessly had important secondary effects on these partners through competition on third markets in Europe and elsewhere. This point applies especially to Eastern Europe: Germany accounted for just less than half of community exports to the region. While the Community as a whole ran a 1 billion units of account surplus with the region, Germany's surplus was 2 billion, leaving the "eight" not only with a small share of this export market, but with a deficit as well.[8]

But Western Europe does more for German trade than provide the surpluses that the country's psychology seems to require. The two thirds of German trade conducted with Western Europe is maintained by a uniquely liberal and reliable system of rules. It is in this area alone that the liberal postwar vision has been realized. The only other partner with whom Germany comes close to having a similar trade regime is the United States, with a modest 6 percent of trade. Even here, the European exporter is dependent on the good will of any current administration, the U.S. Congress, and the judiciary, such as occurred with the anti-dumping cases which have been only narrowly deflected in recent years.

Trade with the other industrialized members of the OECD is even further removed from the GATT ideal. Australia and Canada are still protectionist in key areas, and manage their trade—imports (for example, automobiles) and especially exports (raw materials). Japan is a law onto itself, with imports manipulated out of tradition, and exports out of necessity.

If one looks beyond this group of countries, one finds in the Third World, with few exceptions, a very high level of tariff protection, exchange controls, and government import monopolies or licensing systems, that is, state-trading practices. These countries account for 17 percent of German exports and 20 percent of its imports (1977).

The same, only more so, applies to that group of countries officially described as "state-trading." Their share in German exports rose from around 4 percent in the sixties to around 6 percent in the seventies. Only in the extraordinary years 1974-76 did their shares rise to around 7 percent, 8 percent, and 7 percent respectively. (The reason was a coincidence of a German need for markets for its depressed capital goods industry, and an Eastern modernization drive which is beginning to founder because of the shortage of foreign exchange.)

If we add up the regional export shares of the South, the East, and parts of the North that depart significantly from free trade practices, we come to a sum approaching 30 percent, with perhaps 8 percent of extra-

European trade approximating the ideal free trade world which Germany exerts so much effort to defend.

One can explain this discrepancy in several ways. One would be to describe it as a lag in perception, which seems to have taken in neither the halving of the share of the United States in German trade since the peak year of 1968, when it was 12 percent, nor the establishment of a European free trade area with its own commitments which are in fact stricter and more far-reaching than GATT rules.

An explanation that rests on the proposition of Germans holding an abstract and idealistic, rather than empirical, view of world trade, finds support in German attitudes and policies toward the commodity proposals of the Third World. As in no other country, in Germany the proposals for buffer stocks and the like were seen as make-or-break issues that would decide the future of the entire world trading system. Even the most elementary knowledge of world commodity markets would have dispelled the notion that there was a market system to be destroyed here, at least a system that was relevant to the textbook advantages of markets: efficient allocation of factors, prices that provide useful signals to users, and such. A look at real commodity markets would have found a chaotic coexistence of very strong private oligopolies and monopolies, widespread state trading (including stock piling, price setting, and such), concerted manipulation by big producers and traders of the big exchanges (London and Chicago, for example), and the existence of economic mechanisms that worked toward imbalance between supply and demand in the medium term. Resistance against any form of price stabilization was so great that Germany became the advocate of the vastly more expensive solution to some of the welfare and equity issues raised by commodities, that is, of an extension of compensatory credits on the Stabex pattern (the European Community's scheme for stabilizing export receipts for raw materials under the Lomé Convention). This is a typical example of a side payment offered in the interest of system maintenance.

An obsession with a nonexistent market system in commodities has made the "common fund" a term of abuse, making it very hard for the government to explain to the public why, in the end, it agreed to have such an instrument to finance buffer stocks. The chancellor himself is a victim of this passion, believing firmly that the United Nations Conference on Trade and Development (UNCTAD) scheme bears a resemblance to the Common Agricultural Policy (CAP). The difference between a system with an unlimited intervention commitment, prices set by the producers virtually independently (for example, the ministers of agriculture), and false prices maintained for decades on the one hand; and a system with a strictly limited intervention budget and prices set by consumers and producers each holding 50 percent of the voting power on the other, could not be greater. Yet, with a righteousness that only ideological conviction can bring, Germany isolated itself for years as a hard-liner in North-South negotiations and prevented the world trading system from gaining a much needed element of stability.

To understand Germany's concern with a liberal order for trade in manufactured goods, the ideological explanation can be supplemented by taking into account very concrete interests. We can start again from that third of Germany's export markets accounted for by state-trading or quasi-state trading countries. The ability of these countries to buy German goods is circumscribed by their ability to earn foreign exchange. More specifically, their willingness to buy Germany's preferred exports (that is, capital goods) is conditional on markets being found for the products made with these machine tools and factories. From this perspective, it matters little that these countries are protectionist themselves. What matters is that the United States and the European Community maintain an open trading policy toward the Third World and Eastern Europe.

It is sometimes maintained, however, that there is an unhealthy imbalance in the Community's international division of labor, in which Germany supplies the capital goods while the partner countries, disproportionally, buy the consumer goods resulting from such exports. While a thorough testing of this proposition would need to compare individual sectors (for example, textiles machinery versus textile imports), the global figures show a slightly different picture: in both the EEC and OECD-Europe as a whole, the German share of imports of manufactures from the less developed countries (LDCs) is slightly higher than its share of exports of machinery and equipment (SITC group 7). In trade with Eastern Europe, however, that share is significantly higher, proof of a potential divergence of interests between Germany and its regional partners in the question of open trade with the East (see table 1-2).

Table 1-2
German Share of Imports of Manufactures (SITC 6-8) and Exports of Machinery (SITC 7) in Total Trade of the EEC (and of the European countries of OECD in parentheses), 1975

	Machinery Exports	Manufactures Imports
Less Developed Countries (LDCs)	34% (29%)	35% (30%)
Centrally Planned Economies (CPEs)	42% (36%)	35% (24%)

Source: Adapted from *Statistics of Foreign Trade—Trade by Commodities* (Paris: OECD, 1976).

The core of this divergence of interests, however, does not lie in the maldistribution of costs and benefits associated with the capital goods in a consumer goods type of trade. The real difference lies in the unequal capacity for adjustment which, in the last analysis, determines the perceived costs of free trade. A country's ability to adjust, that is, to shift capital and labor to new activities when old ones lose competitiveness in the international marketplace, is determined, not by the will of the politicians alone, but by deep-seated socioeconomic structures. To mention a few: the margin of profit left to enterprises reflects, inter alia, the bargaining strength of capital and labor, and the national consensus on the distribution of wealth as expressed in the tax system. Where profits are low, capital stock must be amortized over long periods, that is, adjustment is slow. Spatial and sectoral mobility of labor differs according to social values, home ownership patterns, pension schemes, and the fragmentation of trade unions with vested membership interests. The degree of specialization in particular regions may also inhibit the capacity to adjust. Reliance on migrant labor can significantly increase adjustment capacity. On these and other criteria, Germany scores higher than its partners. This country, therefore, will reach (somewhat later than its partners) the point at which a given rate of increase in imports from low-wage competitors, or capital-efficient competitors such as Japan, will cause unacceptable social costs and political pressures.

In a general environment of low growth in Europe and continued industrial dynamism in newly industrialized countries, this particular problem will gain in significance—irrespective of economists' calculations of the net employment effect of trade with these countries. In general, Germany will push for a more liberal policy within the European Community than many of its partners are willing to accept. The same applies to crisis cartels and other measures of financial protectionism, which together raise profound questions of the future economic constitution of the European Community.

Rules, Inequality, and Balance

It has been argued in this chapter that there is an incompatibility between the extraordinary performance of one or more members in a system and the maintenance of a voluntary rule-based order. The strong tend to believe that a system which allows others the freedom to emulate them is the best of all possible worlds. In the real world, however, the weak have to be either bribed or forced to continue playing a game they lose. This point, which is central to an only half-acknowledged policy predicament of Germany in the European Community, needs more elaboration.

Rules are the essence of European and international organization. They create equality, but they also assume equality to exist. Much of the Western political development since the eighteenth century and of the international community since 1944 can be explained by this central tension: the conflict between the need to impose a single standard on a heterogeneous population as the precondition for minimal justice and stability on the one hand, and the perceived need by groups in society or nation states to offset the de facto unequal results produced by common standards.

There are several ways to contain or relieve this tension. One favored by liberal economists domestically and internationally is the side payment: groups of nations that lose in competition are paid enough to cease asking for a revision of the system itself.[9] Bismarck's labor laws and West German Economics Minister Count Lambsdorf's advocacy of vastly increased development aid belong in this category. When the nature of such side payments extends to a broad range of internationally valuable goods, including military security, we approach a system that is hierarchical regarding not only wealth and achievement, but also power in general, that is, a hegemonic system.

Instead of relying on side payments, a second alternative is to adapt the system of rules itself to take account of inequality: from its inception, the international trading system was a multitier system. Until 1958, the United States discriminated against itself by agreeing to mutual tariff cuts which for its trading partners remained theoretical as long as exchange restrictions were in effect. Since 1948, and with increasing formality, less developed countries have insisted on a double standard, benefiting from most-favored-nation (MFN) cuts without reciprocating. In time, under the guidance of the UNCTAD, that double standard came to include positive discrimination, such as the General System of Preferences. Regional policy within nations and in the European Community, the toleration of nonconforming behavior in weaker member states (for example, distortion of competition through state capitalism in Italy and Great Britain)—these are some examples of double standards that are positive discriminations.

A third way of resolving the contradiction between the equality presumption of rule systems and factual inequality is the nonobservance of rules by the weak. In its most dramatic form, this is generally referred to as international anarchy in the economic system and constitutes a major obsession of postwar planners and policymakers. In fact, there is a continuum between more or less tolerated cheating by minor participants (or minor cheating by major participants), and a serious and systematic infringement of rules which tends to be mutually reinforcing. The present concern with nontariff barriers and positive adjustment in the OECD is directed at this gray area of international behavior.

These three possibilities—side payments and hegemony, the acceptance of self-discriminatory double standards, and the deterioration of the European and international rule systems—are the options open to Germany if the present imbalance within the Community persists. In fact, unattractive though they are, all three approaches are already present in today's Community.

There is, of course, a fourth possibility: the reduction of inequality. We can neglect, in this context, transfer payments between the more prosperous and the less prosperous through regional and agricultural budgets. A much more profound harmonization of socioindustrial practices would be required. Here again, we can distinguish three theoretical options: Germany might become more like other countries; others might become more like Germany; or both might meet halfway.

The prospect of Germany becoming more like others—perceived, for example, as people willing to select easy options, such as protectionism and subsidies, and to run balance of payments deficits to finance domestic overconsumption at the risk of landing in the debtors' prison of the international credit institutions—is a rarely acknowledged but real fear which, perhaps more than the fear of the paymaster ending up as in Europe, helps to explain German reservations about the European Community. But by a number of measures—the growing public deficit, the decline in profits and investments, the growing assertiveness of the trade union movement, and an individual resistance toward spatial mobility—the Federal Republic is losing some of its industrial dynamism.

The process of others becoming more like Germany is much more immediately political, as the European Left in particular interprets this as evidence of German hegemony. In mirror-image to some of the German fears, the suspicious attitude of most of the Left toward the Community derives from the fear of enforced convergence. Nevertheless, the ambitious experiments undertaken by M. Barre in France and Mrs. Thatcher in Britain go in this direction. They attempt to forego the easy solutions which consist of throwing good money after bad, and depriving potentially viable parts of industry of scarce capital, skill, and other resources. The success of these experiments is made much less certain by the onset of the second oil recession. But this success is much more important for the continued existence of the European Community than is commonly realized. With a dynamic Britain and France, the majority of the Community countries could follow compatible industrial and trade policies. Italian private industry could well compete and prosper in such a setting. Residual problem sectors in both the old and new member states could be helped by focused, and therefore cost-effective, programs.

At this point, however, we must return to the point made earlier about the unequal adjustment capacity of Community member states and the conflict this raises about future trade and related industrial policies. For the happy scenario just outlined cannot be achieved by converging national industrial and economic policies alone. There will remain, in the most optimistic hypothesis, a substantial gap, and hence the problem of fitting a single commercial policy to a heterogeneous membership. A similar problem is raised in the field of industrial policy.

As long as the common commercial policy was mainly a matter of tariffs, the discipline of a single standard applied to a diverse membership proved tolerable—especially in a context of rapid growth and an overvalued dollar, and when countries with genuinely different cost structures were only beginning to compete on world markets. In a world where, outside Western Europe, quantitative restrictions gain in importance as a tool of commercial policy, agreement on such policies is ever harder to achieve for the members of the European Community. One example was the debate about the Selective Safeguard Clause as a Community bargaining objective in the Tokyo Round. Germany, concerned with the sanctity of the non-discriminatory nature of the GATT system, for a long time resisted efforts from countries like France to gain the right to introduce restrictions against specific exporters whose market penetration increases dramatically in a given year. Apart from such broad questions, the Community must agree in its day-to-day business on quotas to apply within the Multifibre Agreement, and in its trade with the East, and so on.

As the employment situation deteriorates for conjunctural, balance of payments, and perhaps technological reasons, differences in adjustment capacities, sociopolitical climate, and balance of payments positions may translate themselves into bitter disputes about the conduct of the common commercial policy. If Germany in such a situation insists on standards of liberalism which correspond to its own superior adjustment capacity and its own favorable net gain from trade, member countries may be forced to break the discipline of the common commercial policy and even introduce trade barriers within Western Europe (as Italy did in 1974). In other words, Germany's concern with free world trade may undermine the very real free trade on which two thirds of its exports depend. Needless to say, if Germany maintains surpluses in its Western European trade, it will accelerate this process through the impact on the industrial employment and the balance of payments of its main customers.

There is, of course, a second option open to governments that wish to ignore the verdict of the international marketplace: financial protectionism. This term is almost, if not quite, synonymous with the more familiar industrial policy which for most practical purposes consists of subsidies by governments to selected industries and firms. The trend toward increasing subsidies for lame ducks, which has been sharply accelerating throughout Europe since 1974, has been reversed in France and Great Britain. These policy shifts are warmly welcomed in Germany, as they will increase adjustment capacity in the medium term and provide the basis for an overdue exercise of a mutually balanced subsidies reduction (MBSR). The national habits of decades cannot be changed overnight, especially in a conjunctural situation that promises to be very bad indeed.

Notes

1. Compare the similar points made in David Calleo, *The German Problem Reconsidered: Germany and World Order, 1870 to the Present* (Cambridge: Cambridge University Press, 1978).

2. Statistisches Bundesamt, *Lange Reihen zur Wirtschaftsentwicklung*, 1978, p. 175. As the percentages refer to current Deutsche marks, domestic consumption in fact fell sharply during these years.

3. In 1974, Japan had to pay an additional $14 billion for oil, but its current account surplus was reduced by only $4.5 billion. The United States had to pay an extra 20 billion, with a mere 1.3 billion deterioration of its current account. See Bank of International Settlements, *45th Annual Report*, p. 89.

4. *Jahresgutachten des Sachverständigenrates*, 1977/78, p. 248.

5. Compare Priebe's chapter. The Green Mark is the artificial exchange rate administered for purposes of the EC agricultural policy after the currency alignment of 1969.

6. In the category of finished goods (*fertigwaren*) German trade statistics distinguish between *vorerzeugnisse* (cloth) and *enderzeugnisse* (clothes). The 60 percent refers to this latter group. See Statistisches Bundesamt, *Aussenhandel*, serie 7, reihe 3, p. 38.

7. Calculated after OECD, *Statistics of Foreign Trade*, vol. 1, 1975.

8. Trade with eastern Europe, in billion units of account:

	Economic Community	Federal Republic of Germany
Imports	12.2	3.9
Exports	13.2	5.8

Source: Eurostat, *Monthly Trade Bull.*, Spec. number, 1958-1977.

9. Compare the argument presented by F. Hirsch and M.W. Doyle, "Politicization in the World Economy: Necessary Conditions of an International Economic Order," in *Alternatives to Monetary Disorder*, eds. Hirsch, Doyle, and E. Morse (New York: McGraw-Hill for the Council on Foreign Relations, 1977), pp. 56, 59.

2 Germany: Economic Nationalism in the International Economy

Wilhelm Hankel

The Federal Republic of Germany: A Model or a Problem Country?

After nearly thirty years of export-led growth, the Federal Republic has reached the end of a long successful road. Because the world economy has stopped expanding faster than the internal economies of most western (and eastern) industrial countries, Germany can no longer delay substituting domestic demand for exports. Not even the surrogate concept of the European monetary system (EMS), which was in part designed to preserve the German export surplus, at least in Europe, is likely to last very long, unless it is secured from within (through a European structural policy) and from without (through a consolidation of the U.S. dollar and the Euro-dollar markets).

A new type of full employment and structural policy for the future requires less demand management than supply incentives; the sector of medium-sized enterprises of less than five hundred employees, decimated during the crisis of the 1970s, must be revitalized. It is this sector that has the potential for hiring the unemployed, and has the essential demand, price, and cost elasticity capable of steering the production and investment processes within the market economy. Tax incentives for the creation of jobs and rationalization-neutral reforms are, of course, the conditions for the reanimation of middle-class investments.

In today's integrated world economy, we must add to the old problem of the subordination of the individual (and his economic dispositions) to his national order, the new one of the order *between* the different nations and their economies.

The economic, financial, and monetary policies of tomorrow, which cannot be renounced even for national reasons, must therefore *be coordinated and synchronized internationally*. This does not require new goals for economic, financial, and monetary policies, but rather, a totally new distribution of competence among national, regional (in our case European), and supranational decision makers at all levels.

The following analysis concerns itself with the question: is the Federal Republic of Germany still a model country or, rather, a bad example not to be followed by other nations?

The End of the Social Market Order and
Export-led Growth

The Germany economic miracle after World War II is regarded in the German consciousness as the dual outgrowth of the liberal economic reorganization of Ludwig Erhard in 1948-1949, the so-called social market economy, and the resultant policy of monetary-stability-first which was pursued within that framework. Thirty years after the birth of the Federal Republic and its much admired concept, the end of this economically successful road seems to be in sight; certain qualifications have to be made to the Germans' fondest prejudice without in the least diminishing Erhard's historic shift for Germany.

The total bankruptcy of the war and command economy of the Nazi period, and the currency reform conceived and carried out by the allies on June 20, 1948 (eleven months before the founding of the German Federal Republic on May 23, 1949), from which the West German mark resulted, left no alternative to a free market economy. And yet Kurt Schumacher's Social Democratic party (SPD) of the first hour still had to cover the long road to Bad Godesberg (1959) before it accepted the importance of this central concept for German social and economic policy.

After the rigorous and socially unfair currency reform, which in two stages nullified 93.5 percent of all old Reichsmark notes as well as monetary claims denominated in some Reichsmark, there was even then no more stable currency than the West Germany Deutsche mark (DM) which, after only a few weeks of free floating against the East Germany Mark, quadrupled its value: from 1:1 to 1:4!

Two of the most pressing factors in the social consciousness and the political judgment of the postwar Germans were already present in the currency reform of 1948: the identification of even the less-well-off citizens with their national money, and the fear by foreign countries of the competitive pressure exerted by an undervalued Deutsche mark.

Because the Germans unanimously hailed the liberation from the Hitler inflation, they remained almost totally blind to the heavy (and completely avoidable) social injustices of the currency reform which left far more options to owners of property (industrialists, peasants, and investors) than to the badly trapped hoarders of money who alone had to accept the entire cost of the devaluation. The monetary reform of 1948 also engendered the preference for Deutsche mark stability which was as typical as it was unique to the German postwar development among all social strata, and which has until now successfully subordinated all social conflicts, or at least strongly reduced them.

Because the allies, who then still controlled Germany, saw—and feared—the advantage of a strong West German mark resulting from "their" currency reform as compared to their own currencies, they did not allow the newcomer among the established western currencies the 30 percent depreciation against the U.S. dollar allowed to the other currencies at the time of the parity realignment in September 1949; they only permitted 20 percent. At that time, the West German mark parity of 4.20 DM to the U.S. dollar was established, instead of the rate of 4.40 desired by German officials.[1] It was then that the cornerstone was laid for the preference for revaluation which continues to this day.

Thirty years later, the real miracle is that none of the politicians or economists of that time, neither on the German nor the allied side, foresaw that the partial state regenerated in West Germany was condemned to the burden of export. Since I have treated this theme at length elsewhere,[2] only a brief review is offered here. As Bruno Gleitze has shown, the sites of the most important heavy and manufacturing industries, which before the war had 57 percent of their markets in the former middle and eastern German provinces, were in the West[3] (see table 2-1). Furthermore, the western parts of the country had to absorb and employ the greatest part of the masses of humanity which fled from the Russian Army and the Communist rule; a total of about twelve million people.

Thus, the already highly industrialized West Germany had to overindustrialize in order to accomplish the integration of the refugees (an additional fourth added on to the existing population). Above all, West Germany had to find receptive foreign markets to substitute the lost domestic markets east of the Elbe and to absorb overproduction and market shortages. If ever the Hamburg phrase, earlier imported from England, *exportare necesse est* had meaning, it was in the early years of the second German Republic. Germany could only handle the double problem of substitution for lost domestic markets and the absorption of newly added population to normal employment if it established itself in the expanding world market. This meant a complete break with the history and development of the old Reich and the Weimar Republic, both of which had drawn their economic growth impulses from the domestic, not the foreign, market.

But long before Kaldor developed his theory of export-led growth,[4] Germany's chances were judged pessimistically. In his examination of the possibilities of economic survival for West Germany published in 1949, Fritz Baade, director of the reknowned Kieler Institut für Weltwirtschaft, reached the conclusion that the German economy was not even viable without massive economic aid from the allies. This was a judgment to which both the author and the Institut held fast even in the revised edition of 1951, as the miracle was already producing its first successes.[5] And Otmar Emminger, then chief economist of the Deutsche Bundesbank, explained in 1952 that the German positive balance of payments was a short-term "late flowering of the autarky" of the Nazi period, which had set for

Table 2-1

Integration of East and West Germany Economies Before and After World War II

	1936		1957	
	Billions of Reichsmark	%	Units of Account	%
East Germany				
Total exports	5.3	100.0	4.0	100.0
Exports to:				
Federal Republic of today	2.7	50.9	0.4	11.3
Other German territories	1.5	28.3	—	—
Foreign countries	1.1	20.8	3.6	88.7
Total imports	4.8	100.0	3.6	100.0
Imports from:				
Federal Republic of today	2.7	56.2	0.4	11.4
Other German territories	1.4	29.2	—	—
Foreign countries	0.7	14.6	3.2	88.6
West Germany				
Total exports	7.4	100.0	36.8	100.0
Exports to:				
Federal Republic of today	2.7	36.5	0.8	2.3
Other German territories	1.5	20.3	—	—
Foreign countries	3.2	43.2	36.0	97.7
Total imports	6.8	100.0	32.5	100.0
Imports from:				
Federal Republic of today	2.7	39.7	0.8	2.5
Other German territories	1.4	20.6	—	—
Foreign countries	2.7	39.7	31.7	97.5

Source: Berliner Bank nach: Bruno Gleitze: Ostdeutsche Wirtschaft, industrielle Standorte und volkswirtschaftliche Kapazitäten des ungeteilten Deutschland, Berlin 1956; Statistisches Jahrbuch für die Bundesrepublik Deutschland 1958, Statistisches Jahrbuch der Deutschen Demokratischen Republik, 1957.

itself the goal of a wide-ranging substitution for imports of raw materials—a formulation that he later had expunged.

All of this becomes understandable when one keeps in mind that neither in pre-World War I nor in pre-World War II Germany was there ever a trade and current account surplus. Since 1890, Germany's external balance had been negative (with the sole exception of 1926, the year of the British miners' strikes). To its economists and politicians, Germany appeared to be a classic manufacturing country which exported only as many finished goods as it needed to pay for its raw material imports. Its major market was domestic, not foreign. To this day, German economists occupy themselves more with questions of domestic balance than of integration into the outside world. The consciousness of being dependent on the world economy is only now in the crisis of the 1970s becoming more widespread.

As late as the last balance of payments crisis of 1930-1932, a decision for a racially pure economic nationalism—the precursor of a political one—was made. Brüning's foreign exchange and currency regulations of 1931 were readily taken over by Schacht and the Nazi government and developed into a program of domestic autarky and foreign bilateralism. It was hailed by the German producers as "protection from ruinous foreign competition." It joined the oldest tradition of German economic and political theory: Friedrich List's protective tariff in the time before Germany's industrial takeoff.[6]

The German growth success, which already toward the end of the fifties led from full to overemployment, can be regarded as essentially export-induced since 1952, the end of the reconstruction phase (in which investments rose more than exports). In nominal as well as in real terms, exports grew from year to year more strongly than all other components of domestic demand, individually and in the aggregate (see table 2-2).

The share of exports in the gross domestic product indicates a growing trend up to the present. Furthermore, the export growth in all cyclical recessions and economic crises in the postwar period proved to be the built-in demand stabilizer: whether in 1958-1959, 1966-1967, or 1975-1976, the reduced domestic demand was always quickly and almost automatically balanced by increased sales abroad. Because the automatic "export valve" worked more quickly and more silently, all domestic economic programs came too late, and besides, worked in an exaggerated manner. They usually diffused increased internal demand during a phase in which foreign demand had already paved the way back to full production potential, so that they not only worked pro-cyclically, but, even worse in the eyes of the stability-conscious public, they also contributed to inflation.

The unavoidable result was that government activity aimed at maintaining full employment and smoothing the business cycle was considered by the public to be useless at best, and harmful at worst. For decades, Ludwig Erhard could reject or delay every tightening and codification of modern governmental tools of business cycle and call management superfluous, or incompatible with the spirit and the laws of the market economy. And when, in 1967, Karl Schiller finally cleared the parliamentary hurdle and succeeded in creating today's law to promote stability and growth of the economy out of a bill aimed only at stability, he was unable to prove the necessity for his great enlightened market economic policy. The recovery from the recession of 1966-1967 followed much more the accompaniment of renewed export surpluses than the music of Schiller's fiscal programs which worked pro-cyclically—because they were created too late. It was the same old story (see table 2-2).

But why can't we rely on this richly blessed export-value mechanism forever? To that end, what really lies behind this mechanism must be explained. First, Germany maintained a competitive cost and price advantage

Table 2-2
Driving Forces of German Economic Growth: 1950-1977

| Time Span | Gross Capital Investments | | Domestic Consumption (Private and Public) | | Export of Goods and Services | | Current Account (Export Surplus of Goods and Services) | | Share of Exports (Export of Goods to) | | |
| | Nominal | Real | Nominal | Real | Nominal | Real | Nominal | Real | OECD Countries | Eastern bloc-Countries | OPEC Countries |
	(average annual change in %)						(in % of GNP)		(in % of total exports)		
1950-1955	+17.9	+12.7	+11.1	+8.1	+26.6	+20.8	2.1	4.6	76.5	2.1	.
1955-1960	+10.1	+6.8	+8.9	+6.5	+9.8	+12.3	3.0	3.9	74.8	4.1	.
1960-1965	+11.0	+6.8	+9.0	+5.5	+7.7	+6.5	1.2	1.4	80.2	3.8	.
1965-1970	+8.2	+4.5	+7.8	+4.3	+11.8	+10.8	2.0	2.2	82.3	4.4	.
1970-1975	+4.3	−1.0	+10.7	+3.4	+12.2	+5.5	2.9	2.9	75.4[a]	7.9[a]	7.6[a]
1976	+8.5	+5.0	+7.6	+3.3	+14.1	+11.1	2.5	3.2	76.6	6.8	8.2
1977	+6.4	+2.7	+6.6	+2.4	+5.7	+4.2	2.3	3.2	76.5	6.1	9.1
1978 (1st 6 months)		+4.5		+3.0		+4.0			76.9[b]	6.2[b]	8.6[b]

Source: Statistisches Bundesamt, Wiesbaden
[a]1975
[b]January-May 1978

by means of a permanently strong monetary and an occasionally strong fiscal policy. Given the fixed par values between currencies in the Bretton Woods system, this led to a permanent advantage for German exportables with respect to foreign costs and prices. Second, the rate of expansion from domestic to foreign demand in the Federal Republic continued to evolve in an only partially guided (and guidable) way. The external rate of growth of world markets was by and large higher than that of the domestic economy during the entire period.

Two phases of the German stabilization policy may be distinguished: until 1961 (the year of the first revaluation of the DM) the price and cost advantage was supported *domestically* by means of a strong monetary and credit policy. The high interest rate (around 8 percent) in the capital market, although technically not very convincing, was fully accepted by public opinion as being caused by a capital scarcity, and was thus excused. Of course, it is probably closer to historical and political reality that the directors of the Bundesbank, shocked by the balance of payments crisis in the years 1949-51, did everything they could to distance themselves from the notoriety of the beg-and-borrow policy. (Until 1951, the Federal Republic was the biggest debtor, not creditor, in the European Payments Union.)

In that sense, the beginning of the German stabilization policy conformed completely to its balance of payments and thus to the world economy. Of course this was subsequently no longer true, as the "deficit Republic" rose to become the greatest creditor of the European Payments Union. In addition, a policy of involuntary saving through budget surpluses occasionally backed the hard course of monetary and credit policy.[7]

From 1961 on, the stabilization of price and cost levels was shifted to the external exchange rate of the DM. The revaluation of the DM in 1969 and 1971, and the temporary floating periods before the end of the Bretton Woods system in March 1973, were entirely within the priorities of stability.

The double miracle of this domestic stabilization policy and the external revaluation of the DM is that the resultant permanent improvement of the German terms of trade removed neither the competitive German position abroad, nor the German export surplus. Moreover, the permanent growth of export surpluses did not hinder a permanent increase in real income. Because the surplus position produced only money but no real income, there was an inflationary gap. Germany nevertheless combined stability with real income growth through all phases of its "stability first" policy as has no other western industrial country besides Switzerland for the last thirty years (1949-77).

As table 2-3 makes clear, an average annual inflation rate of 2.7 percent prevails as compared to an annual growth in real income of 4 percent; at the other end of the scale is Great Britain with an average inflation rate of 6.4 percent, and a growth in real income of an average of 1.4 percent annually. The middle is held by the United States with an average real income growth of 2.2 percent.

Table 2-3
Stability and Growth in the Western Industrialized Countries: 1949-1977
(average annual increases in percentages)

Country	Cost-of-Living Index	National Income	
		Nominal	Real
Federal Republic of Germany	2.7	10.9	4.0
Switzerland	3.1	9.3	3.0
United States	3.4	7.6	2.2
Italy	5.5	11.3	2.1
France	6.1	11.2	1.8
Great Britain	6.4	8.9	1.4

Sources: Cost-of-living index adapted from Deutsche Bundesbank, Frankfurt a.M., Monatsbericht; nominal and real incomes adapted from International Monetary Fund, Washington, IFS June 1978 and earlier reports.

What explains the German dual successes—the achievement of such a high rate of real growth despite internally lost goods (exports) undisturbed by growing rates of inflation? The solution to the puzzle lies in table 2-4. Each German revaluation compensated for only a fraction of the foreign inflation advantage of the world markets in comparison to the domestic price and cost rise in the Federal Republic itself. The Federal Republic did indeed improve its terms of trade with every revaluation of the DM but never at the full rate of nominal world inflation. In reality, West Germany assured its foreign trade position by means of a relative sacrifice in its real terms of trade, a connection that was always suspected but only recently fully analyzed by the economists of the Kiel Institute für Weltwirtschaft.[8]

Furthermore, table 2-4 clearly shows that even the floating since 1973 has not changed the permanent relative undervaluation of the DM very much. Although world market prices in U.S. dollars have risen 165.3 per-

Table 2-4
Deutsche Mark Revaluations: World and German Domestic Inflation since 1972

Average Annual	Deutsche Mark U.S. Dollar Parity	World Market Price Index	German Export Price Index	German Cost-of-Living Index
			1972 = 100	
1973	83.4	150.0	106.4	106.0
1974	81.2	251.7	124.5	114.4
1975	77.2	229.2	129.4	121.2
1976	78.9	241.6	134.3	126.7
1977	72.8	266.4	136.1	131.7
1978	65.4 (June)	265.3 (May)	137.7 (May)	135.5 (May)

Source: Deutsche Bundesbank, Frankfurt a.M., Monatsberichte.

cent since 1972, German export prices and cost of living (in Deutsche mark) rose only 37.7 percent and 35.5 percent, respectively. A simple computation of the resulting average price and cost advantage of German export products would thus have necessitated an upward float of the Deutsche mark with respect to the U.S. dollar of 165.3 minus 37.7 equals 127.6 percent relative to its 1972 level. In fact, only 34.6 percent resulted which, incidentally, demonstrates more clearly than any theory how little foreign exchange movements are dependent upon or determine real purchasing power. At the same time, the computed difference between 127.6 minus 34.6 equals 93 percent shows how strongly undervalued the DM still is, at least as measured by the purchasing power parity theory of foreign exchange. Stated another way, it demonstrates how successfully the German currency policy has defended the DM foreign exchange rate in the sense of maintaining the German export position until now.

In this connection, the strong monopolistic-oligopolistic position of German big businesses in the domestic market must be examined. More than 50 percent of German exports come from leading or oligopolistically-behaving suppliers who act as price-takers as for their domestic price levels; namely, the machinery manufacturers, the car producers, and the chemical and electro-technical industries.[9] For this reason, the rule at all times was to make good the nominal deficit in proceeds (caused by revaluation) from foreign trade by raising prices at home.

In other words, thanks to its high degree of monopoly in the domestic market, the German export economy could permit itself the luxury of selling its foreign product under the full terms of trade, because the profit that was given away in exports was regained by way of the relatively higher domestic prices. Thus, while exports maintained high employment, the home market produced the needed return to capital.

This strategy continued as long as the world economy expanded faster than domestic consumption and investment in the Federal Republic itself. But this typical constellation for the total growth of the Federal Republic for nearly thirty years is fading away. The country has reached the end of a road where its economic growth was less dependent on the *domestic market* economy than on the *export* economy. In the future, we must first of all count on a decline in export-led growth. Indeed, this is a situation that might have arisen earlier if regional export of offensives aimed at the Eastern bloc (the economic harvest of Brandt's Ostpolitik) and the Organization of Petroleum Exporting Countries (OPEC) (because of old special economic relations with this new world creditor group) had not over-compensated for the loss in the traditional export markets in Europe and North America (see the last two columns of table 2-2).

To this may be added the point that, in the future, the upward float of the DM could become much more explosive than in the past. For beyond

the real purchasing power structure, there are money-investment preferences that are more than ever determined by exchange rate expectations
rather than by interest or yield. An acceleration of the upward trend of the
DM compared to the U.S. dollar as the denominating currency of international capital markets must be expected. As a result, the maintenance of export positions through sacrifices in the terms of trade will become more difficult, if not impossible, in the future.

It is no accident, therefore, that the rediscovery of the advantages of
fixed exchange rates—within and outside of Europe—is occurring just at
the time when the end of the era of export-led growth is beginning to be
perceived as a reality by German policymakers. The notion of Europe as a
currency area is always rediscovered when there is something to be defended. In the two years between 1969 and 1971 (when the Werner plan was
being discussed), Europe's economic stability was to be defended against
the inflation caused by the influx of U.S. dollars. Today as the flight from
the dollar is generating a surplus in both the current account and the short-
term capital account, thus driving the exchange rate of the Deutsche mark
(and the Swiss franc) upward, the Federal Republic is interested in
diminishing the pressure to revalue by enlarging the investment opportunities to other European currencies, through a more stable exchange rate
between them and the DM. In any event, it is not a problem of economic
stability (because this is not threatened but strengthened by the upward
trend of the DM); nor is it a problem of Europe or of the world economy. It
is, rather, a problem of saving what one can of the traditional foundations
of Germany's export-led economic growth.[10]

In other words, it is the problem of a redefinition of the old neomercan-
tilistic growth and employment policy, according to which the Federal
Republic, as a country dependent on exports, cannot aim for satisfactory
domestic growth without a high export multiplier.

Alternatives that are Not Alternatives

As a matter of fact, *all* domestic economic programs and plans discussed in
the Federal Republic since the outbreak of the crisis of the seventies amount
to an effort to gain time until the currently blocked adjustment mechanism
springs into action again.[11] The government and the German Council of
Economic Advisers (*sachverständigenrat*), united as seldom before, are proposing cost reductions (tax, interest, and real wage) which, on rational
grounds, make sense only if one is trying to return to the old level of external competitiveness with all its problems. The trade unions and leftist
groups demand higher public expenditures, higher real wages to boost purchasing power and, in addition, an expansion of employment by reducing

individual work hours. All this makes sense only if it aims to replace the lagging foreign demand with a stronger domestic demand, but at the cost of still higher public deficits and a still higher public burden on the domestic economy. The opposition has no economic concept at all. It reinforces the program of government and its economic advisers, which gives priority to cost cuts over increasing demand, by settling limits on the extent to which the social market economy should be burdened. It sees the economy as being less threatened by the wholesale death of legions of small and medium-sized enterprises (which were also sacrificed earlier under a Christian Democratic Union-Christian Social Union (CDU-CSU) restrictions policy), than by legislation that could well have been introduced by its left wing (codetermination and apprentice training).

The frightening thing about all three positions is their evident distance from reality. The government and its economic advisers are deceiving themselves if they think they can reduce real wages and real monetary interest rates. And even if they were successful in pushing this through against the will (and market power) of the trade unions, and against the preferences (and alternatives) of investors and savers, the result would be fatal. For the new Brüning policy would either increase the pressure for revaluation of the DM (under free floating), or it would strengthen the intervention of the Bundesbank (under managed floating). Both must make investors uncertain; they would lose income either because export proceeds would not materialize (revaluation), or because domestic costs would rise faster than heretofore (because of the internal increase in money supply as a result of the interventions).

In short, as long as investment is too risky, and saving by comparison presents a more comfortable alternative of higher and safer returns—at least for the mass of independent "risk" entrepreneurs—cost credits, no matter how introduced (whether by wage, interest, or tax credits), can mean only that the latitude for higher marginal savings quotas will rise. The economic impulse will fall flat, as it has thus far.[12]

On the other hand, demand programs from the left would certainly not lead to the desired expansion of real demand but, given the price leadership of the market-dominating enterprises, only to the exploitation of existing or imagined price increase margins. The high revaluation of the DM, which lowers the price of imported goods, would of itself set upper limits to domestic price increases. But the more successfully the overvalued exchange rate of the DM plays its role as stabilizer of the domestic price level, the more it will fail to launch a wave of investment that would restore full employment throughout the whole economy, in view of unused capacity in almost all production sectors. In the face of depressed expectations, the government can indeed generate any amount of nominal demand, but it has no influence on its real content (the amount that will not be absorbed by price increases), and even less on its final destination (the amount nominally leaked into savings).

But what is to be made of the fashionable concept of a redistribution of existing jobs? Does the reasoning behind it—the more split jobs, the fewer new ones to be created—hold promise? Unfortunately, this reasoning contains three miscalculations and defects: First, the loss of work time, whether with or without a nominal wage adjustment, raises the real cost of full employment for that portion of real product which definitely can no longer be generated. From a reversible renunciation of real income emerges an irreversible one, because thereafter nobody can expect a higher real income resulting from a higher employment at normal working hours. Second, it is unavoidable that the reduction of working hours and the attempt to increase jobs will create and accelerate tendencies toward unwanted substitution of labor by capital. Very few people note that in capital-intensive large industry, rationalization is less dependent on unit labor costs or wage rates than on the firm's liquidity and total payroll. In the cash flow of large industry, the sum of wages to be paid out has the cost character of absorbing liquidity, whereas the sums representing capital depreciation have the effect of strengthening the budget by accumulation of liquid funds. More computers and microprocessors, therefore, make the self-financing of an enterprise stronger and more independent from outside debt (credit). Besides, during the crisis one can forego depreciation if necessary. But one must, however, pay wages or go to the bankruptcy court.[13]

Third, in large industries more than in the small and medium-sized industries, the potential for saving labor through technical progress plays an increasingly decisive role. Maxi- and mini-computers and microprocessors are already working more reliably than human workers, with no social welfare costs and even less interest in codetermination. Therefore, any partition of jobs would make substitution more attractive, not superfluous.

Because this is so—a result of technical as well as institutional constraints—one cannot hope to win the battle of regaining full employment through wage policy restraint, economic austerity, a reduction of work time, or administered idleness.

Controlling International Liquidity and the Structural Harmonization of Europe

Is there a solution to these problems, which do not afflict Germany alone? Let us first of all say how this crisis cannot be mastered.

The solution cannot be found by increasing external and internal indebtedness of the whole economy, which no longer stimulates real growth but only promotes saving and disinvestment. Nor can the crisis be met through stimulation, without an internal restructuring of the whole economy which in any event would only briefly, if at all, take up the present slack in capacity and reduce the misallocation of resources. The stimulation would be seen by those affected as a fleeting spark whose light would serve to guide their path of flight to save capital; that is, to change their real investments into money hoarding.[14] And finally, the answer is not a reduction of work time to a thirty-hour/five-day work week which would only increase real costs and increase counterproductive rationalization tendencies.

On the contrary, ways must be found out of this crisis that will bypass both dead-end streets marked, "danger, new indebtedness," and "danger, preservation of structures." To spend another 200 billion DM (as they have been wasted by the public authorities of the Federal Republic since 1974) without thereby achieving anything, either in terms of controlling the business cycle or modifying the structure of the domestic economy, must remain a one-time measure. The expenditure represents the cost of an experiment that one had to try, perhaps, but it should not be repeated.

Which possibilities remain for fighting the crisis and for pursuing a full employment policy if domestic deficit spending, foreign Euro-market indebtedness, and a thirty-hour/five-day work week have to be renounced, at least for the present?

The first and, for a limited time, most important measure is the following: Since fighting the crisis requires an *international* and not a national strategy, the balance of payments adjustment of the western industrialized countries must again become a public matter regulated by governmental consultations; for it is the western industrialized countries that are each others' best customers, and they can maintain and manage their common free political and economic order only by working together. The Homeric struggle over the locomotive theory ended when it became clear on both sides of the Atlantic that, although the OPEC countries have taken from the old industrial countries the greater part of their export surplus, they are not themselves in the position of absorbing it for their own imports, at least not in the short run. They have presented an effective demand deficit to the world economy which, as until now, can only be financed through indebtedness or, from now on, through internal and external restrictions.

But if, in the interests of a continuing free world trade and a less acute domestic crisis, neither should be used, there then remains only the concerted balance of payments adjustment: a network of reciprocal balance of payments assistance among all industrial countries, not only among some European countries.[15]

The second task is to recognize the uncontrolled and unconstrained overproduction of international liquidity in the form of privately created U.S. dollars since the end of the Bretton Woods system. The speculator protects himself from the weakness of the dollar by diminishing his dollar claims, if he has any, as quickly as possible (by, for example, selling dollars for DM); or else he assumes (defensive) dollar liabilities, and with these dollars buys strong currencies (DM or other). In each case, however, the private Euro-bank produces these dollar credits, thereby ultimately creating those problems which the speculation is intended to prevent.

The father of the social market economy in Germany, Walter Eucken, once asked: "How is monetary instability to be explained?" He also supplied the answer: "Primarily because the banks have become private mints."[16] Since then, only one new element has been added: the banks' growing multinational exterritoriality and their business base beyond the boundaries of national monetary and regulatory controls.

All the free and private (Euro, Petro, Asian, and Pacific)-dollar markets fulfill every reasonable bank-supported demand for credit, including the necessary hedging and swap operations, because the markets can refinance it, without regard to the receiving country's ability to pay, and without having to consider how its balance of payments is reflected in the strength of its currency. Thus, the freest currency system in monetary and world history until now provokes one currency crisis after another. The common denominator is that the short positions of all currency relationships are always expressed in terms of one currency: the U.S. dollar. The greatest part of the speculation is no more than self-defense: the result is that on the Euro-markets, the greatest turnover is in the form of M2, not, however, as determined by Friedman in his concept F of bank deposit money but rather in the old-fashioned but still realistic concept of the Keynesian speculation money (precautionary balances). A far smaller part of the market consists of M1, in the sense of transaction money, used for working balances.[17]

According to estimates of experts, the share of true (real) goods and services turnover in 1977 represented 8 percent of worldwide international payments, while 92 percent served as protection against currency crises of every kind, most of which were preventive measures whose execution caused the very danger they were intended to avoid.

The weakness of the dollar and chaotic exchange rates can be avoided only if the free international money and capital markets can be brought back from their present exterritoriality and illegitimacy beyond national control and competence to territoriality and legitimacy; that is to say, to a regime comparable to the domestic money and credit-creating controls. Only if it becomes possible to contain the worldwide international liquidity production (largely based on the U.S. dollar), will it be possible to work again successfully with monetary policy on a national level (for instance, for purposes of stability). But above all, only then can an end be expected to the permanent currency unrest and the fatal decline of the U.S. dollar.

From this it will be clear that the world inflation and dollar weakness do not signal a failure of the U.S. national currency and balance of payments policy, but rather, a capitulation of almost all western governments and their central banks in face of the influence and exterritorial expansionary pressure of their private large banks![18]

Only when the production of international liquidity (mainly in the form of U.S. dollars) is again submitted to the control of central banks (or to a world central bank like the International Monetary Fund [IMF]), can today's destabilizing capital movements and exchange variations be reduced to the level implicit in real current account positions and interest rate relations. Only under the condition of an internationally controlled and limited credit supply could one afford a "clean" floating and build upon it. Speculative expectations would thus cause only short-term exchange rate fluctuations and not—as today—a long-term revaluation trend of a currency that can be broken only by a crisis, if at all, just as in the final days before Bretton Woods![19]

In the summer of 1978, the European heads of government decided at their meeting in Bremen to renew the old idea of a common currency for all European Economic Community (EEC) countries. What is this new European monetary system about? Are the Europeans saving themselves from the common danger of the revaluation tendencies imported through the U.S. dollar, which in the past at least meant more stability and not more inflation, by means of purely technical magic, such as the exchange of units of account and intervention currencies? Their problem is to overcome internal difficulties which, depending on the country, include inflation, balance of payments deficits, unemployment, and regional and sectoral underdevelopment. The solution to these problems requires no more and no less than a Europeanization of their growth and structural policy, not a return to the old illusion of a pseudo-exchange union.[20] Today such a union would only seal the intra-European imbalances of underemployment, overproduction in the agricultural sector, and balance of payments deficits and surpluses in the European Community. And even this will be possible only as long as the supply of German Bundesbank reserves for supporting weak currencies holds out.[21]

In the European Community today, the problem is the Europeanization of structural policies by means of a horizontal harmonization between strong and weak countries and regions, and a *European* rather than a Euro-capital market, at whose liberalization France especially tends to bristle. A monetary union can only become topical and functional again after the greatest structural differences within the Community have been adjusted or have found their own path toward financing, which has nothing to do with money, but only with the transfer of savings.

Thus, the problem of the world economy is a double one: a substitute for world demand which has been hoarded in the OPEC piggy bank, and the stabilization of the U.S. dollar as the still irreplaceable monetary measuring stick of all the economic trade, credit, and reserve transactions in the world. To escape into regional monetary bloc solutions, whose failures are unavoidable because of the lack of a real transfer mechanism, is not a true alternative.

Both problems could be solved in one stroke if it were possible to develop an effective management of world liquidity which would avoid both weaknesses of today's world monetary system: the dependence of international liquidity requirements on the accidental deficits of the United States balance of payments, and the profit-oriented Euro-dollar production of private banks. A world liquidity supply controlled by the IMF or a related agency would—as we have already seen—disarm world inflation, the exaggerated capital movements as well as the wild fluctuations of foreign exchange rates.

One need only compare the official U.S. balance of payments deficits according to size, however defined, with the information released by the Bank for International Settlements on the creation of billions of free Euro-dollar money and credit, in order to measure how insignificant a curbing of U.S. balance of payments deficits would be compared to how important a rationing of Euro-dollar money quantities of all shades would be. When banks are permitted to produce their own world money at will, it is only a question of time until this system collapses.[22]

Reflating or Restructuring the German Economy:
The Case for Export Substitution

What is the situation of the domestic economic policy of most western industrial countries (not only of the Federal Republic of Germany)? Practically speaking, the crisis of the 1970s took place only in the area of domestic, not foreign, production. Multinational big businesses were, without exception, able to get by—thanks to their cheap and abundant supply of Euro-credits—and they were able to considerably expand their market position. At the same time, small and medium-sized businesses, oriented toward the domestic market and dependent on credits, fell victim in large masses to the acute competition and hard credit conditions of the national markets. From 1973-77 in the Federal Republic alone, more than 50,000 predominantly medium-sized enterprises "died" of insolvency or from the need to escape it. The number of jobs thus eliminated is estimated to be from 250,000 to 300,000. This is a blood-letting that has nothing to do with rationalization determined by the system, but rather, with the existence of a dual economy: a multinational one for the "big guys" and a national one for the "little guys." The domestic economy is the one in which crises and politics take place and in which, of course, a balancing middle-class policy is missing. This is a situation that is all the more astounding since all political parties in Parliament, without exception, support an active middle-class policy; furthermore, the victims themselves, although organized in various groups, hardly raise their cries of complaint to the usual level of other social groups.

The elimination of so many little guys has without a doubt enormously strengthened the market share of the big guys, and thereby also the degree of monopolization of the German economy during the years of the crisis. This has major consequences for the quality of the market economy which, as is known, thrives on competition and chokes on monopoly. It also applies to the labor market which, as we have seen, is burdened by big businesses, but which is liberated by small and medium-sized businesses.

A full employment policy in our times (not only in the Federal Republic) requires, for the foreseeable future, subsidies to the heavily pressured small-scale enterprise sector. Because only in the still labor-intensive producing enterprises of fewer than five hundred employees do those production and labor techniques thrive, which can only be rationalized in a limited way through automation.

But above all, as long as three-fourths of all investment and employment fall in this sector, and not in the approximate tenth of those enterprises with more than five hundred employees, there would be no more successful program than to encourage small and medium-sized enterprises, regardless of their legal form (see table 2-5). But how, and with what means, can this be done without at the same time creating more public debt?

The first step in this program should be tax equalization. Small and medium-sized enterprises pay no uniform corporate tax rate as do their large competitors. Yet for better cost planning and revenues, they need a uniform rate which, however, should be lower than the rate applied to large corporations in order to compensate for their structural disadvantages. Such treatment should be comparable to the preferential tax treatment of the small German banks (savings banks) whose structural disadvantages are compensated by a 10 percent tax bonus, compared to the large private banks.

The second element should be tax incentives for the creation of more jobs. Small and medium-sized enterprises employ not only more people, but also more professionally trained labor per unit of output than the more thoroughly rationalized large enterprises. Therefore, tax bonuses based on the size of the enterprise would have both a quantitative and a qualitative effect on the creation of new jobs. The demand for qualified professionals would be honored, and at the same time it would become clear to young people seeking employment that training is once again worthwhile.

Table 2-5
Enterprises in the Federal Republic of Germany in 1975

Size	in thousands	%	Employees in thousands	%	Turnover in thousands	%	Investments (capital) in thousands	%
All enterprises and corporate bodies	—	—	—	—	—	—	241.5	—
All enterprises	1,908[a]	100.0	20,782	100.0	2,433	100.0	164.8	100.0
Up to 499 employees	1,906	99.9	15,981	76.9	1,872	76.9	139.1	84.4
More than 500 employees	2	0.1	4,801	23.1	561	23.0	25.7	15.6

Source: Statistisches Bundesamt, Wiesbaden.
[a]1970

Third, the program should include rationalization-neutral tax reforms. Although wage and capital costs (interest and depreciation) are fiscally equally relevant as deductible from earnings, depreciation and reinvestment offer recognized fiscal motives for the overinstitutionalization of the large enterprises, through which the economic productivity of these concerns is again strengthened at the cost of the general public. Every DM saved on industrial wages causes additional social welfare expenditures (unemployment funds), which burden public finances. Therefore, at least those taxes which unintentionally reinforce this effect, such as local payroll and business (capital as well as revenue) taxes, should be changed to depreciation taxes.

Which budgetary resources (beyond the already inflated public) could be placed at the disposal of a spending program that favored the middle classes and created new jobs, rather than at the expansion of demand? For the principal mistake of German fiscal policy is the monetaristic-inspired reduction of government revenue rather than expenditures. This implies at given levels of expenditures governmental deficit spending rather than a reduction of the government share of the GNP. Contrary to this mistaken solution, resources for subsidizing job creation could be taken, at full employment level, from the saved funds for insurance against involuntary unemployment. Instead of burdening the taxpayer with the wages saved by corporations as a result of substituting jobs, the opposite would occur! The unemployment that would have been "rationalized away" as a result of this program would finance the increased employment in the small and medium-sized industries.

Another rich source of fiscal funds for refinancing structural reforms is the subsidy budget. This contains (and not only in the Federal Republic) a set of expensive and false structure-conserving measures that are false and expensive because they aim at price and income fixing. In this area, any country has a financial reservoir which, by a multiple factor, far exceeds the investments in the higher employment and better industrial structure just sketched. The sum of the annual subsidies aimed not at creating new jobs, but rather at preserving earnings and the market shares of agriculture, industry, and services, is almost double that of all crisis-fighting programs of the federal government since 1974!

The salient point is not a set of more or less coordinated single measures, but the mix of policies sketched here: *international* management of world liquidity, a pattern of *regional* (fiscal) adjustment, and a *national*, more supply-than-demand oriented full employment policy concentrated on the revitalization of the medium-sized and small enterprise sectors.[23]

This program is to be understood not only as a part of a anticyclical policy, but also as a new aspect of the domestic and export-substituted (opposed to export-led) growth alternative proposed by Kaldor. At the same time, it is a new page in the book of competition and order policy. It is an investment in the "countervailing powers," as Galbraith calls it, against the monopoly and concentration tendencies of our times which cannot be met only through legal regulations.

Because of our fascination with technocratic solutions, we may have forgotten the simple truth: that the social market economy can live without its conglomerates and their managers, but it cannot live without the legions of small and medium-sized entrepreneurs who risk their capital and private existence; who still, though perhaps not much longer, constitute the main body of its industries, investments, and jobs, even though some politicians imagine that it would be much easier and more rational to govern the world with only a few large industries.

The opposite is true: the market economy provides sufficient goods and jobs only when many entrepreneurs who are neither overly large nor overly strong, compete with one another for customers and markets. They are indeed not only its "guardian classes" (Schumpeter), but also its guardian angels.

Notes

1. Compare Hans Möller, "Die deutsche Währungsreform von 1948," in *Währung und Wirtschaft in Deutschland 1876-1975*, ed. Deutsche Bundesbank p. 431. See also Hankel, "The Deutschemark Turns 30: An Expert for Wrinkles," *The German Tribune* (Hamburg), July 2, 1978, p. 6 (from the *Frankfurter Rundschau*, June 16, 1978, p. 3).

2. See Hankel, *Der Ausweg aus der Krise* (ECON) (Düsseldorf, Wien: ECON Verlag, 1975), p. 105; also Hankel, "West Germany," in *Economic Foreign Policies of Industrial States*, ed. Wilfrid L. Kohl (Lexington, Mass: Lexington Books, D.C. Heath, 1977), chap. 5, p. 105.

3. Bruno Gleitze, *Ostdeutsche Wirtschaft, Industrielle Standorte und Volkswirtschaftliche Kapazitäten des Ungeteilten Deutschland* (Berlin: Duncker und Humblot, 1956). See also Hankel, *Die Zweite Kapitalverteilung, ein Marktwirtschaftlicher Weg Langfristiger Finanzierung* (Frankfurt: Knapp, 1961), p. 24; and Hankel, *Ausweg*; and Hankel, in Kohl, *Economic Foreign Policies*. As Gleitze has demonstrated, before World War II East Germany was the main supplier of West German consumer goods, and West Germany was the main supplier of East German investment goods. After the partition, both economies had to substitute the lost capacities and markets. East Germany built up a new investment industry; West Germany a new consumer industry and an efficient export sector.

4. See Nicholas Kaldor, "Conflicts in National Economic Objectives," *Economic Journal* No. 1 (March 1971):1.

5. See Institut für Weltwirtschaft an der Universität Kiel (ed.), *Lebensfähigkeit und Vollbeschäftigung. Ein Beitrag zur Frage des Wirtschaftlichen Wiederaufbaus in Westdeutschland* (Bonn, 1951), p. 4. See also Hankel's works cited in note 3.

6. See Gustav Stolper, Karl Hauser, and Knut Borchardt, *Deutsche Wirtschaft seit 1870* (Tübingen: Mohr-Siebeck, 1964).

7. Of Kaldor's two parameters of such a policy (exchange and fiscal policy), it must have been primarily the fiscal policy that aggravated the monetary restrictions pressure before 1961; and after 1961, it was primarily the exchange rate policy: from the mid-fifties to the end of the sixties, the Federal Republic created involuntary budget surpluses because it undertook to put aside funds for the stationing of troops and the rearmament offered by Adenauer (Finance Minister Schaffer's so-called *Juliusturm*, the tower in which the Prussian war treasure lay); after payment of the *Juliusturm*, the exchange rate policy played the decisive role in the "foreign economic protection" (Karl Schiller) of German stability policy. See Karl Schiller, "Konvertibilität-Liquidität-Parität. Zum Problemwandel der Währungspolitik in der Nachkriegszeit," in *Festschrift zum 75. Geburtstag Ludwig Erhards* (Berlin: Duncker und Humblot, 1972), p. 215.

8. The Institut für Weltwirtschaft in Kiel has developed a thesis augmenting the earlier research of its director, Herbert Giersch, to the effect that the undervalued Deutsche mark of the fifties and sixties led to a "total block of uncontrolled structural changes" (H. Riese): an overinvestment and overemployment in the export sector which is said to be adding to the severity of the crisis now. Compare to this and to criticism of the Kieler Institut's critique of the earlier and present economic policy in Germany—Hajo Riese, "Strukturwandel und Unterbewertete Währung in der Bundesrepublik Deutschland, Bemerkungen zur Theoretischen Position des Instituts für Weltwirtschaft Kiel," *Konjunkturpolitik* 3 (1978):143. For the consequences of this policy of "monetary dumping," see Hankel and F. Lehner, "Die gescheiterte Stabilitätspolitik und ihre politischen Folgen (Von der Unvereinbarkeit Wirtschaftlicher Monopol- und Politischer Konkurrenzsysteme)," *Hamburger Jahrbuch für Wirtschafts- und Gesellschaftspolitik* 21 (1976); see also Hankel, *Währungspolitik Geldwertstabilisierung, Währungsintegration und Sparerschutz*, (Stuttgart: Kohlhammer, 1972), addition to chap. 4, p. 84.

9. Of the total German export, machine manufacturing represents 16.2 percent, chemicals 13.6 percent, electro-technical products 10.1 percent, and automotive manufacturing 13.4 percent. All four large areas are typical oligopoly-led sectors at home, in which the joint stock companies call the plays as leaders in their fields (such as Mannesmann, Gutehoffnungshutte, the three Farben successors Siemens, AFG-Telefunken, Brown, Boveri and Cie, and the five large automobile makers).

10. Compare Hankel's "Europäisches Währungssystem: Ist das Risiko noch kalkulierbar?" *Frankfurter Rundschau*, September 23, 1978.

11. In the following, Hankel is returning to ideas and definitions already presented in recent publications: "Die Dollarschwäche—Gründe und Hintergründe," in *Aus Politik und Zeitgeschichte, Beilage zur Wochenzeitung Das Parlament*, No. 12 (March 25, 1978); and "Die Grosse Krise kommt noch.—Das Krisenmanagement ist bald am Ende. Was dann?" *Zuckerindustrie* 8 (1978); and "Beschäftigungspolitik muss bei Mittelunternehmen ansetzen," *Frankfurter Rundschau*, August 16, 1978.

12. One of the most fertile, and statistically as well as politically neglected sources of "fear" saving done in times of depression is represented by the earnings no longer invested of entrepreneurs endangered by depression. In the years of crisis since 1972, the (personal) small and medium-sized enterprises in the Federal Republic took more money out of their businesses than they earned. Where did they invest it? A regression in the rate of investment combined with a growing savings rate leads to the assumption that they saved that money earmarked for investment in risk-free but certain earnings: in treasury notes which, in times of crisis, always have record sales. Former investors thus became savers, aggravating the crisis endogenously. By contrast, those large enterprises and investors (joint stock) who are tied to long-range programs do indeed maintain the investment rate at a high level. But, first, they do not proportionally close the gap that the others (whose share represents 70 percent in the Federal Republic) have created. Furthermore, the trend of large investors is away from domestic and toward foreign investment. They are not only conscious of the world market, but also of the exchange rate; that is, they calculate onsite costs which result in the buying of assets and liabilities by means of currency relationships.

13. This forgotten factor of rationalization in large industry was first treated by Hankel in his *Währungspolitik* (Stuttgart, Berlin, Cologne, Mayence, 1971-72), p. 84. It was treated more recently and fully in Bündesanstalt für Arbeit (ed.) "Von der Einkommens- zur Arbeitsmarktpolitik" in *Mitteilungen aus der Arbeitsmarkt- und Berufsforschung*, September 1978; et al., p. 289.

14. Hankel, "Europäisches Währungssystem," 1978.

15. A situation, incidentally, that is disturbingly reminiscent of the German reparations payments after World War I by means of international indebtedness (U.S. credits) instead of public savings (domestic taxes). Because the United States insisted on repayment of war debts incurred by the victors, England and France, these latter countries drew their reparations from the vanquished Germany. But Germany paid them with U.S. credits. In this way, the United States financed its own "debt service" from an expansion of the international credit inflation, a bubble that burst between 1929 and

1931. The crisis might possibly never have occurred if the United States had not followed a "Shylock" policy of exacting payments on its war loans or if the Weimar Republic had followed a more careful domestic financial policy of paying for its reparations with tax revenues instead of installment payments with international credits. See Charles P. Kindleberger, *Die Weltwirtschaftskrise* (München: *DTV* Wissenschaftliche Reihe, 1973), p. 33.

16. See Walter Eucken, *Grundsätze der Wirtschaftspolitik*, 1st ed., 1952 (Tübingen, Zurich, Mohr, Seibeck, Rentsch, 1960), p. 169.

17. John Maynard Keynes, *The General Theory of Employment, Interest and Money* (New York: Harcourt Brace, 1935), p. 199.

18. An "invisible" hand that sometimes becomes visible. Compare the explanations of Anthony M. Solomon, Undersecretary of the U.S. Treasury for Monetary Affairs before the Sub-committee on Economic Policy, Committee on Foreign Relations of the U.S. Senate on July 24, 1978. (Deutsche Bundesbank, "Auszüge aus Presseartikeln," August 8, 1978).

19. With regard to sources and figures, compare Hankel's article: "Der Zerfall des U.S.-Dollar, Diagnose und Therapie: die internationalen Liquiditäten müssen gemanagt werden, nicht die Wechselkurse," *Wochenzeitschrift Das Parlament*, September 22, 1978.

20. See W.M. Corden, "Monetary Integration," *Essays in International Finance* (Princeton, N.J.: Princeton University Press, April 1972), no. 9, p. 2.

21. See Hankel, "Europäische Geldillusionen," *Sozialdemokratischer Pressedienst Wirtschaft*, April 7, 1978, p. 4.

22. See (note 11) Hankel, "die Dollarschwäche," as well as "die Lokomotive zieht uns aus der Krise," *Frankfurter Rundschau*, July 12, 1978.

23. The author first took a position on this policy mix of international monetary policy, supraregional fiscal policy, and national full employment policy in 1970 at the Innsbruck meeting of the Verein für Sozialpolitik; see H. Arndt and D. Swatek, eds., *Grundfragen der Infrastrukturplanung für Wachsende Wirtschaften* (Berlin: Duncker und Humblot, 1971), p. 421. See also (note 13) Hankel, "Währungspolitik," p. 251; also Hankel, "Weltwirtschaft, Vom Wohlstand der Nationen Heute," Düsseldorf and Vienna: Econ 1977, p. 324; and Hankel, "Beyond Keynes and Monetarism," *The German Tribune, Economic Affairs Review* No. 19 (1978):5. For related analysis, but applied to transatlantic relations, see Robert A. Mundell, "Appropriate Use of Monetary and Fiscal Policy for Internal and External Stability," *IMF Staff Papers*, vol. 9, no. 1, 1962; and Mundell, *The Crisis Problem, Monetary Problems of the International Economy* (Chicago and London: The University of Chicago Press, 1969), p. 343, 379.

3 Germany and the World Monetary System

Susan Strange

Pirandello imagined six characters in search of an author. An observer of the unfolding drama of the international monetary system might similarly imagine one of the characters in that drama—Germany—having to choose from five different roles it can play, five different postures it can adopt. One of the five roles has already been played. Others have been imagined and advocated but never put to the test, and others have never been seriously contemplated. Yet a consideration of the full range of conceivable possibilities is no bad device for analyzing Germany's place—past, present, and future—in the world monetary system.

Until now, there have been strong domestic constraints limiting the choice of monetary roles for West German governments. These internal constraints are very important and cannot be ignored, for they are more than likely to continue to circumscribe policy choices in the future. No less important are the external constraints of Germany's political relations with other countries—especially, but not exclusively, the United States—and the dominant position (which to my mind is continuing and undiminished) of the dollar as the focal point and pivot of the international monetary system.

After outlining the five roles, and considering the internal and external constraints, this chapter will consider the implications that follow from these external constraints, both for the general issue of international monetary order and for the particular question of the prospects within the world monetary system of a closer European monetary union. It will suggest some tentative conclusions about which of the five roles would best allow German economic power to serve the future of European union, with the internal and external constraints that we know from experience to exist; and finally, to suggest some policy areas and policy measures that might be considered as necessary adjuncts to such a monetary strategy or as means of putting it into effect.

Five Roles in Search of an Actor

The five theoretically conceivable roles are primarily political rather than economic in nature. That is to say, they are distinguished from each other more by the political character they represent than the economic or financial

45

measures or consequences by which they would be expressed. They are based on a political economy analysis of the question "What is Germany's role in the system?," rather than a purely theoretical economic or a narrowly financial one.

The five roles, briefly described, are those of "leader of the system," "obedient ally," "bigemonist partner," "lone ranger," and "leader of the opposition." Obedient ally is the role most often assumed and most consistently played by German governments in the past. Of the others, leader of the system is the role which, for reasons that can be briefly summarized, is simply impossible—at least in present political circumstances and for the foreseeable future. Lone ranger and bigemonist partner have both been imagined, and there have been playwrights to draft the parts and write the lines. Neither has played on the world stage. Leader of the opposition has not been seriously contemplated so far. But perhaps it is time it were. Let me explain a little more clearly what I mean by these five rather frivolously named roles in search of an actor.

The obedient ally role involves support for the United States as leader and dominant manager of the international monetary system in whatever goals it seeks and by whatever means it chooses to achieve them. The rationale is simply that the Germans need American military protection and can best ensure that it is maintained (and is seen to be maintained) by complying as much as is politically feasible with American wishes; and by making American monetary leadership as easy and nonconflictual as possible. During the 1960s, there were few occasions when Germany failed to give such support. It is true that sometimes, as with the negotiations leading to the General Arrangement to Borrow (GAB) in 1962, a small price was exacted for the cooperation deemed necessary by the United States. In that case, it was so that Germany should be given a blocking vote on the activation of the GAB. Sometimes, as in negotiations preliminary to the Stockholm Agreement of 1968 on Special Drawing Rights (SDRs) for the International Monetary Fund (IMF), German representatives joined the French in stopping the Americans from having it all their own way. Again, the price exacted for ultimate cooperation and support was the granting of additional voting power in the IMF for the European Community—in short, a rather slender insurance policy against abuse of the new reserve asset on the say-so of Washington.

But for the most part, the West German executive director of the IMF in Washington, the president of the Bundesbank at the Bank for International Settlements (BIS) in Basel, and the West German finance minister at the OECD in Paris could all be relied upon by the U.S. Treasury to expand Germany's foreign aid program, subscribe to the gold pool, refrain from converting dollar balances into gold, negotiate offset agreements easing the burden of U.S. defense spending in Europe, and so on. Assisted by other obedient allies—notably Britain, Japan, and Canada—the United States had a relatively easy ride during the 1960s even when U.S. payment deficits persisted and when the foreign exchange and gold markets increasingly questioned the long-run reliability of the dollar as international money.

The role of leader of the system is not one that Germany is able to assume at present, but not because its quota in the IMF is still less than that of the United States. That is merely a mirror held by international organizations to the realities of the international political economy. The leader of the system has to be the possessor of the globally preferred monetary medium (what I have called in the past the top currency).[1] Despite the doubts that foreign exchange dealers persistently express about the valuation to be put on the dollar, it is striking that the bulk of Euro-market dealings is still denominated in dollars, and that no matter where on earth one might drop from the skies and go shopping, it would be easier to use dollar notes to buy necessities than any other national currency. The reason, again, is political more than economic. In the long run, although the United States may mismanage its currency, it is true that its basic political and economic stability, military strength, and therefore supreme place as a superpower in the world market economy is not in doubt. It is just possible to imagine a future scenario in which West Germany is overrun by an exuberant Red Army while Fortress America remains inviolate across the Atlantic, but it is impossible to imagine the converse: a West German state surviving while the United States is overrun or the North American continent laid waste by nuclear attack. As long as this basic political asymmetry persists, there is no chance whatever of the Deutsche mark being the pivot of the international monetary system.

Much more easily conceived is the role of lone ranger—the part already played in large measure by the Swiss. In a crisis, the lone ranger is available to come to the aid of the system. It would never do anything deliberately to undermine or weaken it. But the role is essentially defensive, isolationist, and noncommittal. It would not preclude the use by foreigners of Deutsche marks as a store of value, whether private or official. Nor would it be inconsistent with the linking of other weaker currencies like the Austrian schilling or the Danish kroner as satellite currencies to the Deutsche mark. What the lone ranger role does necessitate, however, is that the domestic economy should be well insulated through various balancing strategies that prevent whatever links it has with the international monetary system (as a result of its evaluation as a strong currency by the markets) from disrupting its domestic economic management. Banks especially must be severely disciplined. Foreigners' transactions must be governed with discrimination and kept under close surveillance. The markets may be allowed substantial freedom to express their appreciation of the strength of the lone ranger currency, but there must be effective insulating fences around sensitive areas, such as employment, investment, and capital movements, which may interfere with internal economic stability.

Bigemonist partner is a term—and by any literary standards a pretty awful one—borrowed from Fred Bergsten, currently undersecretary for international economic affairs at the U.S. Treasury. In an article written in 1974, Bergsten argued that "there are only two important powers in the international monetary system—the United States and Germany."[2] He went on to propose a "bigemony" instead of the U.S. hegemony which, along with other American economists, he believes is weakening as the value of the dollar depreciates relative to other currencies. He defines this as "an hegemony of two. The term is intended to be a bit weaker than 'condominium' but much stronger than 'partnership.'" Although Bergsten acknowledged that others, including the rising middle class of developing countries with commodity power and rapid industrialization, would have to be involved in some ways in international economic decision making, he thought such pluralism was too unwieldy. It introduced too many varied viewpoints to provide a basis for the aggressive leadership needed with the creation of a new international economic structure.

A more sophisticated variation which could possibly be called a "trigemony"—in which the United States and Germany would be joined by a third power, Japan—has also been proposed by American economists, notably by Ronald McKinnon of Stanford University. Noting that the exports of the United States, Germany, and Japan constituted over a third of the world trade in 1973, and that Germany and Japan now hold well over half of the world's official dollar balances, McKinnon proposed an arrangement that looks like an updated version of the Tripartite Agreement of 1936. The aim of the agreement would be: "A parallel and consistent expansion of the domestic monetary base in each of the three countries, supported by official intervention [the terms of which were to be spelled out] to maintain stable rates between the dollar, the Deutschmark and the yen." Characterizing this with admirable frankness as "a strategy for the world's three principal trading countries to strengthen the dollar system,"[3] McKinnon also proposed that the triumvirate would act together to regulate capital movements and the expansion of Euro-dollar dealings.

The role of the bigemonist or trigemonist partner as described by American economists, however, never seems entirely convincing. The United States and its partner (or partners) are supposed to act domestically and toward each other's exchange rate according to certain guidelines. But it is never made very clear what happens if in the future (as in the past) the United States acts in contravention of the guidelines; or if the interests of the bigemonist partner or partners diverge sharply from those of the United States.

As always, the inherent asymmetry between the power of the United States and that of the bigemonist or trigemonist partner is played down. Unless and until a scheme is proposed according to which the United States is prepared to intervene in foreign exchange markets to maintain stable rates in Deutsche marks and in yen and to encourage the equal acceptance by third parties of reserves denominated in these currencies, and unless and until a scheme is proposed that provides for effective sanctions against unilateral decisions on the part of the United States, this role is not one that in any significant particular differs substantially from that of obedient ally.

The fifth and final role, leader of the opposition, is one that was briefly attempted by France under General de Gaulle. As a result, he is (wrongly in my view) caricatured by many American economists as seeking to bring about the collapse and ruin of the international monetary system. On the contrary, the historical evidence suggests a remarkable inhibition in French monetary diplomacy about using any forms of leverage against the United States that would risk damage to the delicate fabric of international monetary confidence. De Gaulle rightly perceived that this fabric, like a plastic bag or spider web, was very easily torn but could be repaired only slowly and with cost and difficulty. The lessons taught by the failures of central bank cooperation in the crucial years 1928-1931 had been well learned in France.[4] Though no French official would accept or even agree that France was primarily responsible for those failures, none was prepared to see them repeated. Interpreted as a strategy to impose long-overdue discipline on an irresponsible top-currency country, the conversions of French dollar balances, the negotiations over SDRs, and the attempt to create a European monetary union in the late 1960s, make perfect sense. That these measures went no further in disrupting the two-tier gold price or in blocking the reform negotiations in the International Monetary Fund suggests that the French opposition was—to use English parliamentary language—that of the *loyal* leader of the opposition party rather than the standard-bearer of monetary revolution. The tone of Rueff's *Le Péché Monétaire de L'Occident* is much more one of sorrow than of anger; his appeal to Americans is to recall and live up to their own high standards of responsible Republican government, and to do so, moreover, in the long-run interests of the United States itself as well as those of Europe and the rest of the world.

The leader's role, however, requires that the leader has followers, and the French, for the most part, did not have them, even before the events of 1968. Only sometimes (and then only briefly) have subsequent French governments been able to muster a confederate army of uncertain volunteers: at the Nixon-Pompidou meeting in the Azores in 1971, and perhaps at the Washington Conference in February 1974. The Conference on International Economic Cooperation (CIEC), feeble though its results have been, was the fruit of such a brief alliance under French leadership. The Schmidt-Giscard agreement leading to the Bremen proposals in July 1978 suggests a French recognition that German partnership, at least for any monetary enterprise, is indispensable. But in monetary matters—perhaps as a result of the experience of 1968, or perhaps for economic reasons—the French seem for the time being to have lost all taste for leadership in opposition. World affairs in France have taken a backseat to domestic affairs, and no major political group is keen to follow de Gaulle's example. Whether Germany could now take over from France the leadership of an effective opposition group within the international monetary system will therefore depend on an assessment of the domestic and external constraints on German policy.

Domestically, German governments survive if there are plenty of jobs, rising incomes, and relatively stable money. By these three means, political stability and democratic institutions have been reinforced, the communist specter has been kept at bay, and the hazards of a frontier situation have been made bearable. The growth has clearly been achieved through successful exploitation of an expanding foreign market for Germany's exports of capital and consumer goods. The accidental legacy of the postwar partition, which left most of the heavy industries to West Germany, enforced an early preoccupation with exports of capital goods. And once domestic prosperity had been achieved, aided by the overflow of refugees from the East, this laid the foundations for later diversification into other manufactured exports—cars, ships, and all sorts of industrial office and domestic machinery. To maintain the momentum of prosperity and employment at home, German governments needed the open world trading system pursued actively by the United States, supplemented by the preferential trading area created by the European Community. In 1975, the investment goods industries, which accounted for more than 55 percent of all industrial exports, were directly and indirectly dependent on foreign markets for 47.4 percent of their total output. In the automobile industry, the dependence was rated at 52 percent; in the machine-building industry, at 56 percent; and in chemicals, 48.5 percent. In short, exports were the means by which industrial peace was maintained through an *embourgeoisement* of the proletariat very similar to that experienced in the United States. One job in five in West Germany now depends on exports.[5] By 1978, Germany's place as the richest, most competitive, most productive economy of the nine members of the European Community was assured. As Michael Kreile has said, it qualifies, in Francois Perroux's terms, as the "économie dominante" of Western Europe. Even allowing for the conversion of wage rates into dollars at current exchange rates, Germany's economic lead is evident, as shown in table 3-1, by the Dresdner Bank.

If the need to maintain uninterrupted progress to higher incomes has been one major constraint on all German governments in the last generation,

Table 3-1
Shares of Industrial Production of Ten Industrialized Countries 1970-1978

	1970	1978
United States	48.0	42.7
Japan	12.9	16.3
West Germany	13.9	15.9
France	7.9	7.6
Britain	7.0	6.4
Italy	5.0	4.9
the Netherlands	1.7	2.1
Switzerland	1.3	1.6
Sweden	1.4	1.3
Austria	0.9	1.1

Source: Dresdner Bank, *Economic Quarterly*, No 58, August 1978. Reprinted with permission.
Note: Numbers are at current August 1978 prices converted at current dollar exchange rates.

the need to maintain stable money has been almost as great. Defending the Deutsche mark from enfeebling infections from abroad—from over the mountains or across the sea—has been a major preoccupation of the monetary authorities, and especially the constitutionally autonomous Bundesbank, for almost a generation. The lesser attachment, in German eyes, of other countries and their governments to the ideal of stable money has made it difficult at times to pursue the goal of both an internally stable value for the Deutsche mark and an external stability as expressed in exchange rates. As recounted by Otmar Emminger, the first serious clash between internal and external balance came in 1957 as surpluses built up on the German balance of payments, the disparity being aggravated (as it so often was subsequently) by inflows of scared or speculative money. Harmony was briefly restored by the two French devaluations of 1957-1958 and the deliberate raising of British interest rates and lowering of German ones, aided by the worldwide slackening of economic activity in the recession of those years. Emminger quotes the Bundesbank verdict on 1958: "The economy probably came nearer than in any previous year to the famous 'magic triangle' of monetary and economic objectives—optimum employment, price stability and equilibrium in the balance of payments."[6]

Almost immediately afterward, the incapacity of German monetary policy to keep these three objectives in view against the contrary forces exerted by the United States was dramatically demonstrated. The "monetary broadside" thoughtlessly but destructively delivered by the Kennedy administration in 1960 showed how fragile the balance achieved by Germany between internal and external stability really was. The Federal Reserve system reduced its discount rate to 3.5 percent just one week after the Bundesbank had raised its rate to 5 percent, intending a restrictive influence on the economy. Its policy was completely "unhorsed" (in Emminger's phrase) by the increasing inflows of foreign exchange that followed. Putting external stability first, the Bundesbank went into reverse and lowered its interest rate. The United States had, in Eric Chalmers's vivid phrase, won a big battle in "the interest rate war."[7] Defensive measures, such as capital controls, were rejected, and German governments accepted the U.S. suggestion, strongly backed by Per Jacobsson for the IMF, that increased German aid and capital exports would ease the burden carried by the United States as well as restore some equilibrium to the German balance of payments. In addition, the Deutsche mark revaluation of 1961, it was hoped, would make imports more competitive, check wage demands, and thus reduce inflation at home as well as serve to restore external equilibrium.

By coincidence, any recurrence of the conflict between internal and external stability was avoided for about six years between 1962 and 1967, largely because of a temporary convergence between U.S. and German inflation rates and thanks to the rejection by the German government of a flexible exchange rate strategy—at that time still heartily disapproved by the United States and avoided by the European Community as conflicting with its integration strategies. From 1968 to 1971 and again in 1972, German domestic monetary policies had to adjust, with frequent agility and considerable ingenuity, to tidal inundations of liquidity coming from abroad and equally heavy outflows drawing liquidity from the German banking system. "Monetary policy," Emminger concluded, "was largely at the mercy of external ups and downs."[8]

These ups and downs, once again, were usually the result of sudden switches in U.S. interest rate policies, reflecting political priorities often dictated by the imminence (or other aspects) of American elections. More than other European countries, Germany was being obliged in effect to accept unusable dollar IOUs in very large amounts. At the beginning of 1970, the Bundesbank's net external assets were a modest 26 billion DM; by the end of May 1971, they were up to 68 billion DM, of which only 5.6 billion DM had been contributed by a surplus on current account. The same kind of tidal wave of monetary movement swept 18.6 billion DM into the Bundesbank in the first week of February 1973 and another 7.5 billion DM on March 1 of the same year. That date marked the final long-delayed end of the Bretton Woods system. Although the effect of its protracted death throes on the domestic money supply was described as disastrous, the end result was to gain freedom from the tyrannical and expensive combination of fixed exchange rates and free exchange markets and to regain at least partial control over domestic liquidity. The one thing floating did not do, of course, was to stabilize the external value of the Deutsche mark.

As in the 1930s, a system of floating rates impelled many countries to seek some stability by linking their currency to a stronger trading partner.

This tendency reappeared in the Smithsonian realignments and became more marked later on. The European Community's "snake in the tunnel," whose dependence on the stability of the dollar was demonstrated in 1971 even before it was formally initiated, was unable to survive any situation of uncertainty about dollar values in the foreign exchange markets. Flight *from* the dollar implied flight *to* a relatively strong European currency—the Swiss franc, the Deutsche mark, or the yen—quite independently of the objective economic conditions within the country concerned. Thus, the snake was rapidly transformed into a constellation of weaker currencies grouped around the Deutsche mark. Far from developing as a means to greater European integration, it became a source of increased monetary division among the members of the Community, separating them more than ever into three groups: those with strong, medium, and weak currencies.

Again, the objective differences between the national economies were not the prime cause of this deeper division. These certainly existed, but the monetary reflection, as in a concave mirror, was grossly exaggerated whenever the foreign exchange dealers had cause to revise their opinions about the prospects for the U.S. economy and the valuation to be put on the dollar. Meanwhile, European hopes—propelled by powerful political motives—were revived, plans were drafted, and proposals (from the French in 1975, the Dutch in 1976, and Roy Jenkins in 1977) were put forward.

But the basic reality did not change. And the increased cost of intervention to hold a weak or medium currency from dropping out of the snake was a further reflection of the same reality. That cost could be reduced, but only by diluting the definition of stable parity; by widening the snake into a boa; by finding technical devices to reduce the conditions on which intervention became mandatory; or by allowing repeated floats, realignments, and defections for deviant currencies. But the greater the dilution of the concept, the greater the centrifugal pulls on national economic management and the greater the prospective division between the strong and inflation-proof and the weak and inflation-prone currencies.

The inevitable conclusion expressed to his colleagues by the chairman of the European Community monetary committee, Jacques van Ypersele de Strihou, in his oral statement of March 1977 was that "for the foreseeable future it would not be feasible to introduce a coherent exchange rate policy system, if such a system were to go beyond consultations and also contain binding obligations whether in respect of general economic policy or exchange rate policy in particular."[9] As the previous annual report had made clear, a major basis for skepticism about the feasibility of adopting "target zones" for intra-Community exchange rates was the recognition by some members of the monetary committee that this involved intervention to maintain the stability of the *dollar* as well as the member currencies, and that this was a truly sisyphean task unless strongly supported by

U.S. monetary authorities and by U.S. policies (including U.S. energy policies) which affected the balance of payments. The resort to floating had not changed the essential characteristic of the international monetary system—that no significant change could be made in its operation without the consent and cooperation of the United States.

As far as Germany is concerned, the record of monetary contortions (especially since 1969)—as presented by several authoritative and knowledgeable economic analysts starting with Emminger—carries a message about the constraints on policy that seems quite clear.[10] There has been a rather remarkable constancy in the domestic constraints. Germany's devotion to stable money, and its determined pursuit of growth, exports, and employment have been some of the more remarkable and persistent features of the European landscape.

There has been a contrasting inconstancy in the external constraints laid down by the special relationship with the United States. In the 1950s, these constraints included fixed exchange rates, a fixed gold price, the conscientious pursuit by all (including the reserve currency countries) of equilibrium in external payments, and free trade within the world market economy but restricted trade with China and the Soviet bloc. By the 1970s, rates floated, the gold price was freed, and the pursuit of equilibrium was abandoned by a central country which solved the adjustment problem by an accelerated accumulation of inconvertible and depreciating dollar assets by others. Free trade has been redefined as fair (that is, managed) trade and the restrictions on East-West trade mostly removed. Whether described by analysts of international organization (such as Nye and Keohane) as a "regime change," by most economists as "the collapse of Bretton Woods" and the "demise of the dollar," or by the late Fred Hirsch and more radical critics as "international monetary disorder,"[11] there is wide and general agreement that a change in the external monetary environment has occurred, and that it is this, more than anything else, which has accounted for a series of defensive reactions by Germany among others. For the first half, roughly, of the Federal Republic's postwar existence as an independent state, the pursuit of its constant domestic goals had closely coincided with the wider goals of the United States and had been consistent with the broad character of the system. But in the latter half, from about 1965 or perhaps 1967, the coincidence disappeared and the divergence has steadily increased.

But for most of this second period, German policy, inside the Community and out, has attempted a defensive strategy suited to external circumstances, seeking to fend off damaging influence and to protect its freedom and capacity to pursue constant domestic goals. The support which at certain points Germany was prepared to give to the European snake has been widely, and I believe correctly, interpreted as primarily a self-interested strategy of trading off some loss of domestic monetary autonomy in order to have stricter discipline imposed on other Community countries. It was a calculated policy to avoid the spread of monetary infection, far more than a public-spirited bid to achieve closer European union through monetary alignment.[12]

The essentially inward-looking nature of German policy was recognized by Michael Kreile in the analysis already quoted. Speaking of Germany's contribution to the loan for Italy and its support for IMF aid to Britain, Kreile said that these acts "do not represent a will to power. Rather they represent defensive measures intended to stabilise trade partners."[13] Such passivity has reflected a profound absence of any sense of responsibility for the global system, a deep indifference to it *except as it affected Germany*. The confident assumption was that the United States could safely be left to get on with running the global system while Germany created for itself an island of stability immune to all that went on outside. The basic assumption was that there was no inherent conflict between the domestic and external constraints, between the pursuit of internal stability and loyal support for the United States—both as leader of the international monetary system and as protector in the international security system.

Whether or not Chancellor Schmidt's initiative at Copenhagen in April 1978 and the Bremen proposals for a European monetary system really reflect a strong wish to change roles, is still open to question. Two considerations may have induced a real shift of attitudes. One is the rising costs of avoiding major changes in the dollar-Deutsche mark exchange rate. From time to time, since the oil price rise in 1973, there have been serious attempts to maintain this axis by deliberate market intervention. It began to be noticeable in the summer and autumn of 1974 when the dollar was getting stronger and the Deutsche mark weaker. It was openly acknowledged by the 1975 annual report of the BIS, which recorded that the degree of success achieved by U.S.-German-Swiss interventions to steady the cross-rates had "not been outstanding—although some stability has been achieved." And it was adopted as a conscious aim by the Rambouillet conference of 1975. But since then, the costs have vastly increased and the results have been more and more disappointing. United States interventions have often been more than a little half-hearted, and the major burden has been carried by Germany. For example, between mid-January and mid-February of 1978, the Bundesbank spent 1.7 billion DM in a support operation for the dollar which proved quite futile against the strong convictions of the foreign exchange markets that it was losing value. In the second half of the year, another 10 billion dollars went down the same rathole. The combined interventions of 1977 and 1978 must have cost much more than 50 billion dollars. The doubling of the swap arrangement with the United States in March 1978 to a limit of 4 billion dollars was also ineffective in restoring confidence. The conclusion could be drawn that holding *any* Deutsche mark-dollar rate was sooner or later likely to be doomed and that stability of the exchange rate required at the very least the full supporting efforts of the United States and perhaps of the central banks of all the rich countries. Some observers have even noted that the "dollar overhang" (that is, of foreign liabilities of the United States over central bank resources) is approaching a four to one ratio and that therefore *any* central bank interventions will be powerless against the convictions of the market operators.[14]

A second consideration that might influence policy in Bonn is that in conditions of slow recovery from world recession, Germany finds that it needs first to work for stable rates with its best export customers. (Next to Britain, Germany's economy is now the most trade-dependent of the major industrialized countries, trade accounting for 22.8 percent of the GNP compared with 18 percent in 1960.) To keep German unemployment down, it is more important to maintain buoyant levels of intra-European trade than to keep open an American market that is not only far smaller but also far more subject to capricious door-slamming under the permissive provisions of the last trade act. Peter Hermes recently pointed out that 50 percent of all German exports now go to other European Community countries (65 percent to Europe as a whole) compared with only 5 percent to the United States and 6 percent to Eastern Europe. Had the Bonn summit raised any strong hopes that the United States would succeed in leading the world economy to full recovery, or had the Carter administration shown convincing signs of meaning to arrest the dollar's decline, the trade figures might not be so important. As things are, it is only logical for Germany to turn more decisively toward its European partners.

But how far, and with what sense of permanent commitment? The basic proposition put forward in the Bremen proposals was for concerted intervention by Community central banks in order to keep (as before) the stronger currencies inside the "snake" but also to keep the weaker currencies inside a wider band (or boa) twice as wide as the snake.[15] The scheme was scheduled to come into operation by January 1, 1979, although it was clear after Bremen that many difficult questions had first to be resolved. (In the event, the formal inauguration of the EMS was delayed not by the British, who refused for domestic political reasons to join, but by the French, who insisted at the eleventh hour on prior agreement with Germany on the issue of agricultural prices.) The earlier arrangement between the four countries and Germany which had been associated in the so-called snake had committed each to maintaining its currency in a grid of bilateral exchange rates, rising no more than 2 percent above the weakest and falling no more than 2¼ percent below the strongest. The EMS arrangement, under French pressure and with support from Britain, instead contemplated the use of a basket of currencies, the European currency unit (ECU), in place of the dollar as a pivot for intra-EMS rates. But the way the ECU worked when used to indicated divergence from a central rate for currencies with a large weight in the basket was different from the way it worked for those with a small one. The compromise reached between the grid system and the basket system inevitably left many practical details unclear. Moreover, the picture was complicated by the fact that Italy, which at first had feared to join the lira to the EMS, later negotiated an arrangement to allow a 6 percent (instead of a 2¼ percent) margin around the ECU. Settlements in the European monetary system were to be made not in dollars or their equivalent, but in ECUs. The participating countries meanwhile would increase their mutual credit commitment and would pool 20 percent of their respective gold and dollar holdings to form a fund, denominated in ECUs and available for coordinated intervention in the foreign exchange markets. The valuation of the gold contributed was one open question. Another more important one was the degree of monetary discipline to be exerted on weaker currency countries when they needed to draw on the fund or to seek the support of the partners.

The basic strategy, however, is clear enough: one of collective self-defense against the continuing and threatened depreciation of the dollar, a kind of Lone Rangers Incorporated role, played jointly by the members of the Community. It cannot, however, succeed by itself in its prime aim of keeping European Community cross-rates stable for reasons that have already been stated in this chapter. Or, at least, it cannot succeed except by keeping the dollar stable, which is too difficult and costly a task for Europeans to undertake unless they have the full cooperation of the United States.

What will happen, as it has happened so often before, is that when confidence in the current valuation of the dollar fails (as it may do in reaction to quite frivolous or arbitrary political events) the seesaw mechanism tips the stronger currencies upward; they bounce as high as the dollar falls low. The weaker currencies are left below with the dollar. The difficulties encountered in achieving the Bremen goal of a "zone of monetary stability in Europe" were well explained by the chairman of the European Community monetary committee, Jacques van Ypersele, a Belgian.

> When people move out of the dollar because there is a lack of confidence, they do not move equally into all the European currencies. They move specifically to one currency in Western Europe, the mark. This pushes the mark up and it widens the relationship between the mark and the French franc or sterling. So one can say that sharp fluctuations of the dollar have also, in a certain way, contributed to sharp fluctuations between European currencies. And when I say "too sharp" fluctuations what I mean is fluctuations much in excess of what would be allowed by differential rates of inflation between European currencies.[16]

Equally, the relatively smooth passage of European currencies in the last month or two of 1978 owed a good deal to the measures announced by

President Carter on November 1. These included an impressive 30 billion dollar reserve of foreign currency for the New York Federal Reserve Bank to draw on, the use of higher interest rates, and (in effect) special guarantees in the form of issues of U.S. bonds denominated in Deutsche marks and Swiss francs. What is still uncertain is, first, whether this package was a response to the EMS initiative or (more likely) to the threatening signs from the markets; and second, whether the November package will be enough; and if not, whether the United States is prepared to act still more positively to maintain the value of the dollar.

For if it is not, the logic of the situation seems clear enough. Only a strategy of concerted opposition to the United States, using all the available means of leverage, to make the United States resist the temptations that beckon every authority capable of controlling a monetary medium, can possibly succeed. The dollar in the international monetary system is somewhat like an ultimate, irresistible weapon in a security system. If those who control it abuse their responsibility, the only chance that others have of arresting that abuse is to use all the means available to them of collective leverage against that country.

To put it bluntly, the only effective strategy of collective security—in monetary just as in military matters—must involve more than passive resistance. There must be some readiness to take the initiative, even to defend one's own security by threatening that of one's opponent or partner. Admittedly, in a monetary system, the fragility of confidence in the whole structure imposes closer limits on the use of coercive threats. But it is still true that collective monetary security for Europe cannot be achieved without some resort to coercive pressure, without some attempt at active initiatives not just within the Community but also in the global monetary system. The concept of coexisting autonomous regional blocs—in money as in trade—is inconsistent with the familiar reality of twenty-four-hour, round-the-world financial markets, with international banking and insurance, with all the innumerable international channels for financial flows. These flows are now so many and various that, like some kind of worldwide underground drainage system, the surface walls and barriers erected by regional blocs have very little impact on the ebbs and flows below. The EMS proposals, therefore, can only succeed as part of a broader strategy of concerted opposition. They cannot succeed merely as Lone Rangers Incorporated; and the strategy requires the transformation of Germany from an obedient ally into leader of that opposition.

Let us now try to translate labels into practical politics and to draw normative conclusions from this analysis. Let us suppose first that the United States administration fails to hold the dollar to a stable value, and that no appeals to American goodwill toward the EMS avail because the failure is a result of weakness and inertia rather than deliberate ill will. The inevitable repercussions are felt in intra-EMS exchange rates. Germany and the Community might then contemplate taking the monetary offensive. Instead of buying dollars or selling Deutsche marks to maintain the rate, some part of the EMS fund might be used to buy a basket of EMS currencies—the ingredients of the ECU. These might then be issued as grants or soft loans to the most severely afflicted in their import policies by the burdens of debt, then to the ACP (African, Caribbean and Pacific) associates of the Community and other selected trade partners in Latin America, Asia, and possibly in Eastern Europe.

At first, this would have the effect of accelerating the dollar's decline in foreign exchange markets and therefore, for reasons just explained, of increasing the disparity between the Deutsche mark and the weaker currencies, especially the lira and sterling. To counteract this, the ECU credits to less developed countries would have to be a form of asymmetrically tied aid, more of which would have to be spent in the weak currency nations of the Community than in the strong. In return for this boost to exports, the weak currency countries would have to agree to observe stricter monetary disciplines and to maintain open trade policies toward the Community members, including Germany. At the same time, the ECU securities so created could be offered to third parties like Japan and the OPEC countries as reserve assets, perhaps index-linked to an agreed basket of traded goods, manufactured goods as well as commodities.

In Germany, no doubt, it will be objected that such an offensive strategy involves the acceptance of the reserve currency role, and that this is something which German opinion from all parties has unanimously and persistently rejected on the grounds that it has had an observable debilitating effect on the economies of those countries—notably Britain and the United States—whose currencies have been used in this way. Perhaps it is time that, instead of accepting unthinkingly this piece of conventional wisdom, Germans should ponder two facts. One is that playing a reserve role from a position of strength is very different from playing it from one of weakness. And even when—as in the early 1960s—both the British and American balance of payments were in deficit, it was the weaker, not the stronger, of the two reserve currencies that suffered. Of course, as in a bimetallist monetary system, the opportunities this offers for switching funds from one type of asset to the other is a source of instability in the system and is not ideal for anyone. But perhaps as a second-best solution, it is better to have one relatively stable reserve currency than none at all.

The second fact is that as external holdings of Deutsche mark assets creep inexorably upward and as dealings in Euro-marks multiply, the reserve role is already being thrust upon Germany whether it likes it or not. Now, therefore, the time may have come when, as leader of a European opposition, Germany could derive some real leverage on the United States through open acceptance in combination with others of such a reserve role.

Such a strategy could also be constructive in shaping European Community policy toward the member countries of the Council for Mutual Economic Aid (COMECON) countries. A glaring weakness over the last five years or so in Community relations has been the total absence of any concerted policy for the surveillance and management of COMECON debt. The political folly of outbidding each other to offer soft loans to Poland and other Eastern European countries to finance their orders for ships and other capital goods is a true example of beggar-thy-neighbor economic policies. But ECU loans on jointly negotiated terms could be a valuable political weapon.

The other policy area to which an effective monetary opposition led by Germany would have to give some attention is that of the regulations governing banks and financial markets. In the aftermath of the Herstatt collapse in 1974, the anxiety of international bankers has been primarily allayed by the actions of U.S. monetary authorities, especially the U.S. comptroller of the currency. On the whole, it was the U.S. banks, seeking to maintain profitability by aggressive lending abroad, especially in Latin America, that were most exposed to risk consequent upon a chain reaction from default. But everywhere, European banks have been associated with them. And now, instead of American and British banks, it is often German banks that are in the lead. It was they, for instance, who took the initiative in arranging consortium jumbo loans of one billion dollars each to Spain and Venezuela in 1976 and to Sweden in 1977. And the outflow of German capital far beyond the confines of the Costa Brava is accelerating yearly. Yet the universal bank principle on which the German banks have been accustomed to operate may carry important risks for the domestic economy of Germany—and, by association, for those of its European neighbors and banking associates. In the nineteenth century, the British found it necessary to separate domestic from overseas banking, as later did the Americans. The Swiss also decided that stricter regulation was necessary when their banks first became deeply engaged in foreign operations.

For its own security and that of others, the surveillance of Community banks engaged in foreign lending may need to be tightened, as may the control exercised over active markets in London or Luxembourg. For Germany to wait until after the 1980 elections (as some political observers have advised) before grasping this nettle may be to wait too long. The assumption that the U.S. monetary authorities would show much concern if German banks got into difficulties abroad is probably not justified even while Germany looks like an obedient ally; as leader of the opposition there would be additional need for self-preservation from the widely recognized dangers of financial panic. It may also be necessary, in order to reinforce the efficacy of national monetary authorities, to initiate collective measures—possibly through the Bank for International Settlements—to monitor the extent and nature of bank lending to particular developing countries, to high-risk sectors like shipbuilding or to individual borrowers.

In summary, the EMS as it stands displays a distressing mentality which in military terms might be called the mentality of the Maginot Line: "sit tight; close the hatches; and hope for the best." But almost a decade of effort to align European currencies has shown the increasing futility of such a strategy in the conditions of the 1970s. It could only work if *either* the dollar were so stable that it created no upsetting turbulence in other parts of the system; *or* if the European Community were so insulated from that system by a common external wall of exchange controls, investment, and trade controls superimpenetrable and so effctive that it would be immune to any economic policy pursued by the United States. Without some such wall at least as efficient as the Iron Curtain around the COMECON group in the 1960s or a wall similar to the barriers protecting the sterling area and the franc zone in the 1950s, European monetary union is either a sham or vulnerable. It is only necessary for the dollar to suffer a sudden slide, for the financial cost to Germany of maintaining snakes and boas to prove too great, and for the political costs to Britain and Italy of keeping the rules to be too severe, for the EMS to collapse and to go the way of its predecessors. A fresh start has to be made—and it has to be led by Germany—but a Germany that has finally shed the fond delusion that it can shut its eyes, keep its nose clean, and leave the problem of managing global monetary interdependence to the Americans.

Notes

1. Susan Strange, *Sterling and British Policy*, (1971), London, Oxford University Press, chapter 1.

2. Fred Bergsten, *Toward a New International Economic Order: Selected Papers of C. Fred Bergsten 1972-1974*(1975), Lexington, Mass., Lexington Books, D.C. Heath, p. 342.

3. Ronald I. McKinnon, "A New Tripartite Monetary Agreement, or a Limping Dollar Standard," Princeton Essay No. 106 (1974), p. 17.

4. See S.V.O. Clarke, *Central Bank Cooperation 1924-1931* (1967), New York, Federal Reserve Bank of New York. Also the essay by C. Kindleberger on secondary financial centers.

5. Michael Kreile, "West Germany, the Dynamics of Expansion," *International Organization* Autumn 1977:785-886.

6. Otmar Emminger, "The D-mark in the Conflict Between Internal and External Stability," Princeton Essay No. 122 (1977), p. 11.

7. Eric Chalmers, *The International Interest Rate War* (London, MacMillan Press, 1972).

8. Emminger, "D-mark in Conflict," p. 24.

9. Annexe to the 19th annual report of the EC monetary committee, *Official Journal*, July 3, 1978.

10. Annexe II of 18th annual report of the EC monetary committee on Community exchange rate arrangements noted (paragraph 7) the reasoning of those opposed to target zones and succinctly summarized the argument as follows: "It was further argued that, both because of the dollar's general importance as a vehicle and reserve currency, and because of its different weight in member countries' external transactions, it will be difficult to achieve a reasonable degree of stability between snake and non-snake member currencies (and even to avoid tensions within the snake) without concerted endeavors to keep exchange rate movements between the snake and the dollar within reasonable bounds." *Official Journal,* August 15, 1977.

11. See R.O. Keohane and J. Nye, *Power and Interdependence,* (1977), Boston, Little, Brown and Company, chap. 1; and Fred Hirsch and Michael Doyle, *Alternatives to International Monetary Disorder.* (1977), New York, McGraw-Hill.

12. See Peter Hermes, "Germany's Responsibility in the World Economy," *Aussenpolitik,* March 1977; Michael Kreile, "Dynamics of Expansion;" Rudolph Herlt, "Der Dollar Schock: Seine Folgen und der Aussichten zu Ihrer Ubervunching," *Europa-Archiv* June 1978.

13. Kreile, "Dynamics of Expansion," p. 807.

14. This argument, however, is based on the assumption that central banks have no control over their reserves. But just as Lloyd George could *if necessary* create unlimited new members of the British House of Lords, so central bankers *if necessary* could create for each other unlimited quantities of foreign exchange. That there would be costs and dangers in doing so is another matter.

15. The "snake" is an exhange-rate agreement whereby the participating currencies cannot fluctuate vis `a vis each other by more than a defined maximum spread, thus giving rise to a joint movement in relation to nonparticipating currencies, such as the dollar. When charted on a time axis, this movement resembles a snake. The first effort to form a European monetary "snake" occurred in the early 1970s, following recommendations of the Werner Plan.

16. *The Listener* (London), October 5, 1979. The tendency of the markets to exaggerate differential consequences for European currencies is also one of the points made in a recent and characteristically brilliant analysis of these issues by Robert Tultin, "Gold and the Dollar Crisis: Yesterday and Tomorrow," Princeton Essay, December 1978.

4

Germany and the Coordination of Stabilization Policies among the OECD Countries

Hans-Herbert Weber

Germany as a Partner in the OECD

German economic performance during the last three decades has met with respect and sometimes been envied by foreign observers. But this attitude has given way to a less emotional and more political one: With growing economic and political stature, Germany is expected not only to live up to its normal responsibilities to itself (of looking after its own growth and stability), but also to assume some kind of leadership in a worldwide context. Can—and should—Germany accept this noble assignment? Leadership presupposes that there is a true chance to exert influence on other countries. Since we do not think in terms of political pressure, the only features that might impress others would be a convincing record of successful economic policy and the persuasive force of argument.

Concerning Performance

Germany has been growing fast and has still kept its inflation rate relatively low. But on both counts, the record has not been so good since 1975. Germany is the second largest trading nation, and there is certainly something impressive about the penetration of world markets. But the persistence of the current account surplus and the fact that Germany is the richest country in terms of foreign reserves gives rise to criticism—and certainly does not qualify it for leadership. Anyway, it would be inappropriate to suggest that a relatively good combination of economic growth and stability, together with an international creditor position, are indicators justifying a rivalry in leadership with the United States. Besides, it would be unwise to seek supremacy in a European context over another member of the Community.

For quite a long period (up to the present day), political and social stability in Germany has been appreciated internationally, but its price stability often has been thought of as a rather quaint peculiarity which cannot be fully explained by sad historical experiences with inflation. In German thinking, price stability is, in fact, considered instrumental in making a market-oriented economy work, keeping competition sufficiently intense, and avoiding misinvestment. In view of this, German policymakers are willing to endure increased difficulties in ensuring enough wage restraint and more difficulties in maintaining or regaining a satisfactory employment level and growth rate.

Prospects of Germany remaining a model economy have become dimmed in recent years. True, the merits of a market economy are still there, bringing with them a good measure of elasticity to adapt to changing conditions. The trade union organization is still acting reasonably, but some of the wage discipline has gotten lost. And the industriousness of German workers and employees has become less pronounced.

Apart from the slow change in the sociopolitical factors just described, it should be remembered that decision making in Germany seems to get more difficult too. It is true that Germany has a law to promote growth and stability, offering a set of instruments instantly applicable under eased parliamentary procedures. But they have scarcely been put to use in just the way outlined in the law. For political reasons, these measures were applied in a modified form and, therefore, had to undergo normal legislative procedures. And the idea behind that piece of legislation; namely, the tripartite consensus about how to attain the target combination laid down in the law, proved very difficult to achieve, despite the famous concerted action. Policy performance consequently was not so good: There have been decision lags and misleading projections causing wrong kinds of behavior. Incomes policy did not really materialize, and fiscal measures were hampered by the federalist structure. But after all, it might be said in all modesty that there probably have been less policy mistakes in Germany than elsewhere. To some persons responsible for economic policy in Bonn, this must have been a consolation whenever they got angry about wrong decisions at home.

Concerning Persuasion

The attitude of German representatives in international bodies is a modest one. They avoid pointing too much to laudable German character traits or policy achievements. They try to explain our own ways to manage our economy and often complain about political obstacles to measures proposed by technocrats. They abstain from lecturing other people, knowing that certain basic sociopolitical structures are too firmly grounded to undergo quick changes. And too often, they feel at a loss about what advice could be given, simply because they do not know enough about foreign countries' legal powers and political possibilities.

On the other hand, the German representatives are reluctant to accept advice from their colleagues if they think these prescriptions could be dangerous to stability or contrary to their convictions about the appropriateness of certain types of measures in a market economy. And it is no use denying that there is another sore spot: Sometimes there is a feeling that certain recommendations are addressed to Germany with the intention of making Germany pay for the deficiencies of other people. In summary, it is no easy task to defend price stability in a world that is not afraid of inflation and is all too confident that cyclical slack can be remedied mainly by more expansion of demand.

The Organization for Economic Cooperation and Development (OECD) bodies normally do not make decisions. Rather, they concentrate on roundtable examinations and discussions. The topics most frequently treated are growth and payments equilibrium. And this means the perennial choice: inflation versus stability; growth and employment versus payments imbalance. The magic word is adjustment, and since the days of the OECD Working Party 3 report of 1966 on the balance of payments adjustment process, the battle of words and convictions is carried on about mutual responsibilities and burden sharing.

I could think of no better method to describe the German position during these policy discussions than to review the following main issues: (1) international liquidity and stability; (2) oil and other deficits; (3) floating and adjustment; and (4) adjustment by demand management.

International Liquidity and Stability

Each time the figures on international liquidity creation are reviewed, "experts" are deeply impressed by what has happened. In October 1964, the Group of Ten (G-10) ministers stated that the total availability of international reserves and financing facilities, supported by the General Agreement to Borrow of 1961 and by the Basel swap arrangements initiated in 1962, was fully adequate to allow the world economy to expand. At that time, G-10 countries and Switzerland owned foreign reserve assets of nearly 50 billion dollars. In addition, credit facilities available to the same group of countries amounted to 13 billion dollars.

In spite of their satisfaction, G-10 ministers asked a study group to look for possibilities to create additional reserve assets (Ossola Group). Six years later (in 1969) the International Monetary Fund (IMF) was authorized to issue Special Drawing Rights (SDRs). Such assets were created to the tune of 9.5 billion dollars between 1970 and 1973.

This issue, according to U.S. views, was not intended to make a net addition to existing international liquidity growth, but merely to compensate for the slowdown of dollar outflows brought about by the expected return of the United States to balance of payments equilibrium.[1] But during the following years, there were more U.S. deficits causing increased pressure on exchange rates and forcing many countries into floating. The newly created SDRs came on top of this. During the years 1970 to 1973, international liquidity increased by about 105 billion dollars, of which 51 billion constituted direct official claims on the United States, and another 20 billion official holdings of Euro-dollars.

A second wave of liquidity creation, totaling 46 billion dollars, followed promptly in 1974 and 1975. Even before this, dollar holdings were considered to be excessive by some central banks. Already in 1972 the G-10 ministers had ordered a study on the reform of the monetary system, including possibilities of controlling this kind of liquidity creation. In the Outline of Reform (1974) we find the idea of substituting surplus dollars for SDRs which were designed to be placed at the center of the system. But after the oil price shock in October 1973, the G-10 in Rome put off this part of the reform and forgot all about excess dollars.

At present we find ourselves in the middle of a new wave of dollar liquidity rushing from a record U.S. deficit of almost 30 billion dollars in 1977, which continued into 1978. Most of this deficit had to be financed by increased dollar holdings of G-10 central banks, intervening in support of the dollar without being able to stabilize it. Net interventions by G-10 central banks led to a reserve increase of almost 36 billion dollars during 1977, accounting for even more than the U.S. deficit on current account (29.3 billion dollars). This allowed the United Kingdom and Italy to replenish their reserves substantially, which was welcome until it began to jeopardize domestic monetary policies. For Germany and Japan, the reserve increase was less desirable from the beginning, and for the same reasons.

Germany felt much concern during all of these years about the tremendous amount and rapid growth of this uncontrolled liquidity creation. Germans are not the only ones who believe that such a pace in liquidity creation has something to do with world inflation which, in fact, reached its peak from 1973 to 1975. Admittedly, the oil price increase made anti-inflationary policies much more difficult to pursue. But the easy availability of reserve assets and credit facilities undoubtedly did more than just facilitate the financing of oil deficits. Under the impact of crisis, it was agreed too quickly that large economies were unable to adjust and, therefore, there should be easy access to deficit financing.

The lesson from this experience evidently has not been learned. In full view of another bout of uncontrolled liquidity creation stemming from the U.S. deficit, another issue of SDRs has been proposed. In German opinion, this does not seem to be justified. However, there is no supreme court to examine the validity of arguments in the context of Article XVIII, section 1a of the IMF statute. Decisions on such creation of controlled liquidity are preceded by staff studies and by an exchange of views in IMF, OECD, and Community bodies. But both the studies and the views are political ones, and eventually there has to be a political compromise.

Oil and Other Deficits

The first burst of international liquidity (1970-1972) was enough to do away with the system of fixed exchange rates, and the oil price shock led to quick agreement among industrial countries that oil deficits had to be accepted.

Germany had no difficulty supporting the view that most countries would have to finance their oil deficits by incurring debt *until* the increased oil bill could be paid for in real terms. The question, however—how long this financing could and should continue—was left unanswered. The following years demonstrated that few countries were able to realize the real transfer quickly. Germany succeeded in turning its trade deficit with the OPEC (including oil) which amounted to 13.3 billion DM in 1974 into a surplus of around 1 billion DM in 1977. A similar success was recorded by the Netherlands and Japan. But other economies failed to capture a larger share of newly opening OPEC markets.

Experts had thought that the United States would be less affected by the oil price increase because of its large domestic energy production. However, some years *after* the crisis, it turned out that the United States developed a particularly large oil deficit, accompanied by a rising trade deficit with Japan. This was certainly not considered a beneficial contribution to adjustment. But it is interesting to note that international experts, thinking more in terms of growth policies than in terms of adjustment, tended to feel that it would be rather dangerous if the United States tried to redress its current account. Even in 1977 they advised the United States not to slow down its cyclical upswing, in spite of the emerging record current account deficit of about 20 billion dollars and the downfall of the dollar in exchange markets. The United States was excused from quick adjustment, with the exception of energy policy. And even this was not criticized regarding the efficiency of the measures envisaged, but merely regarding the legislative delay.

Time and again, the German representatives had stated that Germany would accept a deficit in the current account, a reduction of its exchange reserves, an appropriate measure of appreciation of the Deutsche mark rate, and a reduction in the German share in world markets. Germany did expect its partners to really *earn* their way by normal competition. But evidently most countries, even when benefiting from currency depreciation, seemed unable to exploit growing markets for themselves, with the exception of the United Kingdom—although the export rise looks limited to oil—and

Italy, where the improvement in the current balance had to be paid for by too little growth in the gross national product.

Recognizing the needs of other countries less able to react, Germany cooperated fully to make the financing of oil deficits easy. The government refrained almost completely from approaching the Euro-markets for budgetary financing, well aware of more urgent needs on the part of neighbor countries. Recycling of funds through official channels was approved wholeheartedly. Germany was ready to participate in the OECD support fund (which was deadlocked in the United States Congress) and it presented a scheme of its own for an investment fund for oil dollars (an idea originally proposed by Treasury Secretary G. Shultz but also discarded soon). Germany was among the first that contributed to the IMF oil facility, agreed to the extended fund facility (1972), subsidized the trust fund (created in 1976 out of IMF gold sales), and voted in favor of the Witteveen facility.

Germany felt the only concern related to the stability of Euro-market operations. In 1974, there was uncertainty about the ability of Euro-markets to handle the recycling problem. Rechanneling oil dollars to where they were most needed was officially supported by giving relevant information to banks. But there was less coordination between banks and governments than some thought necessary. For a while at least, Euro-markets became more cautious after the Herstatt failure. This failure surely was a warning against overextension in general. German officials seemed to be more concerned than others about possible overexposure of individual banks. Failures could have led to chain reactions. We looked, therefore, for measures of improving market transparency and bank supervision. But since the authorities in other centers of Euro-market activity (London and Luxembourg) did not share our concern, international action has not been taken yet.

In all, deficit financing from official and private sources did not pose too many problems during 1974 and 1975. In the following year, some countries began to feel the limits of their credit worthiness. This soon induced them simply to ask for more official financing facilities. If they continue to succeed with this line of thought, easy financing of deficits will go on and balance of payments adjustment will, in all probability, have to wait.

Floating and Adjustment

When the oil crisis came, Germany was happy to see its exchange rate already floating with other "snake" currencies. Since the end of 1972, the Deutsche mark had been appreciating against the dollar; it had appreciated 33 percent by September 1973. This had been called overdone, that is, it was more than what was required to offset changes in relative export prices. But Germany did not counteract and, as a consequence, expected a noticeable reduction in the current account surplus. At that time, nobody dared to expect that five years later (in September 1978) the Deutsche mark would have risen by 66 percent against the dollar. The 1977 surplus, however, still equaled that of 1973.

After the oil crisis, floating was considered quite useful to absorb shocks like this. On the other hand, there was a widespread desire for rules and surveillance. It was also felt that economies might be pushed apart and additional inflationary impulses generated, since the effects of exchange rate changes were likely to show less quickly on current accounts than on prices. As sterling and lira became very weak, experts argued that depreciation resulting from actual or anticipated high rates of inflation could tend to perpetuate through the effect of high import prices on wages. This vicious circle proves particularly vicious, indeed, when there is an automatic price-wage indexation or escalator clause, as is the case in Italy.

In German opinion, the vicious circle theory does not go very far because no exchange rate change can have the intended effect on the balance of payments if complementary domestic demand policies are missing. According to German views, monetary policy, although it should not and need not be directed exclusively and always toward external objectives, can have a strong effect on the exchange rate. In the countries concerned, there is a well-recognized need for monetary restraint on purely domestic grounds, and this would also be helpful in limiting any overshooting by the exchange rate.

Germany was not overly afraid of the Deutsche mark appreciation. Only when the dollar began its rapid decline in relation to the Deutsche mark in October 1977 was there some nervousness on the German side. Partly this was an uncertainty about how long it would continue. Partly it had to be seen as a reflex of United States teachings on which growth policies would be appropriate for Germany. Generally overshooting was seen as something to complain about. In other cases, the same phenomenon was named real exchange rate change, and then—curiously enough—it was welcomed because only such changes could be expected to help in the adjustment of current accounts. There was even disappointment about the failure of floating to bring about lasting real exchange rate changes that could really reduce the imbalance of current accounts. This judgment is not easy to understand. Floating exchange rates could not be expected to do more than just reflect the relative competitive positions; they could not change these positions. And as long as there is no practical way to enforce real exchange rate changes by policy measures, or to make them last, countries can hardly do anything but rely on domestic measures bearing on the current account.

Adjustment by Demand Management

Disappointed with the role that floating rates were able to play in balance of payments adjustment, and recognizing the fact that easy deficit financing tends to delay adjustment, the international leaders took a new turn late in 1976: The recession that was so stubbornly plaguing most industrial and developing countries perhaps was to be remedied by differential demand management.

Without any doubt, demand management is to be regarded as an appropriate policy complementary to exchange rate changes. It has the advantage of showing effects on rather short notice, while exchange rate changes need around two or three years to work themselves through. But it was not simple demand management that was recommended, but a somewhat refined version called differential demand management. According to this prescription, the main responsibility would rest with countries in a strong balance of payments position, while weak countries would more or less be excused from applying any kind of demand restraint as long as their GNP growth was less than modestly positive. Here again, we were confronted with the old theme of burden sharing. When this idea was first mentioned, Germany could still point to a 5 percent GNP growth prospect and an increase of 16 percent of import volume (as against a mere 13 percent for export volume). The call for differential demand management in Germany did not seem imperative.

More important, however, was the feeling that the exemption for weak countries from applying monetary restraint lacked credibility, as it is well known that several countries suffering from strong inflationary pressures are badly in need of some monetary restraint, but are unable or unwilling to apply effective measures. They should not be excused simply because their legal and political structure leads to an institutionalized habit of having fiscal expenditures financed directly by their central bank. If this argument is acceptable in international discussions, it is only fair to accept arguments presented by the German side which explain that demand management, in certain cases, does not seem to be a very promising way to cope with economic slack.

Recent German experience has shown that demand is not so easy to manage. What *can* be managed is bank liquidity and, by tax relief and deficit spending, liquidity in the hands of consumers and investors, including public authorities. Whether or not this liquidity will and can be transformed into effective demand is an open question.

Our recent programs for public expenditure have proved difficult to set up. In conditions of present-day Germany, the preference is for public investment. But once a country has gone through a decade during which public investment projects have been carried out massively, it is not easy to recommend still more additions to infrastructure to those levels of government where, in a federal system, building and construction projects are planned and executed. Even if, for general economic reasons, such projects are called for, it is difficult to persuade local authorities to incur still more debt when they feel overburdened already—when there is some overinvestment in house buildings, and surplus capacity in kindergartens, elementary schools, and high schools; when municipal receation facilities and modern town halls are plentiful, and when there is even a surplus of hospital beds. In a situation like this, the German government in its program of 16 billion DM for four years, concentrated on environmental improvements and technological research. But even such a program would appear to be a feeble attempt at relaunching an economy in which investment expenditure by all public authorities amounts to only 16 percent of total investment.

The private sector, too, seemed to need some impetus to step up investment. In fact, there had been hardly any net real investment in industry since 1970. But undeniably, there is a widespread hesitation to make additions to industrial capacity while existing capacities still are underemployed, and there is a tendency to focus investment on labor-saving projects, given the fast increase in labor cost (wages and social contributions) during recent years. In all, there seemed to be no great chance to step up investment through tax measures.

Finally, there is a possibility of increasing consumer demand. Germany had been told to try this, in view of its propensity to import which seems to have increased noticeably during recent years. In this way, much of the supply would come from foreign countries—a prospect fitting nicely with the locomotive theory. It can be seen easily that in this case, the main benefit would not go to German production and employment, but to other countries.

The desire to see the German external surplus vanishing is understandable and even justified in the interest of international equilibrium. As already mentioned, Germany agreed to accept a current account deficit for a number of years, and to accept loose exchange reserves. This was and still is an official attitude and not just lip service. However, it is extremely difficult to envision an economic scenario in which Germany would run a trade deficit. A large part of German industry has been producing for world markets. This export-oriented capacity has been created over the last two decades, partly because of a long period of undervaluation of the Deutsche mark. This part of industrial capacity would go unutilized, implying unemployment, or would have to be converted to produce goods for domestic use. Both solutions would cause major problems.

No expert or international organization would be able to describe a pattern of production for Germany that would correspond to a trade or current account deficit or even to equilibrium, and, at the same time, remain compatible with an appropriate level of employment. There would have to be industrial or tertiary sectors expanding enough to assure sufficient employment. But it would be very difficult to define them, and more so to describe policy measures that would reduce capacities in one branch and, at the same time, give expansionary impulses to other sectors with medium-term growth prospects.

Similar problems would arise in an attempt to stimulate imports up to the point of near current account equilibrium. This clearly cannot be achieved through specific import stimulation. And it still has to be explained to us how this could be done through demand management.

Note

1. The early availability of SDRs removes one of the concerns as to the impact of the U.S. balance of payments program, namely, a slowing of reserve growth and a consequent adverse effect on world trade and income.

> *If new reserves* of the appropriate kind are flowing into the system, it *is* possible for some countries to satisfy their preferences to reserve increases without necessitating that other countries be in corresponding deficit.

From *Maintaining the Strength of the Dollar in a Strong Free World Economy*, U.S. Treasury, January 1968, pp. 9 and 36.

5 Bonn and European Political Cooperation

Reinhardt Rummel

Compatibility of German and European Foreign Policy

In the second half of 1978, the Federal Republic of Germany was holding the presidency in the Community. Hans-Dietrich Genscher was chairman of the Ministerial Council of the European Community as well as of the European Political Cooperation (EPC). If one had asked the German foreign minister about his views on Germany and European political cooperation, the answer would probably have been as follows:

> European unification remains the first priority of German foreign policy. This creates no conflict with our readiness to assume a greater share of responsibility—in keeping with the political and economic impact of the Federal Republic—throughout the world and in the United Nations. Our response to problems in other areas of the world fits into the co-operation among the EC States. European Political Cooperation, which we and our partners are continually developing, reinforces the international profile and impact of the Nine.

> The on-going exchange of views and the close coordination of the positions which the Nine take on all important international issues are to us a point of departure and a source of support in bilateral relations and in our activities in international organizations and at international conferences. Just as European Political Cooperation helps to strengthen the Community it, in turn, requires a strong European Community as the base. Sound progress towards European unification therefore remains one of our fundamental interests.[1]

This statement is remarkable above all for its reference to the broad agreement between German and European policies which are seen largely as an entity. In the past when a country held the presidency in the European Community, it often turned out very difficult for the official representatives of the presidency to represent and promote national and Community positions at the same time. Not so with Bonn. Not in the second half of 1970, the first half of 1974, or the second half of 1978 have complaints been voiced by any of the partner countries regarding the German execution of office. The Bonn diplomacy seems to be quite at ease with the state of "two souls dwelling in its breast"—even when it does not hold the presidency.

73

Bonn has good reasons to keep national and community affairs compatible. For the Federal Republic, the nation state has not been as central a yardstick as it has been to other member countries. Germany had more the psychological problem of belonging to somebody somewhere. Of course, there is also the objective fact of being involved in a highly interdependent world. All these factors have produced a background in favor of cooperation and unification with other nations.[2] But the more Germany became stronger economically, the more it was perceived as giving up its European-mindedness.

The general topic of Germany's role in the Community is hardly a major nor a desired issue with the German Foreign Office, much less the subject of this chapter. Those people working on the EPC within the Foreign Office today are hardly aware of how important the establishment of the EPC in 1970 was for their Ministry as well as for their foreign minister.[3] Successively Walter Scheel and Hans-Dietrich Genscher have tried to profit from the EPC in representative terms. This was especially important for domestic reasons, both serving as vice chancellor and chief of the smaller coalition party alike. The Foreign Office received with the EPC an exclusive voice on European politics in the German administration. Other Community affairs had been and still are managed cooperatively with the responsible section of the Ministry of Economics.

But there was more important cause for German satisfaction with the start of foreign policy cooperation, which had been conceived and organized with active participation by Germany from the very outset. The EPC was pursued primarily as a step toward political union, an objective that could only be pursued, in German eyes, on a pragmatic basis. The technical argument put forth was that foreign policy cooperation would help shape the necessary basic orientation for the Community's increasingly expanding foreign trade policy. It is this concomitant function, however, which the EPC so far has lived up to the least.[4]

What has been achieved within the Nine (the nine members of the European Community) is at best a common outlook on several policy areas: Atlantic alliance, East-West detente, relations with southern European countries and the Arab states, development processes in southern Africa, and several United Nations topics. The actual extension of identical or compatible attitudes of the Nine is difficult to outline. Although it goes beyond public declarations of the Nine, the consultation mechanism takes only limited account of the national elements of the member states' foreign policies. EPC activities are furthermore restricted by three factors: first, the EPC lacks a binding nature, for cooperation is based solely on political commitments; second, foreign policy concertation remains confined to noneconomic and nonmilitary aspects of foreign policy, which means that the only means of action is the diplomatic "software"; and third, the EPC's internal rules of the game are largely geared to a policy of responses, and lack the institutional support to generate initiatives.

Despite all this, the EPC is always mentioned in the forefront whenever the successes of European policy are reviewed, perhaps because the benefits of this instrument for the respective foreign policies of all member countries were about evenly divided. It appears that the mode of cooperation is sufficiently flexible and efficient to allow for individual support of the individual actors, thus promoting the Community cause as such. In this way, the decline of the European identity on the global level (along with the loss of European empires) was probably slowed down somewhat and now comes up here and there in different terms with the EPC. To the extent that there is a general success story of the EPC,[5] Germany, of course, took its share. In addition, participation in the EPC gave Germany an opportunity to gradually penetrate the realm of international diplomacy after some of the major barriers had been removed following the Ostpolitik of the Brandt-Scheel government. Bonn had to cope with a significant extension of its foreign policy in terms of substance and counterparts. It had not put in a great appearance as a foreign political power so far and, because of its status quo philosophy, had not had much scope for major initiatives in that respect.

On the other hand, Germany could not conceal its economic and political stability, and with every new step it faced latent suspicion—not least because of its past. By virtue of its information and consultation facilities as well as its joint analyses and occasional actions, the EPC has been a suitable framework for a mutual adjustment process within the Nine. The questions to be asked at present are: how far has this process advanced, and what type of a member in the club has Germany become? In answering these questions, it should be kept in mind that political cooperation is, after all, a foreign policy instrument with very selective functions and fragmentary outcomes. One has to be aware of the fact that the EPC is a narrow field, and in contrast to the European Community, it has had a short career.[6]

European Political Cooperation—A Multilateral Tool for a Political Dwarf

The Conference on Security and Cooperation in Europe (CSCE), which lasted almost three years until the final act was signed in Helsinki on August 1, 1975, was the first test of the EPC. Through their continuous coordination in Geneva and Helsinki and at the Belgrade follow-up meeting (1977-1978), the Nine have made an important contribution to opinion forming and coherence among the western democracies. The successful cooperation on the CSCE among the Nine in the framework of the EPC made the Community in the East and West a real element of equilibrium in Europe. It has at the same time formed the basis for common positions among the Community member states on the major aspects of eastern and detente policy.

Germany continues to have vital national stakes in the broad field of eastern relations. However, implementation of these interests presupposes comprehensive western concentration and support. Next to the North Atlantic Treaty Organization (NATO) and the Four (the three western allies plus Germany), the EPC assumes functions for consultation and activities in this field that can be used by German diplomacy. Thus it was possible to embed sensitive elements of Germany's Ostpolitik into a framework with reassuring implications in three respects. First, it put the Bonn government in a position to effectively counter domestic opposition by pointing to the coordination of its policy with the West European partners. Second, by maintaining constant consultations within the Nine, it was thus able to explain the particularities and limitations of the German objectives in its eastern policy. Third, it made it easier for Bonn to demonstrate to Moscow and the eastern states that its eastern initiatives were backed up by a broad western consensus.

It should be clearly understood, however, that the EPC was just one of several multilateral instruments in the East-West relationship. Still, even to the surprise of Moscow, the EPC developed into a major asset in all-European negotiations. The eastern literature reproached Germany, for exploiting political cooperation of the Nine to pave the way for aggressive nationalistic forces. Bonn, these authors pointed out, is determined to utilize its high economic and military potential, as well as its enlarged foreign political leverage, to enhance its growing self-reliance within the imperialistic camp. Moreover, the German government, they claim, tries to capitalize on the process of West European political integration in order to violate the Four Power Agreement on West Berlin of 1971 and to extend the competencies of the European Community to West Berlin.[7]

Indeed, Germany profits from the fact that the extended western platform allows for an endorsement of German concerns. This was exemplified by the controversy about West Berlin's representation in the directly elected European Parliament. However, as far as the Nine are concerned, the "eternal" German issue appears to be more of a strain on them. That may apply less to London and Paris than it does to the other EPC partners. Compensation by means of special capabilities—for example, Bonn's diplomatic experiences in dealings with the East—though difficult to assess, is not without merit for collective East-West negotiations. On the other hand, this asset may have ambivalent implications for Bonn's partners if it entails (economic) advantages mainly for Germany.[8]

A second challenge in the early seventies was to establish the Community's position on relations with the United States, following the call for a constructive dialogue at the Paris summit of 1972, and the appeal by Secretary of State Kissinger on April 23, 1973, for a restructuring of the western alliance. The dialogue between the Nine and the United States, begun in September 1973, has made it clear, without any need for the originally proposed formal declaration, that European unification and Atlantic partnership are conditional upon each other. In the Gentlemen's Agreement reached at Gymnich (near Bonn), the Nine decided to inform and consult allies and friendly states in the process of evolving common positions on foreign policy. The significance of the policy of European unification for the Atlantic alliance was acknowledged in the statement issued by the NATO council with regard to Atlantic relations on June 26, 1974. On the basis of that informal agreement among friends, the practice of close mutual consultations between the Community and the United States has taken shape.

The Federal Republic surely has both a major say and a vital interest in this practice. There is no need to repeat why Bonn will neither be forced into an antagonistic position with Washington nor be suspected of assuming the role of executor of U.S. interests in Europe.[9] Although Bonn played an active part in elaborating the declarations in response to the Kissinger initiative in 1973, it did not act as forerunner of the Nine. Even the success of the Gymnich agreement, conceived under the German presidency, cannot simply be credited to the German account. Rather, the fact that this agreement was never seriously put to the test during the ensuing four years indicates the degree of a general relaxation of tensions in the European-American relationship after the days of Michel Jobert.

In realistic recognition of its own situation and the abilities and inabilities of the Nine, the federal government contributed to collective European efforts regarding the Middle East, the Mediterranean area, and Africa, while advocating "very close concertation" with the U.S. administration in each case. This approach is not tantamount to Atlantic uniformism. The EPC activities offer sufficient evidence of Bonn (together with other partners) taking positions different from the American administration (on the human rights issue at the CSCE at Belgrade) and the U.S. Congress (on the Cyprus question). In these cases, Germany need not resort to the solidarity of the Nine to underline such independent stands, much less so whenever questions of detente and European security are at stake.

With a declaration of November 6, 1973, the Nine opted for a policy of solidarity regarding the Middle East and the oil crisis and embarked on a balanced common Middle East policy. On June 10, 1974 at a meeting in Bonn, they took the initiative for the Euro-Arab dialogue and thus created a

comprehensive political framework for long-term regional cooperation between the Community and the countries of the Middle East. The federal
minister for foreign affairs, Hans-Dietrich Genscher, emphasized in this
context that the Nine were willing to develop relations with Israel as well.
This balanced Middle East policy was further developed by the Nine in,
among other things, United Nations debates and is set out in the statement
by the European Council of June 29, 1977, which also emphasized Europe's
own interest in peace in the Middle East. With their statement of November
22, 1977, the foreign ministers therefore supported the new peace initiative
which began with the meeting between the Egyptian and Israeli heads of
government in Jerusalem. The outcomes of the Camp David meeting were
welcomed likewise.

Contrary to the Atlantic context and the eastern policy where Bonn
played a major part in shaping EPC policy, the Middle East position of the
Nine saw Germany relegated to second rank. Perhaps this is the area in
which Germany benefited the most from cooperation within the EPC (as
well as the European Community). The advantage for Germany is particularly obvious here because it is difficult to conceive of another way to
sustain the historical responsibility it has to shoulder. In this sector Germany moves like a snail without a house, unlike its position toward the
Soviet Union within the detente context. Compared to Paris, for example,
Bonn faces a more complicated Middle East relationship. For anything
hinting at progress in German statements is conducive to hard feelings on
the part of the Israelis, whereas any respective French step would simply be
explained in terms of France's well-known hard line. The following example
may illustrate this: After Chancellor Schmidt, while talking to the Saudi
Arabian foreign minister in Bonn in June 1978, mentioned the rights of the
Palestinians "to organize a state of their own," Foreign Minister Genscher
took three full days explaining to Israeli officials during his visit there that
this statement did not imply German deviation from the position of the
Nine. Fortunately, Genscher's agenda included negotiations about trade
concessions requested by Israel in the context of the forthcoming European
Community enlargement. These talks gave Genscher the opportunity to
make a few reassuring remarks. Thus, it is extremely helpful for German
diplomacy to be able to refer to the European level and the solidarity of the
Nine in bilateral discussions with Israel.

On the other hand, this two-level policy is equally indispensable to Germany's relations with the Arab states. In its bilateral dealings with the Arabs,
Bonn is more generous than within the framework of the Euro-Arab
dialogue. There is displayed a much more hesitant attitude in economic as
well as political questions. The dialogue conducted by the EPC is largely
restricted to issues of mutual economic development. Rejection of a noteworthy financial fund, however, affects the political goals of the dialogue.

As far as the Mediterranean policy of the Nine is concerned, Bonn took a more community-oriented stand regarding the pursuit of political aims by financial means. Thus in 1975, within the EPC efforts, Germany favored support for the new Portuguese regime from Community funds (thereby ignoring EC credit rules) in order to strengthen the democratic process there. Furthermore, the federal government engaged in bilateral activities with similar objectives and means. It also showed special interest in a joint declaration of the Nine heads of government in this context.[10]

The establishment of pluralistic democratic systems in Portugal, Greece, and Spain made the orientation of these countries toward the Community a new, important factor in European politics. The Nine coordinated their views of this development and in some cases announced their position in public statements. Meanwhile, a second round of accession negotiations began. All three countries submitted applications for membership to the Council of the European Community. Negotiations with Greece are already well advanced, whereas in the case of Portugal and Spain preparatory work is still going on in the Community's institutions. Regarding EPC membership for the three applicants, the Nine have agreed on a transitional arrangement. During the accession negotiations, current information on EPC work will be given to the applicants. After the signing of the treaty, there is a period of consultation in EPC matters. The day of entry then brings participation in EPC bodies. Turkey, which is not an applicant but an associated country with a treaty-based accession perspective, is offered—for the time being—intensified information on any question of interest to Ankara. After Greece's entry in 1981, this line of communication will be maintained by a rotating group of three Community members. Such complicated mechanisms are sufficient evidence of the highly sensitive situation prevailing in the eastern Mediterranean. Incidentally, Germany was prepared to tie Turkey even more closely to the EPC club.

With regard to the Cyprus crisis, Germany tried to maintain a balanced position toward the conflicting parties. The main EPC activities at the beginning of the crisis were led by Great Britain (as one of the guarantors) and France (as holder of the presidency). Immediately upon the outbreak of the conflict in July 1974, the Nine formulated their common approach as the basis for diplomatic talks between the Nine and the three parties of the conflicts, Greece, Turkey, Cyprus, all associated with the European Community. Only during the more recent stages of the Nine's mediation attempts did Bonn assume a more prominent role. The German Foreign Office points out that the Turkish chief of government, Bülent Ecevit, during his Bonn visit in May 1978, for the first time demonstrated a clear willingness to make concessions in the Cyprus question. Yet, Germany was far from stimulating a genuine EPC initiative. When the U.S. Congress lifted its October 1974 embargo in August 1978, this was probably a consequence of new American assessments rather than of West European influence although Chancellor Helmut Schmidt pleaded to Congress on the television program "Face the Nation" to lift the embargo as soon as possible. Despite a certain amount of crisis management cooperation between the EPC and Washington in the Cyprus case, it was obvious that both sides remained relatively helpless. Nonetheless, Germany repeatedly drew on the EPC in addition to other forums to demonstrate that its interest as a central European power in restabilizing the situation at the southern flank of the alliance has to be taken seriously.

In the United Nations, the Nine have gradually become an important negotiating partner. By common statements and votes, they expressed European policy in the General Assembly and its committees as well as in Special Sessions. Since 1975, it has been the practice of the President of the Community Council to make a comprehensive statement on the common policy of the members of the Community at the beginning of the annual General Assembly. The impact of the Community, which received observer status in 1974, made it a negotiating partner in the worldwide dialogue for a new international economic order. Since becoming a member of the United Nations in 1973, the Federal Republic of Germany has strongly advocated a common Community policy within the world organization. In a sense, Bonn strengthened the European position in New York in a twofold manner: In some cases, it was instrumental in sponsoring West European initiatives and others. In other respects, it had to fight off criticism directed at almost every western state, for example, concerning relations with South Africa.

As holder of the presidency of the Nine, the federal government took an active part in promoting two resolutions of the thirty-third session of the General Assembly. The first project aimed at reinforcing the U.N. human rights stance. The second project involved proposals to expand the peace-keeping role of the world organization. German membership in the U.N. Security Council since 1977 has increased willingness and possibilities for coresponsibilities in resolving worldwide problems.

A case in point is Bonn's participation in the Namibia contact group. The federal government joins such enterprises less as a result of current assessment than in compliance with the decision of 1971 to become a U.N. member. Although the Group of Five did not emerge from the EPC, a feedback channel to the club of the Nine does exist. From time to time, the contact group draws on the EPC to back up its proposals by public declarations. The same procedure is followed in the British-American initiatives concerning the Zimbabwe-Rhodesia case. The intervention of foreign troops in the civil war in Angola prompted the Nine to counteract the danger of a comprehensive racial war in southern Africa with its repercussions for world peace.

In their Luxembourg declarations of February 23, 1976, and April 18, 1977, the nine foreign ministers came out in favor of a policy of independence and self-determination for the Africans. They condemned the policy of apartheid as well as any other form of racial discrimination, and opposed all attempts by foreign powers to establish zones of influence in Africa. On this basis, they have supported diplomatic endeavors to bring about peaceful change in Rhodesia and Namibia and have stated their position on specific problems concerning southern Africa, especially within the framework of the United Nations. In a critical dialogue with the Republic of South Africa, the Nine urged to change the policy of apartheid, which they are trying to encourage through their own measures (for example, by the code of conduct for establishment of European firms, adopted in September 1977).

The Federal Republic of Germany is emotionally involved, especially in the Namibia case. For the rest, it finds itself in the same defensive position as Paris and London—all three try to protect their massive economic interests, while going as far as they can in bringing about peaceful solutions in that area. Bonn hardly has an independent African policy. It prefers to leave Salisbury to the British and Shaba to the French. Germany tries to avoid any action that might make it the subject of a collective attack, as was the case in the 1977 Organization of African Unity (OAU) meeting. Clearer stands are taken by the smaller Community countries—Ireland, Denmark, and Holland—which because of traditions and convictions have less ambivalent sympathies for movements of liberalization in Africa. Not for domestic reasons did Foreign Minister Genscher have a hard time following the evaluation of Belgian Foreign Minister Henri Simonet, for example, who acknowledges the increasing stabilizing function of Cuba in Angola. In those instances, Genscher prefers to refer to a possible Angolan participation in a Lomé II convention.

To the same extent that the Nine endeavor to acquire a common profile on African issues, the Federal Republic attempts to develop a "German" African policy. In the perspectives of the Nine, Bonn tends toward an in-between position. It endorses basic demands of a general nature. By the same token, it appreciates opportunities (in its bilateral Middle East relations) to refer to the multilateral level—the Community and the EPC. In concrete cases, such as Namibia, Angola, Zambia, and Tanzania, it will not hesitate to show its readiness to offer major economic support. To have several levels of action at its disposal is all the more important for the German government as its actions are increasingly watched on the international level; such as in the North-South conflict, the United Nations Conference on Trade and Development in May 1976, and the Conference on International Economic Cooperation in Paris in 1976-1977.

Readiness for a Greater Share of Responsibility

The EPC has helped enhance the European impact on international events. However, it has not been able, of course, to stop the process of growing intra-European heterogeneity and the rise of Europe's external dependency. All the EPC was able to do was make these weaknesses more tolerable. Apart from the EPC's limited effectiveness as such, there is the consideration that the Nine—even collectively—do not really have enough to offer to counterbalance the threat by the one superpower and the dependence on the other, and take appropriate account of the demands of the Third World. This fact is part of the environmental conditions of any kind of West European foreign policy in the foreseeable future. To that extent, political cooperation of the Nine is less a tool that can effect major changes in the structure of the international environment than a method of adaptation of one's own country to this environment with the chance to help shape future structures.[11]

In this sense Germany no doubt has profited from EPC membership, which has enabled Bonn to make the outside world familiar with the dynamics of its foreign policy. At the same time, it has facilitated the process of Germany's assuming a more active role in world politics. Apart from these general evaluations, the value of the EPC to Germany varies considerably with the issues at stake. The advantage of greater bargaining power by virtue of the cooperation of the Nine is helpful where Bonn finds itself paralyzed by psychological strains (in its Eastern relations, and the Middle East). In such cases, inevitable shifts in German politics become easier, externally as well as domestically. Additional support from the Nine of a moral political nature will also assist Germany in subjects like African policy, where there is a different type of pressure. Moreover, the EPC has promoted German objectives where there are technical restrictions on its freedom of action. German diplomacy profited from the fact that the Nine's consultation body combines a larger sphere of influence and broader international experience than is nationally available, an asset that paid off in particular in relations with the Mediterranean, the Third World, and the United Nations. Hence, the EPC not only serves as a common point of reference in resisting pressure from domestic and foreign sources, but also is useful in promoting German interests of a different kind. The advantageous development of the Nine's concertation has coincided with a new active period in German foreign policy.

Compared with Germany's gains from EPC membership, the disadvantages are minor. The necessity of showing consideration in return and not disrupting the new solidarities of the Nine has produced less difficulties for Germany than for other member states. There have been no major linkages between political goals and financial demands. Yet Bonn's own contribution to the EPC so far has been limited. The special relationship the Federal Republic has with Washington, as well as with Moscow and Paris, surely constitutes a valuable input for effective EPC policy, although by virtue of their specific nature these relations also mean a certain strain. Such unavoidable implications are easier to accept for the partners as long as the German foreign minister refrains from lecturing his allies, as Helmut Schmidt has done on occasion, in the economic field. Thus, German diplomacy plays a stabilizing and balancing role within the Nine.[12]

As far as the procedural process of the EPC is concerned, Bonn is backing the present line of pragmatic development and has provided valuable inputs, including the idea to organize informal meetings, so-called Gymnichs. But as for everyday business, German diplomats have a harder time now and then (be it only for reasons of the language barrier) compared to smaller countries. The German government has always favored extending the subjects of consultation and has interpreted—unlike other member states—the EPC as an open-ended process.

Concerning the binding nature of the jointly prepared foreign policy positions, however, the limits are relatively clearly outlined. A legal fixation of common foreign policy envisaged in Tindeman's report on the European union has been rejected (even for limited areas). Although collaboration of the European Community and the EPC in European foreign policy is pursued informally, Bonn has not overexerted itself in concrete situations (for example, whether to involve the European Community Commission in the dealings of the EPC if, say, Paris was against such participation). A typical contemporary example of the integrational creed of the federal government is the following statement:

> The pragmatic beginning of a common foreign policy in the EPC and the EC's foreign relations are to the Federal Government, besides the enlargement of the Community, the establishment of the European Council and the decision on direct elections to the European Parliament, important stages in the evolution of the European Community into a political union. In unison with its partners in the EC, it regards the EPC as leading step by step towards a common foreign policy which will be a cornerstone of European Union. The Federal Government will therefore play its part in the development of an increasingly comprehensive common foreign policy of the Nine.[13]

How these statements will be realized in the future remains to be seen. Bonn seems to be ready to favor European Political Cooperation in two fields: (1) to assume more worldwide responsibility, and (2) to incorporate more security matters in the concertation process. These lines are illustrated by recent initiatives in the United Nations (peace-keeping forces, Namibia contact group, and disarmament). Another example is—besides ongoing activities with respect to Africa and the Middle East—the opening of a Euro-Asian dialogue with the group of the five Association of South-East Asian Nations (ASEAN) countries. This dialogue was a favorite subject of Genscher who was president of the first joint foreign ministers meeting in Brussels in November 1978. In addition to economic interests, the dialogue with several Third World regions demonstrates the willingness to contribute somehow to a policy of equilibrium outside the immediate East-West context. By way of the EPC, Germany thus might tend to play a part in worldwide diplomatic management more than it has in the past. In company with some other West European capitals, Bonn is showing a cautious readiness to engage itself in areas where the United States used to go it alone but now displays more restraint.

The Bonn administration is pragmatic enough to know that foreign policy and security considerations cannot be separated. As long as there is no chance (and there is none) for a European defense, security questions of special interest to the Nine should be included in the EPC framework. This is true in particular for foreign policy aspects of security—crisis management, disarmament and arms control, weapons export, and armament cooperation. In principle, the German government could be inclined to channel such security-related considerations within the Nine, but it would go too far to speak of a distinct German policy or desire—for on the one hand there is the resistance of the partners and, on the other, Bonn takes care in any case to keep all security considerations close to the NATO assessment process.[14]

Nevertheless, it is a fact that crisis management, disarmament, and diplomatic aspects of security policy have been discussed in EPC bodies recently. The Nine presented a common position in the May 1978 U.N. Special Session on disarmament as well as at the General Assembly. So far, however, the EPC has never dealt with strategic questions as such, although general aspects have certainly been touched upon. Even crisis management activities have not been incorporated in a fundamental and comprehensive way, and there has been hardly any operational common action up to now. Armaments cooperation and weapons exports, though potential topics, are more outside than inside the EPC agenda. In sum, Bonn is not ready to push security questions too hard or too fast.[15]

Although Germany considers the EPC as an important concertation body of West European states, active participation in other multilateral frameworks could increasingly identify the EPC as only one of several levels of action. Similar to Bonn's habit of not always regarding the Community as the central realm of its economic policy orientations, the German government is likely to rely more and more on Franco-German consultation, the U.N. Security Council, the Group of Four (Guadeloupe), economic summits, and other bodies. This line of development is even more likely if there becomes a community of twelve. Within this context, the function of the EPC might shift. It could increasingly constitute the West European pool for the various bilateral and multilateral activities of the West European states outside the regular club of the Nine. The Federal Republic could take a growing interest in such a development. Its foreign policy fares quite well in informal groups. Contrary to European Community bodies, where the status of a member is tied up in written rules, these informal institutions offer room for a smooth change in status. In a future period, Bonn could perceive the EPC less as an instrument for catching up on diplomatic experience than as a platform for influencing the policy of its partners. In any case Germany, like other members, will continue to use the European Political Cooperation network to promote national interests. There are specific domestic and psychological reasons for Bonn to prefer multilateralism to unilateralism in pursuit of its foreign policy goals.

Part of the success of the European Political Cooperation has been a result of its concern with those aspects of foreign policy which least often involve direct costs. Thus, the member governments were able to concert their policies without being forced to consider the budgetary consequences and the distribution of costs and benefits among different governments.[16] There is no substantial sign of a change concerning practice. Once foreign policy moves out of this strictly diplomatic field into using economic levers for political ends or provoking financial consequences from diplomatic actions, the problem of differential distribution of costs and benefits immediately arises (for example, in the Euro-Arab dialogue). So far, Germany favors a combination of economic and foreign policy aspects more in terms of an integration policy in order to concert the two strings, the Community and the EPC, than in terms of mutual leverage. As long as the EPC does not cost anything, the possibility of Germany increasing its influence there remains limited.

The gap that has emerged between the economic strength of Germany and its Community partners has not been fully interpreted so far. Germany is as much aware of its strength as it is embarrassed about it.[17] It has not yet come to grips with its foreign policy potential. It has developed a tradition of concentrating on its vulnerabilities. The decision as to where this potential should lead Germany is an open question; there is not too much consensus among the domestic political forces on this point. Equally open is the question: to what extent will Bonn's partners try to influence these options? Notwithstanding the answer to this question, the Federal Republic will use every opportunity to diversify its need for diplomatic protection and its willingness to take initiatives in world affairs. In many respects, its scope is not confined to the West European context. Bonn searches for a way of living with an old problem: Community-building is pursued in terms of a regional entity, whereas most of the vital national dependencies exist in a larger framework. Is there a compatibility of national, community, and multilateral orientations for Germany in the future? To answer this question properly, a lot of empirical and theoretical work still remains to be done.[18]

Notes

1. See Federal Republic of Germany, Press and Information Office, European Political Cooperation (EPC), Bonn 1978, p. 230.

2. Bernd von Staden, "Politische Zusammenarbeit der EG-Staaten," *AuBenpolitik* 23:4 (1972):200-209.

3. Gunther van Well, "Die Europäische politische Zusammenarbeit in der auBenpolitischen Sicht der Bundesrepublik Deutschland," *Europa-Archiv* 28:27 (1973):643-49.

4. Reinhardt Rummel and Wolfgang Wessels, eds., *Europaische Politische Zusammenarbeit. Strukturen und Leistungsvermögen* (Bonn: Europa Union Verlag 1978).

5. For a comprehensive assessment of the EPC, see Heinz Kramer and Reinhardt Rummel, *Gemeinschaftsbildung Westeuropas in der AuBenpolitik* Nomus (Baden-Baden: 1978).

6. The EPC department in the German Foreign Office makes clear that for the time being, a European foreign policy does not exist, and that Germany's participation in EPC activities has to be seen in the wider context of all sorts of cooperative endeavors in Western Europe. Immo Stabreit, "Aufgaben deutscher Europapolitik," *Rissener Rundbrief*, November 1978, pp. 111-117.

7. Siegfried Schwarz, "Tendenzen der Politischen Integration in Westeuropa," *IPW-Berichte*, No. 6, June 1977, p. 28.

8. See the handling of the Brezhnev initiative for an all-European conference on environmental, energy, and transport questions. Ilka Bailey-Wiebecke and Paul J. Bailey, "Decision-making at the CSCE. The Case of the Federal Republic of Germany within the Context of the European Community and Political Co-operation," May 1978 (unpublished).

9. From a U.S. perspective, Bonn might fit a broker's position best. See Peter Katzenstein, "West Germany's Place in American Foreign Policy: Pivet, Anchor, or Broker?" in *America as an Ordinary Country*, ed. Richard Rosecrance (Ithaca and London: Cornell University Press, 1976), p. 110.

10. "The European Council reaffirms that the European Community is prepared to initiate discussions on closer economic and financial cooperation with Portugal. It also points out that, in accordance with its historical and political traditions, the European Community can give support only to

a democracy of a pluralist nature." (Statement by the 2nd European Council, Brussels, July 17, 1975).

11. This rationale seems to form the background of the recent EPC-Presidency annual report to the European parliament. See Bulletin of the European Communities, Report on Political Cooperation, vol. 11, no. 11, November 1978, pp. 125-30.

12. See Hans-Dietrich Genscher, "Bilanz der deutschen EG- und EPZ-Präsidentschaft, in Presse- und Informationsamt der Bundesregierung, ed., *Bulletin* no. 150 (December 15, 1978), pp. 1289-1393.

13. See *Federal Republic of Germany*, Press and Information Office of the German Government, Bonn, p. 18.

14. Concerning the limitations of a foreign policy consensus of the Nine, see Rudolf Hrbek, "Integrationsschub durch gemeinsame Au-Benbeziehungen?" in *Auf dem Weg zur Europäischen Union*, ed. Herbert Schneider and Wolfgang Wessels (Bonn: Europa Union Verlag, 1977), pp. 117-142.

15. Otto von der Gablentz, "Wege zu einer europäischen Außen-politik," in *Auf dem Weg zur Europäischen Union*, ed. H. Schneider and Wolfgang Wessels (Bonn, 1977), pp. 85-115.

16. William Wallace, "A Common European Foreign Policy: Mirage or Reality?" *New Europe* 5:2 (1977):21-33.

17. Almost the same feeling prevails in Germany's perception from outside. See M.C. Brandis, "The Federal Republic—Economically Strong, Politically Blocked, No Major Chances in Foreign Policy?" (Paper submitted to the Trans-European Policy Studies Association Conference on The Role of the Federal Republic of Germany in the European Community, Bonn, October 27-28, 1978.

18. A few attempts in this respect have been made recently. See Ernst-Otto Czempiel's chapter in this book; Roger Morgan, "West Germany's Foreign Policy Agenda," The Washington Papers, No. 54, 1978; Peter A. Busch, "Germany in the European Community: Theory and Case Study," *Canadian Journal of Political Science* 11:3 (1978):545-73.

6

The Atlantic Community, Europe, Germany: Options, Objectives, or Contexts of German Foreign Policy?

Ernst-Otto Czempiel

Introduction

The most interesting thing about the question of the orientation of West Germany's foreign policy is the fact that it is even being asked. Has Bonn's foreign policy changed? Or has the world political context in which the Federal Republic pursues foreign policy changed? In the *Frankfurter Allgemeine Zeitung* of February 3, 1979, Rüdiger Altmann states that under "Helmut Schmidt . . . the national traits of German foreign policy have been more prominent than ever before." One sentence later, he ascribes to the German chancellor an "open internationalism." Has German foreign policy changed? Has it become more national?

The idea advanced here is that Bonn's basic policies have not changed, but they look somewhat different today because West Germany's place in the world has changed. The Federal Republic has remained faithful to its steady ties to the West, its collaboration with the European Community, and its cooperation with the United States. But the situation has changed decisively: the small, weak Federal Republic of the fifties has become an economic giant whose political and military significance is correspondingly great. Its cooperation is no longer, as earlier, an unnoticed matter, taken for granted; but rather, an event. Bonn's freedom to maneuver has increased because the importance of the Federal Republic has grown.

This increase in freedom to maneuver has nothing in the least to do with nationalism. Imprecise concepts always result in imprecise perceptions. It is not the nationalism of the Federal Republic that is under discussion, but its unilateralism. Both must be distinguished clearly. Nationalism signifies a goal; unilateralism a process. The nationalist wants to maximize his profit; the unilateralist negotiates alone. Of course, there are connections between goals and processes, but they are not clear. The nationalist can negotiate only unilaterally. The unilateralist need not pursue only national goals, but can very well pursue common ones. This is exactly the case with the Federal Republic—in fact, all West European countries and the United States act in this manner because they can only behave individually for common goals. There is perhaps the concept, but not the practice, of multilateralism in which common goals are negotiated in common. NATO and EEC matters, if one looks closely, reveal the principle of unanimity: each country must agree individually. The West (to say nothing of the East) has not developed procedures to correspond to the growing community, to interdependence. The contradiction between a common goal and a unilateral method is evident, and it is general. That it is particularly evident in the case of the Federal Republic has no objective reasons, but rather, psychological ones. For a long time, German unilateralism was not conspicuous because it was of no great importance. Now it is more important, nothing more. The Federal Republic continues to work unshakeably with the West. But it shows the signs just now of what has always been evident in the example of the United States, France, and Great Britain: the contradiction between common goals and unilateral behavior. Here lies the answer to the question regarding the orientation of West German foreign policy.

Security and Detente

Security Policy

"That the Atlantic Alliance, in which America plays the most important role, is the indispensable basis for the common security and defense policy,"[1] continues to be an axiom of West German foreign policy. That the security of the Federal Republic is threatened is for Bonn a certainty. To be sure, the image of the Soviet Union has somewhat changed in the meantime. Its military expansion represents an exception, a "worst case" which is possible, but not probable. The Soviet Union uses its great and increasing military potential far more to assure for itself its position and sphere of influence in central Europe; and, when possible, it uses it to expand its influence toward the West in order to displace the United States in Western Europe.[2] The NATO reacts to this double threat in that through its deterrent function it assures the continuing renunciation of aggression on the part of the Soviet Union, and through its own military strength it prevents the Soviet Union from taking political advantage of its military potential. Without the United States, neither of these functions can be carried out. Only the United States disposes of a sufficient nuclear deterrent potential; only it can guarantee the security of Western Europe on the strategic level. Neither the French nor the British nuclear force is capable of it. The Federal Republic's political freedom to negotiate and maneuver depends on the nuclear protection of the United States. Beyond all (more important) points shared between the United States and Western Europe, this military fact presents a point of orientation that is binding for every concept.

For the Federal Republic, additional factors are present. The freedom of West Berlin and its ties to the Federal Republic depend completely on the willingness of the United States to maintain its presence there and to politically guarantee the security and freedom of West Berlin in relation to the Soviet Union. The Berlin Agreement of September 3, 1971, was solely dependent on the United States not only with regard to its genesis, but also for its realization and continuation.[3]

There is no alternative. Of course, theoretically the West European countries would be capable of developing and providing a military potential the size of one of the two superpowers.[4] But that does not solve any problems. A European military force, if it is to be taken seriously, would have to have an integrated structure, a common supreme command, which is unthinkable without the unification of the political decision-making processes. Neither France nor Great Britain is interested in such a construction and the concomitant reduction in their freedom of action. The Federal Republic has not taken an interest in it. It would therefore be much more topical to preserve the American-European defense alliance and to look for new possibilities within it, to solve the differences of interests, and to compensate for those power shifts which have arisen.

A critical difference of interests concerns the codetermination to use atomic weapons. It is fundamental, but not new.[5] The Social Democratic party (SPD) rightly warns against the tendency in certain sections of the Christian Democratic Union-Christian Social Union (CDU-CSU) to let Germany become a nuclear power within, and via, a European atomic force. This policy would be dangerous to the security of the Federal Republic and the rest of Europe. As Schmidt says, "It cannot be approved by us."[6]

Less weighty but more numerous are the differences in interests of the NATO partners outside the alliance. The Vietnam War of the United States was the greatest example, the Middle East conflict the most current, and the conflict in southern Africa the future example. In contrast to Vietnam, the Middle East and Africa involve not only American but also European interests—in the Federal Republic, the Social Democrats are watching the conflicts with concern;[7] the Free Democratic party (FDP) apparently with a willingness to participate.[8] In a way quite different from that concerning an atomic force, these conflicts clearly reveal the shifts of power within the NATO. The American refusal to intervene in Angola was taken by the German foreign minister as a sign of increasing American restraint.[9] The Federal Republic is active as an intermediary in southern Africa, especially Namibia, but also in the southeastern flank of the NATO, in Greece and Turkey. It is aware of the "growing political importance of the Third World" and offers them "a fair partnership."[10]

It is not easy, of course, for the United States always to tactfully consider the transformation of Bonn from a dependent small country to a partner willing to cooperate.[11] The decisions concerning the neutron bomb, made by the United States and the Soviet Union in the course of the Strategic Arms Limitation Talks (SALT) negotiations,[12] or its demands in the unpleasant offset payments affair, which almost reached a point of pressure, have evoked in Bonn a corresponding discomfort.[13] When Germany openly and critically resented the American use of German ports and airports for U.S. shipments to Israel, this reaction must be taken as an (unnecessary) demonstration of power.

Although German-American relations may occasionally be "rubbed raw"[14] through delays in adjustment, although there may be differences of opinion concerning the tactics for the implementation of human rights, although there may be antipathies between decision makers—the alliance will not be affected. Its importance to the Federal Republic was reiterated by Willy Brandt before the U.S. Chamber of Commerce on June 20, 1978: "The stronger the bonds of common risk, the greater will be our security. Anything that could uncouple us in danger would mean less security first for us, quickly for all. I think the implication is clear . . . for Europe and for America, for each of us, the alliance has become indispensable."[15] The Atlantic policy of Bonn has remained unchanged; but the decisions of the Federal Republic have increased in importance.

Detente and the Ostpolitik

Both detente and the Ostpolitik of the Federal Republic are determined by the same interests. The Ostpolitik swings, though with certain time lags, to the same rhythm as the relations between the United States and the Soviet Union. To behave anticyclically is not possible for Germany. Chancellor Schmidt rightly sees the historical role of his predecessor Willy Brandt in the fact that he just barely "achieved the German Ostpolitik and secured it through treaties before the big powers had gotten together right over our German head."[16]

If German detente and Ostpolitik depend on the state of Soviet-American relations, they depend also on the consent of the European partners. On the other hand, there is no unified policy of the Nine with regard to goals and means, let alone coordination with the United States. The European Political Cooperation (EPC) within the framework of the European Community is necessarily reduced to broad guidelines with regard to detente and Ostpolitik. But within this "conceptual synchronization" it has "proved itself relatively well."[17] The Nine have maintained and improved the practice adopted at the founding of the Conference on Security and Cooperation in Europe (CSEC) in Helsinki to develop and present common points of view.[18] No European country, least of all the Federal Republic, could confront Moscow unilaterally. It is precisely the attempt to negotiate individual interests with the East European countries and the Soviet Union that demands a solid anchor in the collectivity of the Nine.

This has been axiomatic for all German governments since Adenauer. The Federal Republic's detente policy and Ostpolitik must be adjusted with the allies, and it must not endanger the security of Western Europe, the Federal Republic, or West Berlin.[19] A tendency toward self-Finlandization, toward the abandonment of the NATO in return for a Soviet promise of security and the prospect of a German reunification, is not discernible.[20] For the Social-Liberal coalition, the Ostpolitik is irrevocably tied to detente. It holds not only the "hope for a turning point in our national destiny,"[21] but also the possibility of stronger contacts with socialist countries within the Soviet perimeter. Above all, it reflects the self-perception of the Social-Liberal coalition in the same way the policy of strength must be ascribed to the Adenauer cabinet. Concept and interest direct the social-liberal Federal Republic toward detente.

It is unavoidable that such a policy encounter the criticism of those who do not wish detente with the Soviet Union.[22] Among these, one may include certain members of the Christian Democratic Union who neither supported nor opposed the principal items of the Ostpolitik.[23] It is difficult for the party to adapt itself to the changed context of detente. This context is surely more difficult to deal with than that of the Cold War. Since the Atlantic alliance and the European Economic Community were formed under its auspices, the idea that both might be endangered by detente could arise. The concern that the Soviet Union could derive tactical advantages from the detente is understandable.[24] But the consequence of this cannot mean a return to confrontation; rather, it should lead the solidarity and cohesion of the West into the changed context of detente.

Here lies the actual nerve center. If unilateralism goes beyond the inevitable limit which reflects the complexity of western positions, that limit which is safe, the cohesion of the West will fall apart and each country will be damaged in its isolation. This is not a German problem but rather one for all West European countries. Furthermore, the Federal Republic must be asked whether it successfully combined detente and Ostpolitik, (in which it undoubtedly had specific German interests to gain) with a European Economic Community policy which, though not yet aimed at the elimination of unilateralism, was directed at its reduction in favor of multilateral procedures.

The assessment is not easy and not clear. At the very beginning of his Ostpolitik, Chancellor Brandt had made an active western policy its most essential prerequisite.[25] If one regards the visit of the secretary general of the Communist party of the Soviet Union, Brezhnev, in May 1978, as an additional test case, it is evident that the Federal Republic has in this, as in other examples of its Ostpolitik, "close if not to say the closest feeling with our partners" in the West.[26] Far from trying to appear as the leading power in Western Europe, Germany tried to convince the Soviet Union that the continuation of European integration was not directed against detente in Europe. Bonn sees itself as an integral part of the European Economic Community and the Atlantic Community, and it presents this image to the Soviet Union. This self-perception of the federal government is not disputed even by the opposition.[27] Of course, this could also be a self-deception. Nevertheless, a long-term economic agreement was concluded during the Brezhnev visit—despite the fact that the authority to conclude trade agreements actually lies with the European Economic Community. This raises the question for the Federal Republic about how far such unilaterally initiated collaboration with the Soviet Union, for which Chancellor Schmidt attested "good prospects," can be brought into harmony with economic cooperation in the Community.

It is again evident that the real problem lies not in German policy but in the lacking expansion of multilateral procedures in the Community. Its competence to conclude trade agreements is weakened and not strengthened by all members. Multilateralism is diminishing instead of increasing. Whether the Germans show a particular inclination toward unilateralism cannot be determined clearly from the Ostpolitik. There are goals here which, like that of German reunification, are of necessity unilateral and which must, therefore, be pursued in that way. The real test should be made in those situations where there are common goals; that is, in world and economic policy.

Policy of Prosperity and World Policy

Policy of Prosperity

In trade policy, the Federal Republic is dependent on Western Europe; in monetary policy, on the United States. Its policy of prosperity is thus embedded in the strained relations between the United States and the European Community which is fully treated in other chapters of this book. Although there is no question of making a choice between the Community and the United States, the Federal Republic has nevertheless preferred the European Community. It has not only resisted every temptation toward "bigemony"; it largely promoted a step forward of the Community toward a monetary union at the European Council summit in Bremen in August 1978. The uncoupling from the dollar, the lessening of monetary dependence on the United States, has thus come into the realm of possibility.

The option for the European Community lies in the tradition, the situation, and the interest of West Germany. It should not be mistaken for an alternative to American-European cooperation. American-European problems are of a temporary nature,[28] and result from the necessary adjustment of the United States to the relative economic power shift between it and the Europeans, as exemplified by the fall of the dollar.

In this transitional stage, the real possibility exists of yielding to the American tendency to negotiate bilaterally with West European countries. Instead, the European option is to strengthen cooperation among the European partners and together to enter into negotiations with the United States.

Of course, this says nothing about whether these will be managed unilaterally or jointly. The Federal Republic is currently the strongest economic part of the Community. It could use this position to be the paymaster and pace setter of Europe,[29] in other words, to produce an integrating effect. In like manner, it could be tempted to assume the position formerly held by the United States: that of the hegemonial power.

The policy of the Federal Republic is not uniform and not clear. On the one hand, it can be said that it exercises no particular economic pressure on its partners. Many German interests—for example, a common energy policy or agricultural policy reform—have not yet been fulfilled. The Federal Republic has not even been successful in attracting the jet project to West Germany; it went to Great Britain. On the other hand, even Chancellor Schmidt had to admit that, given their economic strength, some Germans "feel a lust for power because they think they hold a lever in their hands."[30] Schmidt delineated his own position on both sides. The Federal Republic need neither "cultivate inferiority complexes nor . . . make the mistake of adapting new rich attitudes."[31]

With that he endorsed a moderate unilateralism. The Federal Republic does not take advantage of its economic power to create a position of hegemony, nor does it use it to further European integration. The result is an unclear situation in which the Federal Republic is, to be sure, the paymaster of Europe inasmuch as it finances 36.5 percent of the Community budget, but it does not want to be the pace setter of European integration; it is a situation in which the Federal Republic does not directly take advantage of its economic power, but suffers from the fact that it is felt indirectly. Whether or not the Federal Republic is an *économie dominante* in the sense of Perroux[32] remains open to discussion. What is certain is that the Federal Republic, with the highest gross national product in Western Europe, provides economic indicators that set standards for its Community partners and cannot be overtaken. Even the president of the Bundesbank had to admit that West German stability presents not only a support and a spur for the world, but also "a challenge and occasionally a vexation as well."[33] In France, they already speak openly of Deutsche mark imperialism for that reason, at least with regard to the political hegemony of the Federal Republic, which is said to want to impose its "Germany model" on its European partners.[34] However, many psychological elements—reminiscences of past domination or worries about the future—may be mixed into these assessments; it is undeniable that the German stability policy, in the face of involvement already present in the Community, influences the negotiating latitude on economic and social policies in neighboring countries, and also determines it.[35]

Economically, the Federal Republic is a pace setter in Europe whether it wants to be or not. It cannot evade the question of where it is directing its steps. Since it has not gone exclusively and clearly in the direction of Europe up to now, it has disclosed two things. First, its actions are less European than its speeches. Second, it prefers unilateralism, or in any event has not been intensely active in the expansion of multilateral procedures.

Such a criticism, if it is to be valid, must first of all point to the fact that the practice of the Federal Republic is no different from that of its partners. Above all, one must ask how multilateralism can be constituted as a process, and in which direction it could aim. An answer to this can be only briefly sketched here.[36] A European regional state cannot be constructed so as to resemble an enlarged national state because such a concentration of power could not be taken as progress either from inside or outside. Such a superstate also is not able to be created because it is rejected by many of its future parts, not least because of the possible German predominance in it. No one can say exactly what is currently being played out in the Community, or which direction the process of collaboration is taking. Calleo is certainly correct in saying that it is not a federation that is growing in Brussels, but rather a confederate bloc in which the states do not surrender their sovereignty but protect it.[37] That would mean that unilateralism, which is the characteristic procedure of sovereignty, will continue to increase. All the more pressing would be the development of multilateral procedures which, although not removing sovereignty in principle, would restrict it to the degree that has become necessary because of growing interdependence. How much this is lacking may be seen in the German economic policy toward Western Europe.

To be sure, Germany has already used its economic weight to help its partners. In this it has also used multilateral institutions, although it decidedly preferred bilateralism. It is conscious of the fact that it cannot be an island of prosperity in the middle of a sea of economic problems, but until now it has undertaken no organized multilateral efforts to enlarge the island or to fill up the sea. This is not a question of whether such a policy would best be attained through stimulation of the German economy, or through the elimination of inflation among the European partners. It means that the Federal Republic must help in every strategy variant, and multilaterally, through the European Community. Germany knows that it must not only contribute financial means but also, if necessary, give up parts of its latitude in social policy and reform policy to such a European strategy, that it must help the partners follow, and that it must wait accordingly. It knows that it cannot merely discuss partnership, but must also pay for it.[38] It is not enough to urge the other Community countries to "immediately fight the pressing intra-European problems, especially unemployment, effectively."[39] It must contribute, through its own economic, financial, and social policy, so that the conditions for such a fight against unemployment in other countries may be created.

Such aid cannot be bilateral, but must be multilateral; it cannot be borne by the Federal Republic alone, but must be divided among European institutions. Only in this way can the appearance of a West German hegemony be avoided; only in this way can unilateralism become multilateralism, can precedents be created, and ways of behavior be ingrained that will bring the European Community closer together.

The Federal Republic took a decisive step in this direction at the Bremen meeting of the European Council in August 1978, where it was decided to create a European monetary system. German currency reserves will be its most important base, but they will not be left solely in German hands.

This will not solve all problems of economic cooperation, it will not create all the preconditions. Whether and to what extent countries of such a heterogeneous social structure and diverse political tradition can even be brought together remains an open question. There are sociopolitical differences within the countries themselves, as between the parties, which are carried over into Euro-political concepts.[40] Such differences also decidedly influence relations among countries. France and Germany are very different with regard to their social structures. The SPD, like the Labor party, for instance, cannot be interested in a conservative capitalistic Europe. On the other hand, it cannot dictate a social democratic Europe. In this situation, the temptation is great to withdraw into unilateralism, to limit the "Germany model" to the "Island of Germany." For German prosperity, such a policy of unilateralism can be quite acceptable. Until now, it has only reaped profit from the fact that it has not been more strongly integrated into Western Europe.

World Policy

The function of the European Community for the world policy of the Federal Republic has the same denominator in that it eases and encourages German unilateralism. Such an observation, of course, can only be made very cautiously. To begin with, there is no recognizable multilateral or even synchronized world policy among the Nine, all successes of the EPC notwithstanding. Bonn, therefore, behaves no differently from all other Community partners. Added to this is the special dependence on the United States, demonstrated by the stationing of troops and monetary behavior; added to this is a special competition with the United States concerning the nuclear reactor exports. These specifically German problems could be handled by the Federal Republic only unilaterally; the Community did not enter into them.

The energy policy unilateralism of the Europeans also results partly from the position of the United States, [41] which places a higher premium on its interest in controls than on the development and easing of a common oil policy for the European countries. Generally, it has been said that the tendency of the Federal Republic (as of all other Community countries) toward unilateralism cannot be appreciated without taking into account Washington's preference for selective bilateral negotiations with the individual European countries. Whether the Federal Republic is considered to be a "turn-table, an anchor or a broker" by American foreign policy,[42] it certainly is not considered as part of the Community that preferably should be reached and addressed through Brussels. However, West German unilateralism is not a consequence of American decisions, but a result of German decisions. But it is precisely in the energy sector that it becomes evident how much such behavior preferences are influenced and can be guided by the policy of the leading western power.

Outside the energy sector, the Community acquires a completely different meaning for German world policy. To the African, Pacific and Caribbean (APC) countries, Germany largely appears as a complete Community member; only through the strongly coordinated policy of the Lomé convention and its predecessors was it possible to participate in the aftermath of European colonial affairs, as demanded by France, without suffering for it. As a European Economic Community member, Germany could and can appear in areas of the world where it has not been present before, and where it would perhaps not be welcome as the West German national state. If Bonn has until now restrained itself globally in order to remain faithful to its intention of being a dwarf in world policy, then the Community offers a welcome context for the mediation and embellishment of the German presence which is felt to be increasingly urgent, and in any case, unavoidable. The Euro-Arab dialogue permits the restoration of the traditional German-Arab relations without damaging the German-Israeli ones. Through the European Economic Community, Bonn can also appear in Asia; for instance, among the Association of South-East Asian Nations (ASEAN) members, to which Germany has traditionally had little access. In this way, the European Economic Community acts as a gate to the world, as the open door of German foreign policy. It is not the only one, but it is an important one. Through it Germany can profit from those ties which have for so long connected the European world to the countries of Asia, Africa, and Latin America. It becomes all the more easier for Bonn to overcome Germany's traditional continental orientation.

The European Economic Community not only can facilitate German world policy, but also can strengthen it. A monetary policy toward the United States in any case can be pursued only as a European policy. But even Germany's South African policy can be made more legitimate if it can show a European code of conduct.

How is German world policy to be judged? The Federal Republic finds itself in a dilemma. On the one hand it is economically, and thus also politically, a world power (only militarily a regional power); on the other hand, a German world policy would evoke dark memories in other countries that still recall the actions of the Wilhelminian Reich. Bonn is thus forced to play a world political role without being able to do so. There are two solutions to this dilemma: namely, to pursue world policy as European policy,[43] or to use European policy for the purpose of world policy. The first leads to multilateralism and the strengthening of European integration; the second leads to unilateralism and the degeneration of the Community to a purely tactically managed instrument. As indisputably as the Federal Republic may advocate the first solution, its practice indicates that as a result of the Community's weakness, it increasingly chooses the second.

Bonn cannot make the decision alone. The development of the Community depends not only on the Federal Republic but also on the corresponding willingness of all other Community countries. As far as world policy is concerned, it is practically nonexistent and thus would first have to be created by the Federal Republic. Given the difficulties connected with this, the inclination to restrict itself primarily to instrumental cooperation within the Community is understandable. German foreign policy cannot be evaluated or interpreted autonomously, but rather, within the framework of the foreign policy of its partners. Unilateralism is neither an invention nor a monopoly of the Federal Republic. He who criticizes it must be prepared to explain how far he legitimized it through his own example and how he made it unavoidable through his own behavior. One cannot remain aloof from the integrational initiatives of the Federal Republic while at the same time criticizing them, and then condemning their lack of success.

The question of whether the Federal Republic has an Atlantic, a European, or a unilateral orientation cannot be settled with a survey of its behavior in the three areas. Foreign policy cannot at all be interpreted as an isolated decision process, nor even adequately as part of an action-reaction process between individual countries. Much more, even if not primarily, it must be understood as the fulfillment of social requirements of the political system of the unit concerned. The analysis of the foreign political options of the West German state must therefore be concluded with a view to the relative demands of West German society.

Demands and Orientations

Demands

In a relevant and politically acute sense, there are no demands for an intensification of West European integration. There are demands on the part of the big political parties and social groups. Nevertheless, they apparently play no role in the political behavior of these groups. Pronouncements are made whenever attention is directed toward Europe. But as soon as policy becomes a concrete and real business, it is difficult to find specific proposals for action.

On the other hand, the pertinent party programs must not be mistaken for pure window dressing. They reflect much more the rational political perception that the West European state of middle size is no longer capable of acting alone, that West Europe has become so interdependent in the ideological, social, economic, and political spheres, that the relations among European countries themselves have to demonstrate a different and higher quality than that between them and the external world. The consequent challenge for European integration, therefore, must certainly be considered as real. *It is latent only inasmuch as nobody knows how to make it into a reality.* The cardinal problem of Europe lies not in the determination of European goals but in the strategies for its realization. The structure of this Europe lies as much in the dark as the concrete decisions with which it could be brought into being. The rationality of European integration fails because of the blindness of integrative processes. As a result, integration remains verbal and policy unilateral.

The programs of the three big parties differ less in the degree of their commitment to European unification than in the varying demands concerning its internal organization. The Social Democratic party, which had placed the political accent on reunification during the first postwar years,[44] declared European unification a primary goal in connection with the Bad Godesberg program. Since then, it has strived for the advancement of western integration. The oil crisis somewhat diminished its enthusiasm because it revealed all too clearly the vitality of unilateralism in almost all European countries. Nevertheless the Social Democratic party continued unabatedly to promote the challenge toward a continuation of European unity, and it particularly dedicated itself to an economic and monetary union.[45] Its party chairman, Willy Brandt, vigorously sought a seat in the European Parliament elected for the first time in 1979.

In this task, the SPD knows itself to be in harmony with its tradition, in which the necessity to overcome the nationalism responsible for so many wars in Europe has always played an important role. Accordingly, the party entrusts two goals to European unification: the creation of a European climate of peace "which will remove the fear of possible war for all Europeans," and the establishment "of a social democracy . . . in the union of freedom and justice."[46] The party broke down this general program into separate planks for the platform developed together with the other social democratic parties in the Community on June 6, 1977.[47] It calls for a Europe of full employment, economic democracy, improved social security, and corresponding conditions for life and employment; it calls for a Europe that will realize detente in the East-West conflict, and solidarity in the North-South conflict. This program is very vigorous: just as the social and democratic level was improved in the transition from feudalism to the nation state, so it will have to be raised to a higher level in the transition to a regional state.

Nevertheless, the program contains nothing that is addressed to the decisive question of how to realize these goals other than the very general exhortation to a corresponding cooperation of political and social groups. Given the visible disparity in social structure and social political concepts that prevails in Europe, such a program has primarily a declaratory value. It is again evident in the SPD "Orientierungsrahmen 85," passed by the party executive committee in 1975. In its general part, it contains the very correct perception of the "necessity for European solutions . . . in view of a more just formation of the internal ordering of society."[48] But the resulting enumeration of concrete political proposals is almost exclusively devoted to the national framework; it is not directed toward Europe but toward the Federal Republic.

The same pattern appears with the other parties. The Christian Democratic Union and the Free Democratic party are dedicated to European unification and have joined together with their respective ideological partners in the Community countries. Of course, they differ with regard to their preferences for the internal structure of this Europe. The CDU accentuates freedom and economic growth;[49] the FDP tries to tie both of these to a call for equality of opportunity and social leveling.[50] These parties do not demonstrate a practical political way to realize these goals either. Not even the German Trade Unions Association (DGB) is capable of finding it. Of course, it is prepared to make sacrifices for European integration if the demands are not biased, and if they really serve the goal of full integration.[51] It works together with the European Trade Union Association founded in 1973, whose first chairman was Oskar Vetter, the DGB leader. Just as the European Trade Union Association sails high above the political waters of its member branches, so too, the European program of the DGB is not concretely linked with the practice of the trade unions in the Federal Republic. As before, it is primarily tied to German realities.[52]

It must be said that parties and trade unions are ready for integration and are interested in it. Nevertheless, they neither know nor take the path that leads to it. More important is the fact that they do not apply much energy to the search for such a way. They are much more directed toward the political unit in which their short-range goals are to be realized. Unilateralism is not nationalism; it is a practice for want of something better.

If one looks to the ministerial bureaucracy and to the managers of the economy—in other words, to that economic-political cooperative structure which makes most European decisions—then a sharper image results. In any event, Werner Feld has noted a clear resistance to political union among the bureaucrats he interviewed;[53] stronger, incidentally, among Germans than among other Europeans. They are afraid of the elimination of careers. By contrast, it was the same German functionaries who were strongly in favor of the strengthening of economic cooperation to the point of economic union.[54] But since an economic union must be a de facto political-economic union, it is probably not wrong to assume that the resistance, or at least the disinterest, of the bureaucrats arises at the point where cooperation shifts to organization. The functionaries would present no resistance, but neither would they foster such a development. Feld states, "They are not so much guilty of treason as they are of anomy."[55]

What claims do the managers make? German managers, especially in the higher echelons, are less enthusiastic about integration than those of other European countries. On the other hand, those who favor integration would work harder for it than would their European partners.[56] The lower levels are more inclined toward integration than the higher. The commitment to Europe grows (as does orientation to the SPD) as the level of managers gets lower. In general, the majority among them is in favor of a construction in which an integrated structure is provided with a true decision-making capability. They are more reserved only in their own field, economy, and the majority favors nationally mixed integrated competency structures. The maintenance of exclusively national decision-making competence is claimed by only a disappearing minority.

Thus, even the managers would not be against an increased European integration, should it occur. Nor would they bring it about; first, because it is not in their power to do so; and second, because their own interests would not thereby be served. They have settled into a "Europe of top managers." Why should they work for a Brussels Europe? Thus, it is also evident that their unilateralism does not stem from necessity or conviction, and least of all from a nationalistic orientation. It is much more a comfortable and manageable practice which nobody would hesitate, but nobody would commit himself, to abandon.

Orientations

The orientations of the public, its attitudes, can be assessed only with difficulty and judged with even greater difficulty. Opinion polls have questionable value and, at least in the Federal Republic, they concern themselves only rarely and unsystematically with international questions. Within this limitation, it can be said that public commitment to European integration has constantly increased. As late as 1965, the majority considered German reunification more important than European integration. But since the seventies, almost three-fourths of the German population has been in favor of a continuing development of the Community even to the degree of a United States of Europe.[57] Almost half (41 percent) favored European unification over an alliance with the United States, and was thus much more oriented toward Europe than to the Atlantic.[58] This option must not be interpreted as a disregard or underestimation of the NATO. In 1971, 71 percent of the West German population was in favor of continued membership, with the correct assessment that the current Europe is not capable of assuring its own security. On the other hand, the continuing support of Atlantic cooperation within the framework of the NATO is marked by a noticeably constant interest in neutrality. In 1951, 48 percent declared themselves in favor of such a position for West Germany, in 1965 42 percent, and in 1975 still 36 percent.[59] The genesis and meaning of this interest are difficult to evaluate. It is probably because of a desire to stay out of the great power conflict, to assume a marginal position in world policy. People feel almost no need for a renewed position of German leadership. The majority of Germans polled were of the opinion that the Federal Republic should have nothing to say in world politics, and only a third was in favor of a claim to leadership by the Federal Republic within the European Economic Community.[60]

These data, as mentioned earlier, are difficult to assess. They are not uniform and, above all, they are incomplete. Quite evidently there is no articulated demand for an intensification of European integration; but there is an evident willingness to accept and develop it further. Nobody is against it; most are for it; hardly anyone commits himself.

Thus, the unilaterally-behaving decision maker is not forced by anyone to strengthen his European options. There is no insurmountable necessity for it, no socially relevant group that would vigorously foster the political realization of the European option. This claim is latently present and broadly dispersed. It is shared by the business world, interest groups, managers, functionaries, and even political decision makers. They would gladly bring economic and social policy into the European union if there were an occasion for it, a real necessity for it. But that is lacking. Since economic and social policy can successfully be managed in the German framework, unilateralism remains. It can be carried out all the more easily as long as the guarantee of security within the American-led Atlantic Community is without problems. The NATO offers collective security without harming unilateralism too much.

In that sense, unilateralism proves to be not the best but the only possible policy. It is an instrument; not an ideology, not a concept. It is practiced because there is no fully developed strategic or tactical alternative; of course, nobody works on it either. Unilateralism is easily tied to cooperation with other countries that have not developed alternatives either. As long as no domestic or foreign political crises force a change, unilateralism will remain the instrument for "muddling through."

The Federal Republic should, however, not be satisfied with this. As a result of its past, it cannot unilaterally consume the successes gained by unilateralism. It cannot behave as others do. Making unilateralism a declared concept instead of using it for the purposes of "muddling through" would isolate Germany externally. It would destroy the internal consensus that is based on the orientation toward European cooperation.

To be sure, there is a coalition of "grandsons and grandfathers" on the fringes of German society, between those who remember a national policy and those who dream of it. But in the broad spectrum of German society, an entirely different tendency is noticeable, as the latest electoral analyses show. As a result of the increasing prosperity of postindustrial society in the Federal Republic, the value system is changing from an emphasis on materialistic values to preference for nonmaterial ones, analogous to Ronald Inglehart's thesis.[61] Self-realization is more important than the maintenance of the obsolete social structure. interest in participation and partnership exceed the interest in tranquillity and order; understanding and the willingness to tolerate minorities are increasing instead of the insistence on the security of one's own group from within and without.[62] The followers of such "new politics" are clearly evident since the sixties; they distinguish themselves from the supporters of "old politics" who had oriented themselves to the value system of the prematerialistic society. It is true that the majority of the German population still belongs to the latter group. But it will decrease to the extent that industrialization is accomplished. Interestingly enough, three-fourths of the followers of the new politics support the Social Democratic party,[63] while only 37.5 percent of the guardians of the old order gave it their vote. It should, therefore, be the first priority of the SPD to transfer its aspired domestic progress to the area of foreign policy.

Above all, this means that unilateralism as a process must be overcome. Common goals cannot be pursued separately; the danger is too great that the method will one day influence the goals. The European Economic Community could drift apart because the Community has no common strategies.

This is a problem not only for the Federal Republic, but also for the entire European Community. It is the Federal Republic's increased freedom to maneuver that has again (even if not always adequately) posed the problem. Why should not the Federal Republic begin with its solution?

Notes

1. Helmut Schmidt, *Kontinuität und Konzentration* (Bonn-Bad Godesberg: Neue Gesellschaft, 1976), p. 49.

2. Bundesministerium der Verteidigung (Federal Ministry of Defense), *Weissbuch 1975/76: Zur Sicherheit der Bundesrepublik Deutschland und zur Entwicklung der Bundeswehr* (Bonn, 1976), p. 14.

3. The historical development of the Four Power Agreement on Berlin is described in Presse- und Informationsamt der Bundesregierung (Hg.), *Das Vier-Mächte-Abkommen über Berlin vom 3. September 1971*, Hamburg 1971, p. 114.

4. See Czempiel, "Organizing the Euro-American System," in *The Euro-American System; Economic and Political Relations Between North America and Western Europe*, ed. Ernst-Otto Czempiel and Dankwant A. Rustow (Frankfurt: Campus Verlag; Boulder: Westview Press, 1976), p. 206.

5. See Dieter Dettke, *Allianz im Wandel; amerikanisch-europäische Sicherheitsbeziehungen im Zeichen des Bilateralismus der Supermächte* (Frankfurt: Metzner Verlag, 1976).

6. Schmidt, *Kontinuität*, p. 49.

7. Hans-Dietrich Genscher, *Deutsche Aussenpolitik* (Stuttgart Verlag Bonn Aktuell GMBH, 1977), p. 37.

8. Ibid., p. 38.

9. Chancellor Helmut Schmidt in the German Bundestag, 8. Wahlperiode, 93 Sitzung, June 1, 1978, in *Stenographisch Bericht*, "The Declaration of the Federal Government on the Special General Assembly of the United Nations for Disarmament Held in New York and the NATO meeting of Leaders and Heads of State and Government in Washington," p. 7289.

10. Hans-Jürgen Wischnewski, "Europa vor den Wahlen," in Vorstand der SPD (Hg.), *Internationale Politik*, Sozialdemokratische Fachkonferenz, April 9-10, 1976, Bonn 1976, p. 40. Wischnewski was under-secretary in the Foreign Office.

11. Ernst-Otto Czempiel, "Die Bundesrepublik und Amerika: Von der Okkupation zur Kooperation," in R. Löwenthal und H.-P. Schwarz, eds., *Die zweite Republik* (Stuttgart: Belser Verlag, 1974), p. 554.

12. See Gert Krell und Peter Schlotter, "Zur Diskussion über die taktischen Nuklearwaffen," in *Europa, Analyse und Dokumentation* (Frankfurt, 1977).

13. See Eugene J. McCarthy, "Look, No Allies," *Foreign Policy* No. 30 (Spring 1978):3.

14. Manfred Knapp, "Politische und Wirtschaftliche Interdependenzen im Verhältnis USA—(Bundesrepublik) Deutschland 1945-1975," in *Die USA und Deutschland 1918-1975* Manfred Knapp et al. (Munich, 1978), p. 153.

15. Willy Brandt, "Europa und die Vereinigten Staaten: Die Unentbehrliche Allianz." Speech before American Chamber of Commerce in Germany, Düsseldorf, 1978. Bonn, mimeographed.

16. Schmidt, *Kontinuität*, p. 153.

17. Klaus Ritter, "Zur Weiterentwicklung der Ost-West-Beziehungen: Der konzeptionelle Spielraum," in *Amerika und Westeuropa, Gegenwarts- und Zukunftsprobleme*, ed. K. Kaiser und H.-P. Schwarz, (Stuttgart: Belser Verlag, 1977), p. 204.

18. *Bulletin* der Europäischen Gemeinschaften, (Beilage 8, 1977: Europäische Union), p. 9.

19. Erklärung der Bundesregierung zur Lage der Nation vor dem Deutschen Bundestag, in *Bulletin* 13, January 30, 1976, p. 136.

20. For example, Evans and Novak, "West German Move toward East Feared," *International Herald Tribune*, August 14, 1978.

21. Schmidt, *Kontinuität*, p. 237.

22. To compare this context in the United States, see Ernst-Otto Czempiel, "Die Vereinigten Staaten von Amerika und die Entspannung," in *Aus Politik und Zeitgeschichte*, Vol. 37 (1977), p. 3.

23. Christian Hacke, *Die Ost- und Deutschlandpolitik der CDU/CSU, Wege und Irrwege der Opposition seit 1969* (Cologne: Verlag Wissenschaft und Politik 1975).

24. See Alois Mertes, Member of Parliament (CDU) who presents a consistent and thorough argument in *Deutschland-Union-Dienst*, August 11, 1978.

25. See Willy Brandt, *Begegnungen und Einsichten, Die Jahre 1960-1975* (Hamburg: Hoffmann und Campe 1976).

26. Chancellor Schmidt before the Deutschen Bundestag, 8. Wahlperiode, 90. Sitzung, May 11, 1978, p. 7064.

27. Leader of the opposition, Helmut Kohl, ibid., p. 7067.

28. See J. Robert Schaetzel, *The Unhinged Alliance: America and the European Community* (New York: Council on Foreign Relations, Harper & Row, 1975).

29. Klaus Otto Nass, "Der 'Zahlmeister' als Schrittmacher? Die Bundesrepublik Deutschland in der Europäischen Gemeinschaft," *Europa-Archiv* 10 (1976):325.

30. Schmidt, *Kontinuität*, p. 144.

31. Ibid.

32. This thesis is disputed by Joachim Hütter, "Die Stellung der Bundesrepublik Deutschland in Westeuropa. Hegemonie durch wirtschaftliche Dominanz?," *Integration* No. 3 (1978):103.

33. President of the Bundesbank, Ottmar Emminger, "Die internationale Bedeutung der deutschen Stabilitätspolitik," *Europa-Archiv* 15 (1977):509.

34. Frieder Schlupp, "Das Deutsche Modell und seine Europäischen Folgen," *EG-Magazin* 5 (1978):8.

35. Michael Kreile, "Die Bundesrepublik Deutschland—Eine 'économie dominante' in Westeuropa?," in *Aus Politik und Zeitgeschichte* 26 (1978), p. 3.

36. For further details, see Ernst-Otto Czempiel, "Europa—integrativ oder national? Koexistenz, Kooperation, Integration," in F.-M. Schmölz, *Christlicher Friedensbegriff und europäische Friedensordnung* (München und Mainz, 1977), p. 65.

37. David P. Calleo, "The European Coalition in a Fragmented World," *Foreign Affairs* 54:1 (1976):98.

38. Schmidt, *Kontinuität*, p. 140.

39. See the statement of the Hamburg Party Congress of the SPD, November 1977, in *SPD: Dokumente zur Europapolitik*, Bonn o. J., p. 7.

40. Genscher, *Deutsche Aussenpolitik*, p. 155.

41. Werner J. Feld, "West European Foreign Policies: The Impact of the Oil Crisis," *ORBIS* (Spring 1978):63.

42. Peter J. Katzenstein, "Die Stellung der Bundesrepublik Deutschland in der Amerikanischen Aussenpolitik, Drehscheibe, Anker oder Makler?," *Europa-Archiv* 11 (1976):347.

43. William Pfaff, "Bonn: A Shift Away from U.S.?," *International Herald Tribune*, June 6, 1978.

44. See Rudolf Hrbek, *Die SPD—Deutschland und Europa* (Bonn 1972).

45. Charles R. Foster, "The Social Democratic Party and West German Foreign Policy: Continuity and Change," in *The Foreign Policies of West European Socialist Parties*, ed. Werner J. Feld (New York 1977), p. 17.

46. Declaration of the SPD Party Executive on the European elections, 1978, in *SPD: Dokumente zur Europapolitik*, p. 4.

47. Ibid., p. 15.

48. SPD, Zweiter Entwurf eines ökonomisch-politischen Orientierungsrahmens für die Jahre 1975-1985 (Bonn, 1975), p. 21. But see the report of the European Commission to the SPD in 1975, *Sozialdemokratische Europapolitik*, which also includes a three step plan, even though it is very general.

49. See das Programm der (christlich-demokratischen) Europäischen Volkspartei vom März 1978, in *CDU-Kokumentation* 8 (Bonn, 1978).

50. Europäische Liberale Demokraten, *Thesen des Wahlprogramms* (Bonn, 1977), p. 16. See also the survey of party programs and their conclusions in Rudolf Hrbek, "Parteibünde in der Europäischen Gemeinschaft auf dem Weg zu programmatischem Profil," *Europa-Archiv* 33:10 (1978):299.

51. Ludwig Rosenberg, "Die Westpolitik der deutschen Gewerkschaften," in *Gewerkschaftliche Politik: Reform aus Solidarität*, U. Borsdorf et al. (Köln, 1977), p. 553.

52. Kreile, "Deutscheland-'économie dominante'" p. 3.

53. Werner J. Feld and John K. Wildgen, "National Administrative Elites and European Integration, Saboteurs at Work?," *Journal of Common Market Studies* 13 (1975):264.

54. Ibid., p 249.

55. Werner J. Feld, "Political and Administrative Elite Attitudes in the European Community," 1975, mimeographed, p. 23.

56. Karl P. Sauvant and Bernard Mennis, "Corporate Internationalization and German Enterprise: A Social Profile of German Managers and their Attitudes regarding the European Community and Future Company Strategies," (mimeo) University of Pennsylvania, 1973, p. 44.

57. Elizabeth Noelle-Neumann, *Jahrbuch der Offentlichen Meinung, 1968-1973* (Allensbach: Verlag für Demoskopie, 1974), p. 211. For the public opinion data, I am grateful for the assistance of Werner Damm.

58. See *Allensbacher Jahrbuch der Demoskopie* (München, 1976), p. 285.

59. Ibid., p. 279.

60. Ibid., pp. 293, 287.

61. Ronald Inglehart, *The Silent Revolution* (Princeton: Princeton University Press, 1977).

62. Kai Hildebrandt and Russell J. Dalton, "Die Neue Politik, politischer Wandel oder Schönwetter-Politik?;" *Politische Vierteljahresschrift* 18 (November 1977):237.

63. Ibid., p. 247.

**Part II
German Policies in the
European Community**

7 German Industrial and Labor Policy and the European Community

Alfred Steinherr

Der Aberglaube ist die Poesie des Lebens—Goethe

Introduction

The task assigned to me for this chapter was formulated as how and whether the evolution of European Community policies or other effects resulting from the formation of the Community have modified the structure of Germany's economy. Moreover, how has German policy responded to the formation of the Community?

In such general terms, it is quite impossible to give conclusive answers. First, the question of the impact of the Community on the German economy depends on what would have happened otherwise. Most analyses take the status quo as benchmark, but it is not unthinkable that Germany might have unilaterally opened itself up to foreign trade. Another reasonable hypothesis is that tariff concessions within the General Agreement on Tariffs and Trade (GATT) would have liberalized world trade more without the Community than with it. Of course, less optimistic speculations are also permissible. A second difficulty with my task is that what one would ultimately like to know are the effects of the formation of the Community on the welfare of German citizens. To show, for example, that tariff reductions on trade within the Community have increased intra-Community trade is not enough for proving that there are economic gains. But to track down welfare effects is not an easy exercise. Unfortunately, the difficulties do not end here. Industrial policy covers such a wide range of actions that one cannot analyze all of them in detail; nor is it obvious how to delineate industrial policy, since most policies have effects on industrial structure and performance.[1]

In this chapter, I shall cover a vast array of policies, obviously not all in depth. In some cases, it will be possible to arrive at precise welfare statements, in most cases not; this should be no surprise. I shall first analyze the effects of what may be considered the major achievement of the

Martina Priebe helped in collecting material for this chapter. Frank Wolter was a very lucid commentator while M. Norro and G. Basevi raised useful questions. My thanks go to all of them without implicating their responsibility.

Community, the customs union. Second, a variety of national and Community policies will be discussed. Then, I will turn to labor policies; and the main conclusions will be drawn in a final section. The analysis in this chapter is nontechnical; when necessary, references are given to technical studies and statistical sources.

Germany and Market Integration within the Community

The Treaty of Rome laid out a step-by-step process of integration from a customs union via an economic union toward, eventually, a political union.

The customs union had been achieved, through several stages, by 1968. It represents a geographical area within which goods circulate free of tariffs; imports from nonmember countries are penalized by a common tariff. To create a common market would require, in addition, absence of discriminatory measures (such as subsidies, differential tax treatments, and so on) applied to producers from the different countries of the Community. In this analysis, we shall assume the existence of a Common Market; integration effects are therefore overstated. Only in the next section of the chapter is this assumption relaxed. The reason for this procedure is that tariff policy has created a customs union while other measures of industrial policy are necessary to achieve a common market.

The creation of and adherence to the Community have always been supported by German governments primarily for political reasons; economic considerations clearly have been secondary. Nevertheless the general view prevailed, for example, within the Spaak Committee and German industry, that a common market would be highly beneficial to Germany's manufacturing section. Such a view also led France to claim compensation through an arrangement for agricultural products.

Whether or not the Common Market, in fact, has been beneficial for Germany or for German industry depends, among other things, on what one considers the adequate basis for comparison. The minister for economic affairs of the 1950s, Ludwig Erhard, was never a staunch supporter of the Community on economic grounds. He rightly defended the viewpoint that worldwide trade liberalization would be welfare not only for the world but also for Germany. Of course, worldwide tariff reductions might have encountered greater difficulties than formation of a common market for Europe.

However, it can be shown that even unilateral tariff reductions are welfare to a customs union.[2] From this point of view, it seems that Germany's membership in the Common Market cannot be rationalized primarily on economic grounds; political considerations must have been predominant.[3] If this argument were true, however, it would be difficult to believe that no major interest group objected to joining the Community. In particular, since German industry strongly supported the Community, one would think that at least industry expected to gain. It appears therefore worthwhile to look at the possible gains or losses for Germany and German industry, and their distribution among factors of production.

Traditionally, analyses have been focused on static effects that are a result of improved efficiency brought about by a reallocation of resources. They shift the growth path without, however, affecting the growth rate. Let us start with this argument.

Within the Community, domestic industry is not protected anymore from competition arising from other member countries. More efficient producers might be expected to capture market shares of less efficient ones. A useful distinction can be made between trade creation, where production shifts from one community country to another, and trade diversion, where production moves from a nonmember country to a member country. I illustrate the argument for the case of trade creation.

Figure 7-1 depicts supply and demand for a particular product in Germany. Suppose that before the creation of the Community, imports from

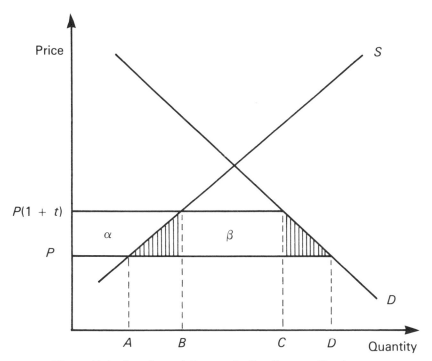

Figure 7-1. Supply and Demand of a German Product

other Community countries are offered at a price P, on which a tariff rate t was imposed. Domestic consumption was equal to C, production occurred at B, and the amount BC was imported. In a common market, imported goods are offered at price P (assuming that costs remain constant). Domestic consumption increases to D, imports to AD, and production drops to A. What is the gain from integration? It is the sum of the two hatched triangles, since part of what consumers gain is compensated by a loss of producers' surplus (α) and a loss of tariff revenues (β). Thus, increased competition leads to a reallocation of resources in favor of more efficient producers. Moreover, this leads to a redistribution of income from industry and government to consumers.

There are at least two disturbing facts about this analysis. One relates to the size of the gain from integration; the other to income redistribution.

Empirical studies of the trade creation and trade diversion effects all reach the conclusion that the gain is inferior to 1 percent of the gross national product (GNP) for the Community and for any individual country.[4] From figure 7-1, we get an idea why these gains are insignificant. We can compute the surface of the two triangles very easily if we assume that the slope of the supply and demand curves are identical (the results will not be much affected by a violation of this hypothesis). We now simply multiply the increase in imports resulting from the formation of the Community with the tariff rate and divide by two. Prewo (1974) has estimated that by 1970, trade creation was completed and amounted to 40 percent of total imports. Applying the average tariff rate of 10 percent (before joining the Community), and dividing by two, the result is 2 percent. This figure can be related to the GNP using the weight of imports in domestic absorption. This has been between 20-25 percent in Germany, so we obtain 1/2 percent or less of the GNP. Prewo's results are rather on the high side compared to others. Moreover, higher production in the rest of the Community requires higher prices. On both accounts, these results are therefore an overestimation. On the other hand, an effective protection rate might exceed the 10 percent of the average tariff rate by as much as five percentage points. Anyhow, the gains seem fairly small and insufficient to warrant integration efforts.

How has Germany fared compared to partner countries? According to Prewo, German imports increased more (in relative terms) than Dutch and Belgian imports but less than Italian or French. This is because German tariff protection before 1958 was intermediate to these two sets of countries. Hence, the gain from trade creation is roughly uniform for all countries.

Within Germany, who benefited from trade creation? According to figure 7-1, consumers gained while producers lost. How then is it possible that industry supported the Community while consumers had no particular attitude?

I think several important aspects for assessment of the gains accruing to any member country are neglected in figure 7-1 and some of them also in the literature.

First, I have only considered trade creation so far. It is often argued that the interest of German industry is in trade diversion. Since some of the most important competitors of German industry are outside the Community (United States, Japan, Canada, and until 1973, all European Free Trade Association [EFTA] countries), the Common Market discriminates in favor of German industry. Similarly, the Common Agricultural Policy (CAP) discriminates in favor of French agriculture and to the detriment of overseas producers. I tend not to give too much weight to this argument. First, the structures of Community economies are quite similar, so there is a high degree of potential competition. Second, for most manufactured goods the common tariff does not provide significant protection. This viewpoint is also supported by the available empirical studies that reach the conclusion that there has been very little, if any, trade diversion for industrial products.

Second, when the overall gains from trade creation are computed for the EC, it is sufficient to analyze imports since the assumption of a constant price in the rest of the Community keeps surplus from those producers constant. When we look at a particular country we have to consider exports as well. Resources that are shifted by import competition are being absorbed by those industries, or product lines, which increase exports to preserve trade balance.

Figure 7-2 (a) shows supply and demand in the rest of the Community, while (b) shows demand and supply in Germany. Suppose for simplicity that tariffs before forming the EC were such that they prevented trade. The price in Germany was P, the price in the rest of the Community, P_r. After

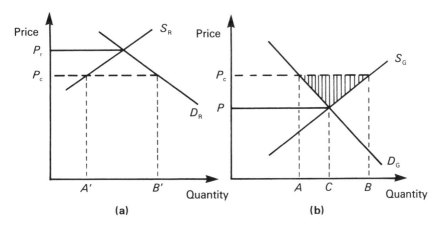

Figure 7-2. (a) Demand and Supply in the Community (Excluding Germany); (b) Demand and Supply in Germany

elimination of the intra-Community tariff, Germany exports to the rest of the Community the quantity $AB(=A'B')$ at the equilibrium price P_c. The net gain for Germany is equal to the hatched triangle. German consumers experience a drop in welfare that is, however, exceeded by the gain of German producers.

This elementary consideration is important because it provides at least partial answers to the two problems posed in the previous analysis.

First, the overall welfare gain for Germany is not adequately measured by looking at imports only. We have to add the gains from higher exports. They are equal to the increase in exports (AB), induced by intra-Community tariff reductions, times the increase in German export prices necessary to generate larger supply, divided by two. The gain obtained on the import side may then be doubled. But even then, the total gain is still fairly small.

Second, and more important, income is redistributed toward producers. However, since German industry loses on some products and gains on others, it is not possible a priori to assess net gains. At any rate, they cannot be substantial; so we still need more convincing reasons.

Finally, even if industry is considered a homogeneous interest group (which it is not!), an important asymmetry has to be noted. Not the entire increase in imports corresponds to a shift of local producers. An important part satisfies increased demand. These imports compete, of course, for the consumers' expenditures, but this indirect competition is probably less directly felt by German producers. The advantage of integration, then, may be perceived by German industry as more substantial than it actually is.

Third, so far it has been assumed that demand and supply curves are unaffected by integration. This may be a useful assumption for demand but less so for supply. Two types of efficiency may be distinguished: allocative efficiency (that is, how resources are attributed to different activities) and X-efficiency. The latter concept applies to the organizational efficiency within firms. It is indeed often argued that market integration does eliminate slack, forces firms to search for new products and the best production methods, and so on. In other words, the supply curves in figures 7-1 and 7-2 shift downward, thereby increasing producer surplus. This is shown by the hatched area in figure 7-3. It is assumed here that foreign productivity remains constant; otherwise consumers and producers would benefit. Similar efficiency improvements may be realized on the export side where they would also affect extracommunity trade.

It is difficult to obtain numerical estimates for this gain in productivity. Balassa (1975) uses an estimate by Walters (1963), according to which in the first half of the century a doubling of inputs in the U.S. nonagricultural sector was accompanied by an approximately 130 percent increase in output. This estimate includes the effects of intensified competition and

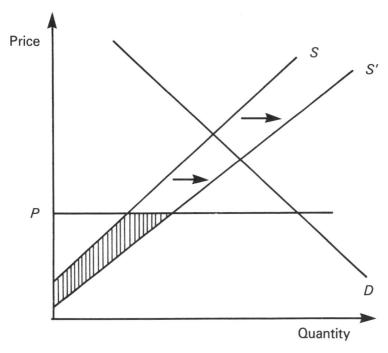

Figure 7-3. Efficiency Effects of Integration

economies of scale. Balassa then calculates a 2.3 percent of GNP gain for the Community. I consider this estimate too high for Germany. First, the German market and available export markets, even in the absence of the EC, are large enough to allow German industry to fully exploit potential economies of scale.[6] There are a few exceptions, such as nuclear energy, aircrafts, and computers, but for those products an integrated market does not exist anyhow. Second, with regard to X-efficiency, the gains are certainly substantially lower for German industry than for the French and Italian industries. Germany was less tariff-protected than those countries, has been less interventionist on internal markets, and less defensive toward foreign investments. Because of this more liberal environment, competition in most German markets has been fiercer than in Italy and France, allowing less slack to exist. However, we have to again add something to the total welfare gain—perhaps as much as 2 percent.

Fourth, another possible source of gain is the following. Suppose that because of rigidities and distortions, the values of the marginal productivity of factors of production are not equalized throughout the economy. For example, unskilled agricultural workers tend to earn less than unskilled construction workers. Now, those sectors where value-added per unit of capital is lowest are the most liable to see their activity reduced through integration. If we assume that the amount of labor and capital released shown in figure 7-1 is used to expand production shown in figure 7-2(b), then this argument amounts to saying that the area under the supply curve with base AB in figure 7-1 is less than the area under the supply curve with base CB in figure 7-2(b). Total value-added thus would be augmented, increasing either the real wage rate or profits, or both.

Again I am agnostic about the numerical importance of this argument for German industry.[7] There are perhaps fewer distortions in German industry than in most partner countries. And precisely in those sectors where productivity is low have employment reductions been slowed down. For example, a shift of resources from agriculture to industry could have significantly increased value-added. But this process is being counteracted by national support policies as well as the Common Agricultural Policy. Other examples can be found, such as the railways, and naval constructions.

Fifth, integration allows a higher degree of specialization. If comparative advantage leads to a resource reallocation toward those industries that are fast-growing, then integration affects not only static efficiency of the economy but also its growth rate. Balassa (1975) shows, however, that there has been very little interindustry reallocation of resources (but substantial intraindustry reallocations) in the Community. In the next section of this chapter, which deals with industrial structure, I shall argue that the share of fast-growing industries has not increased in Germany since 1958, in contrast to what happened in other countries of the EC. It seems, therefore, that reallocations may not have had a significant impact on the growth rate, which has been fairly low in Germany since the mid-sixties.

Sixth, resource reallocation through higher competition should obey the dictates of factor-proportion theory. Since Germany is generally considered as a capital-rich country, the Stolper-Samuelson theorem implies that real rates of return to capital should have benefited from intra-Community trade liberalization, to the detriment of wages. Labor immigration had similar effects.

More important than the Stolper-Samuelson theorem, assuming full mobility of factors of production, is certainly the result that can be obtained from the assumption of factor immobility. In this case, both labor and capital in export industries would benefit from integration, to the detriment of the import-competing and nontradable sectors of the economy.[8] Incidentally, this, together with the strong dependence of employment on exports, is a rational explanation of the support the EC received not only from capital owners but also from workers in Germany.

Although not a counterproof of these propositions, table 7-1 shows that profit rates in most industries have been following a downward trend since 1958. Other phenomena, such as higher competition, increased union power, and increased taxation may have more than offset the Stolper-Samuelson effect.

Table 7-1
Profits in Industry 1958, 1964, and 1970
(in percent)

Industry	Gross Return on Sales			Gross Return on Capital[a]		
	1958	*1964*	*1970*	*1958*	*1964*	*1970*
Pulp, paper, and paperboard	16.7	11.5	11.3	21.0	10.0	8.1
Nonferrous metal manufactures	12.8	17.7	18.3	17.9	24.0	25.9
Pulp and paper products	13.9	15.3	18.8	41.4	33.9	29.3
Wearing apparel, except footwear	11.4	9.7	10.8	50.6	31.7	29.2
Textiles	12.3	12.9	16.0	22.9	10.3	17.6
Iron and steel	14.8	12.1	8.6	25.1	14.3	8.7
Pottery, china, and earthenware	18.8	18.7	15.0	30.1	23.5	14.8
Iron and steel foundries	13.0	13.4	15.7	19.2	15.9	15.9
Leather products	13.0	16.8	18.7	50.0	55.0	43.1
Furniture and fixtures (wood)	11.8	16.7	10.0	30.4	37.4	35.0
Glass and glass products	14.2	17.7	23.5	30.8	27.1	26.1
Rubber products	18.7	13.9	8.0	35.4	23.0	11.0
Chemicals	20.7	16.8	15.4	19.9	10.2	10.0
Footwear	11.6	0.0	3.1	32.4	23.7	15.6
Wood, plywood, and wood products	15.5	14.5	18.3	26.1	19.6	18.8
Office equipment	10.8	16.0	13.7	40.0	54.6	22.3
Leather	−1.0	0.0	16.9	−3.9	2.1	18.6
Musical instruments, toys, jewelry, and sporting goods	19.5	21.1	21.2	82.9	63.4	43.8
Plastic products	22.3	17.9	16.6	66.0	36.8	25.4
Road transport equipment	23.5	16.4	11.7	47.7	25.8	13.6
Printing	20.6	28.2	20.6	29.4	34.8	30.2
Electrical machinery	18.3	10.0	8.0	41.0	20.8	13.5
Steel drawing and cold rolling mills	14.3	10.6	16.0	30.1	13.1	25.7
Precision and optical goods, clocks, and watches	15.1	13.9	12.3	29.1	23.0	18.4
Stones and earthen goods	27.8	28.4	20.3	37.8	30.0	15.5
Machinery except electrical	17.4	15.8	12.1	33.6	26.5	17.7
Construction steel	9.1	6.3	6.2	32.4	17.5	17.2
Mining	28.0	31.4	36.3	14.2	12.8	13.1
Industry (total, without shipbuilding and aerospace)	16.6	14.8	13.5	27.3	21.1	16.2

Source: Donges et al., *Protektion und Branchenstruktur der Westdeutschen Wirtschaft* (Tübingen: J.C.B. Mohr), 1973. Reprinted with permission.

[a]Adjusted for cyclical variations.

Seventh, formation of a common market also affected the terms of trade. Petith (1977) situates the terms-of-trade gains for the Community between 0.3 and 1.0 percent of the GNP. It is easy to show (see Petith, p. 266) that the largest terms-of-trade gains belong to those members that are either small or had the lower initial tariffs. An estimate for Germany is thus well below these figures and can be considered insignificant.

Eighth, integration effects on investment and saving are often mentioned in the literature. I shall not review them since no strong theoretical argument or empirical finding is available; I will only show the evolution of investment from 1950 to 1976 on a global and a sectoral basis (see tables 7-2 and 7-3). This evolution is, of course, influenced by other factors besides the formation of the Community. But, at any rate, investment rates in most sectors have declined, in some sectors substantially, from 1958-1964 to 1964-1970. Also, the rhythm of replacing labor by capital has slowed down (we return to this problem in the third section of this chapter).

Ninth, in order to show the interest for industry to join the Community, it may be more relevant to compute gains relative to industry's share in the GNP rather than relative to the GNP itself. This share is roughly equal to 50 percent, so that all results should be doubled to obtain the relevant gain for industry. Adding point one to point eight then yields a non-negligible percentage of value-added by industry.

Tenth, the customs union was only considered as a step toward an economic union. German industry might have expected that policy makers at the Community level would understand and represent the interests of industry as has been the case in the national framework. The benefits from a European representation in international issues, such as trade agreements, and North-South dialogues, potentially could be substantial; of similar importance is the harmonization of the European business climate and the sociolegal framework.[9]

From this discussion, I derive the following conclusions. There are overall gains from integration compared to the status quo. The traditional calculations of static reallocation gains is certainly an underestimation of

Table 7-2
Net Investment as Percentage of Net National Product

1950	1951	1952	1953	1954	1955	1956	1957
16.5	15.5	16.1	16.0	17.5	20.5	19.8	18.7

1958	1959	1960	1961	1962	1963	1964	1965
18.0	19.0	20.5	20.5	19.7	18.4	20.4	21.0

1966	1967	1968	1969	1970	1971	1972	1973
18.3	14.0	17.5	19.1	20.1	18.1	17.3	16.6

1974	1975	1976	1977
12.3	10.2	12.8	12.9

Table 7-3
Investment and Labor-Saving Effects of Investment in Selected Industries 1958-1970

Industry	Share of Investments[a]		Investment Rate[b]		Labor-Saving Effect of Investments[c]	
	1958-64	*1964-70*	*1958-64*	*1964-70*	*1958-64*	*1964-70*
Pulp, paper, and paperboard	17.5	16.3	70.8	50.3	0.94	0.00
Nonferrous metal manufactures	14.8	13.8	57.8	54.0	0.40	0.36
Pulp and paper products	10.8	10.9	143.3	57.4	0.64	0.69
Wearing apparel except footwear	5.6	4.8	91.0	57.6	0.00	0.77
Textiles	11.3	10.0	66.0	40.7	1.08	0.94
Iron and steel	20.3	14.0	51.2	40.5	0.63	0.07
Pottery, china, and earthenware	9.4	8.9	77.3	57.7	1.01	0.95
Iron and steel founderies	11.2	6.7	66.0	40.1	0.61	0.67
Leather products	4.5	3.9	63.9	45.0	0.77	0.72
Furniture and fixtures (wood)	7.7	7.3	86.3	69.3	0.70	0.01
Glass and glass products	11.9	11.6	173.1	89.7	0.78	0.63
Rubber products	10.2	11.1	87.3	81.7	0.44	0.47
Chemicals	16.0	13.8	72.1	76.1	0.38	0.46
Footwear	5.9	5.4	61.2	41.2	0.93	0.84
Wood, plywood, and wood products	12.7	12.2	70.0	56.6	0.02	1.00
Office equipment	0.1	8.6	107.4	73.7	0.67	0.61
Leather	8.8	7.1	61.8	33.6	1.23	4.02
Musical instruments, toys, jewelry, and sporting goods	5.7	6.8	113.9	103.0	0.01	0.75
Plastic products	15.1	11.3	233.8	142.7	0.33	0.31
Road transport equipment	17.7	14.6	147.0	83.5	0.44	0.36
Printing	11.1	8.5	98.5	63.3	0.67	0.54
Electrical machinery	10.1	7.7	99.6	66.8	0.53	0.43
Steel drawing and cold rolling mills	12.1	10.0	63.7	32.4	0.76	0.42
Precision and optical goods, clocks, and watches	8.8	8.4	49.7	71.7	0.76	0.51
Stones and earthen goods	15.7	13.1	128.1	71.8	0.66	0.04
Machinery except electrical	9.0	9.1	80.0	62.8	0.57	0.42
Construction steel	6.5	6.0	82.8	53.9	0.09	0.80
Mining	15.0	10.7	48.3	26.2	1.62	2.14
Industry (total, without shipbuilding and aerospace)	12.2	10.4	81.8	61.3	0.66	0.58

Source: Statistiches Bundesamt; and Donges et al. *Protektion und Branchenstruktur der Westdeutschen Wirtschaft*. Tübingen: J.C.B. Mohr, 1973.

[a]Gross investment over net volume of production at prices of 1962.

[b]Gross investment over capital stock of the base year, in prices of 1962.

[c]Rate of change of capital intensity.

those gains and fails to show what motivates German industry to support the Community. I then argued that there is a variety of possible additional gains for German industry, some representing income redistribution toward industry. Hence, German industry was favorable toward joining the Community. However, adding up all possible gains still does not yield impressive sums for the German economy as a whole (especially when the trade-diverting effects of the common agricultural market are included). Moreover, in our discussion, existence of a true common market has been assumed—whereas reality is much less perfect and the integration gains correspondingly lower.

It also seems that while the adjustment to an integrated market was less painful to the German industry than to others, because structure and performance were high at the outset, the gains cannot exceed those of other countries. Moreover, since I deemphasized the trade diversion argument for German industry, a free trade arrangement (multilaterally or unilaterally) might have been still better.

Industrial Policy in Germany and the European Community

In the preceding section, I argued that the gains from the integration of product markets cannot have been substantial for Germany although more important for German industry. The arguments have to be extended in two directions. First, increased competition tends to shift factors, and reallocation of economic activity is often lengthy and costly. Therefore, we have to discuss changes in economic structure and the policy measures aimed at easing the adjustment process. Second, more than a customs union has been achieved by European industrial policy. Indeed, although for manufacturing the treaty retained the market as the main regulator of economic activity, coordination of national economic policies is considered a supplementary means of integration. Member states are to carry out their economic policies, in principle, autonomously. But the autonomy is limited by Articles 103 to 109; that is, by the principle of a free common market. However, on the question of the role of industrial policy, that is, planification versus the market economy, continuing debates demonstrate that no definite form of integration has been found yet. However, a resolution of the Council of Ministers of 1971, reconfirmed in 1972, states that a common economic policy should be enforced not later than 1980. Recent proposals for monetary integration are perhaps steps in that direction.

Factor market integration is relegated to the next section of this chapter. Other domestic or Community policies are discussed in this section.

Changes in Industrial Structures

As mentioned in the preceding section, the Community has not led to vast interindustry shifts. In no country have entire industries disappeared because of lower productivity. Partly the explanation can be found in defensive measures taken by governments. Although the Treaty of Rome allows for such measures to ease adjustment, the extent to which national governments have recourse to such policies is clearly beyond the spirit of the treaty. Another reason is that, in general, technology, factor proportions, and market structure vary substantially from product to product so that relative competitiveness also varies from product to product, leading to intraindustry specialization.[10] Reallocations can often (but not always) be carried out within existing firms and at existing locations. The speed of adjustment is then much higher and the cost substantially lower than with interindustry specialization.

In the late fifties, Germany already had a widely diversified and competitive industrial structure with concentration in (at the time) fast-growing industries (automobiles, chemicals, machinery, and electrical equipment). The structure of other countries, less diversified initially than Germany and less oriented toward fast-growing sectors, moved during the sixties and seventies closer to the German structure.[11] This means that more important interindustry shifts occurred elsewhere besides Germany. The importance of certain sectors, such as steel or automobiles, has risen much more rapidly in Italy and France than in Germany. Table 7-4 gives an overview for broadly aggregated groups.

Another way of showing the changes that occurred in the Community (but not necessarily as a result of integration) is to calculate an indicator for sectoral adjustments. In a report to the Commission, a group of experts has calculated an indicator.[12] The difference between the contribution to the gross domestic product (GDP) in 1960 and 1973 is calculated for different sectors. Their arithmetic averages are taken as indicators for sectoral adjustments. If sectors are broadly aggregated (eleven sectors), Germany shows by far the lowest adjustment. On the basis of twenty-five sectors, however, the United Kingdom indicator drops substantially while the German indicator increases to the level of the United Kingdom. This can be interpreted as follows: in broad categories, the structure of the German economy was much more adequate in 1960 than that of other countries. Fewer adjustments perhaps were necessary; but it is also likely that leadership has been lost through reduced dynamism and lack of innovation. However, within broad groups, the German economy has been more flexible and adjusted—more than, for example, the United Kingdom economy.

In the same study, a distinction is made between fast-growing industries and others. Considered as fast-growing are those industries whose average growth rate from 1960-1973 has been superior to the average growth rate of the economy by at least 30 percent. In Germany, this group consists mainly of oil, chemicals, precision instruments and computers, plastics, gas, and transport equipment. A comparison with other Community countries (based on their proper fast-growing industries) is shown in table 7-5.

Table 7-4
Contribution to Domestic Value-added in 1960 and 1973 at Constant Prices of 1970

	1960						1973					
	West Germany	France	Italy	Great Britain	the Netherlands	Belgium	West Germany	France	Italy	Great Britain	the Netherlands	Belgium
Agriculture	4.1	8.9	12.3	2.8	7.5	7.8	3.1	5.6	7.8	2.9	6.1	3.7
Energy	5.0	5.5	4.6	5.0	3.8	4.5	4.9	6.6	6.1	4.6	6.2	6.2
Intermediate products	7.2	6.1	5.2	5.4	4.5	6.5	8.8	7.3	7.2	6.3	6.8	9.8
Investment goods	16.4	9.1	6.3	12.9	9.0	5.7	16.9	12.9	8.0	13.1	9.6	9.3
Food, drinks, and tobacco	5.6	5.6	4.3	3.1	5.7	5.8	5.5	4.7	4.6	3.2	5.1	5.3
Consumer goods	9.0	8.6	7.7	8.1	7.1	7.6	8.6	8.1	8.5	8.0	6.1	8.1
Construction	8.2	8.4	10.4	6.6	6.9	3.4	8.2	9.6	7.5	6.8	7.4	7.6
Services	44.5	47.9	49.3	56.0	55.5	53.2	44.1	45.1	50.2	55.1	52.6	50.1

Source: Commission des Communaute's Europeennes, Rapport der groupe d'experts d'analyses sectorielles. *Les Mutations Sectorielles des Economies Européenes de 1960 à la Récession* (Brussels, 1978).

Table 7-5
Production, Exports, and Imports of Fast-Growing Sectors
(current prices)

	1963			1970		
	Value-added[a]	Exports	Imports	Value-added[a]	Exports	Imports
West Germany	28.2	41.6	19.8	37.1	47.1	37.5
France	33.2	35.8	32.5	39.3	43.8	47.7
Italy	30.7	33.4	37.8	36.4	35.3	43.9
United Kingdom	30.2	39.4	25.6	35.5	40.6	35.8
the Netherlands	28.2	44.1	44.7	37.9	52.9	49.1
Belgium	38.8	66.8	64.4	54.8	66.1	69.5

Source: Expert report to the European Economic Community (1978).
[a]Value-added with services and constructions excepted.

Table 7-5 reveals that France and the Netherlands were most successful in increasing the share of exports of fast-growing industries in total exports. Particularly striking is the increase of those imports which compete with the fast-growing sectors in Germany. This suggests gradual elimination of structural differences in the Community.

Industrial Policy in Germany

Structural changes in the Community have not been purely the result of market forces but have also been influenced by policy measures. Two useful distinctions may be considered: defensive versus activating policies, and national versus Community policies.

In particular, France and Italy have had recourse to defensive measures in order to alleviate some of their industries from increased competitive pressure and to give them enough time to achieve their adaptation. Individual measures will not be discussed here since imagination sets no limits to policymakers in this area.

In Germany, because of a relatively high degree of competitiveness and the basically market-oriented philosophy of the government, no sizable defensive measures have been taken.[13] Exceptions fall outside of my subject definition. One is agriculture. Others are the supports given to coal mining, shipbuilding, and textiles. Problems in those industries, however, have not arisen from market integration within the EC but from outside competition (overseas coal and oil, Japanese shipbuilding, and so on).

Industrial policy was used in Germany, as elsewhere, to assist firms in future industries. Three major tools have been used: subsidies of various kinds, support of research and development, and support to economic concentration. Let us start with the last approach. Servan-Schreiber was perhaps the first to argue that one way of taking up the challenge of U.S. industry is to concentrate economic activity in firms of a size comparable to the largest U.S. firms. He saw in the EC the chance to combine resources in different European countries to eventually rival U.S. companies. These arguments are suspect, since size does not often correleate with efficiency.[14] On an a priori basis it is quite obvious that, at least for Germany, domestic markets and export outlets are sufficiently large to allow firms to operate at optimal size. A process of increasing concentration of course, has occurred in Germany, partly to adjust to a larger market, but it is doubtful that beyond that this process has increased performance. This doubt is supported by an empirical study of the effects of concentration in the EC by Jacquemin and Cardon (1973) who conclude that "the actual increase in economic concentration does not bring superior results in terms of profit or growth rates along with it."

Italian and French governments have frequently lent their support to mergers. So has the German government, but only in a very few cases—perhaps because mergers and internal growth of large firms have been high even without aid. One example is Ruhrkohle AG, into which several former coal companies were merged together. Another example is the (partially unsuccessful) effort to create a national oil company. At present, subsidies to the aircraft industry are tied to the recommendation for the two major producers to join hands. In those cases, sensible economic interpretations can be made. Thus, with few exceptions, the German government preferred to rely on market forces. This also applies to takeovers of German firms by foreign enterprises, sometimes even in sensitive areas, such as the one of Deutsche Erdöl by Texaco which was not opposed by the government.

German governments did not believe in Servan-Schreiber's policy recommendation; quite to the contrary, German competition laws are, by European standards, quite severe and the Kartellamt has shown itself vigilant.[15] The Kartellnovelle (1973) has introduced the possibility of controlling mergers so that Articles 85 and 86 of the Rome treaty, eventually amended for control of mergers as proposed in the memorandum of 1973, would not increase the severity of competition laws for German firms.

A second approach involves subsidizing industry. Instead of discussing various forms of subsidization, I shall use the concept of effective protection. Donges and colleagues have computed the effective protection rates shown in table 7-6.[16] These rates take account of tariffs, subsidies, indirect taxes, depreciation rates, and such.

Table 7-6 yields information regarding imports from the EC. Only two sectors enjoy high protection: nonferrous metal manufactures and nonmetal castings. Particularly insignificant is protection for investment goods. These computations suggest that for producers from other EC countries, access to the German market has been extensively liberalized.[17]

Such conclusions would not hold for Third World countries. Protection rates are very high for some industries (aircraft industry, 73.2 percent; oil

Table 7-6
Effective Total Protection Rates on Imports from European Economic Countries and Third Countries

	Total Effective Protection			
	1958		1968	1970
	Third		EEC	Third
Industry	Countries		Countries	Countries
Mining	0.8	53.2	3.6	102.1
Coal mining	0.8	65.6	4.1	128.3
Lignite mining	− 2.2	− 3.4	−0.2	− 2.9
Crude oil and natural gas	—	—	—	—
Other mining	5.4	3.1	2.0	2.5
Raw materials and basic commodities	23.5	30.2	5.3	16.4
Stones and earthen goods	1.6	12.0	0.4	4.4
Iron and steel	33.3	39.4	5.5	23.8
Iron and steel founderies	13.4	23.4	2.7	18.7
Steel drawing and cold rolling mills	5.6	3.5	3.5	7.3
Nonferrous metal manufactures	31.4	68.2	22.8	30.3
Nonferrous metal castings	35.6	73.7	14.8	37.4
Petroleum refineries	—	60.5	0.8	103.4
Chemicals	18.0	24.6	5.1	16.0
Wood, plywood, and wood products	15.9	19.0	3.0	13.1
Pulp, paper, and paperboard	51.3	53.5	5.6	42.1
Rubber products	27.8	20.3	5.1	15.7
Investment goods	5.5	9.3	1.0	7.4
Construction steel	0.6	5.8	0.2	3.0
Fabricated metal products	16.6	21.0	3.9	12.3
Machinery and equipment	0.8	4.0	0.4	2.7
Road transport equipment	11.0	14.3	2.3	9.4
Shipbuilding	− 14.9	− 14.6	−2.6	− 10.9
Aircraft	24.0	1.8	3.4	73.2
Electrical machinery	5.1	9.2	− 0.4	8.1
Precision and optical instruments	3.4	7.9	1.2	6.9
Clocks and watches	2.7	5.6	1.2	4.5
Office equipment	8.4	15.3	2.5	11.0
Consumer goods	20.4	24.4	3.6	20.0
Pottery and china	9.5	18.3	1.7	18.7
Glass and glass products	16.7	22.8	3.0	15.1
Furniture	23.1	24.3	2.1	17.3
Musical instruments, toys, and sporting goods	6.3	13.8	2.8	10.6
Paper products	29.7	20.3	5.0	27.4
Printing	4.3	9.6	1.3	8.3
Plastics	8.8	13.0	1.6	9.5
Leather	11.6	13.0	3.1	11.2
Leather products	21.0	26.3	3.8	19.1
Shoes	26.2	30.6	4.4	15.1
Textiles	24.9	24.3	5.2	25.6
Wearing apparel	20.9	26.0	3.2	25.1
Industry (total)	14.9	22.1	3.4	19.3

Source: Donges et al. (1973), Protektion und Branchenstructur der Westdeutschen Wirtschaft (Tübingen: J.C.B. Mohr), 1973. Reprinted with permission.

refining, 168.4 percent; coal mining, 123.8 percent). While protection has decreased for Community trade, protection from Third World country imports has increased in most industries after the formation of the EC.

A third way to assist industry is in financing research and development. Public expenditures on R&D increased substantially from 5.6 billion DM in 1969 to 12.2 billion DM in 1974.[18] Three sectors of the economy have most benefited from this aid: computers and telecommunications, energy, and aircrafts. Because of the various forms of support (research financed at universities, subsidies given to firms, government purchases, and so on), it is, however, difficult to make sense out of these figures and compare them internationally or assess their effects on growth.

European Industrial Policy

Industrial policy is not explicitly covered by the Treaty of Rome. A comprehensive treatment of industrial policy had to await the memorandum on industrial policy (1970) and the summit meeting of Paris (1972) where the necessity of a common industrial basis for the economic and monetary union was stressed. However, the global approach of the 1970 memorandum was already abandoned in 1972, partly because of the political difficulties of such an approach, partly because of some unrealistic aspects. By 1972, it had already been realized that the fear of the American challenge was overrated and that some of the measures proposed were of dubious effectiveness. In particular, the negative effects of increasing concentration of economic power received increased attention; while the importance of competition and the efficiency of small and medium-sized firms for activities such as R&D became better appreciated. The need for a more rigorous competition policy was stressed rather than reliance on industrial concentration.

In the Action Program of 1973 (Spinelli-Memorandum) the part of active industrial policy was correspondingly much reduced and mostly confined to aid in future technologies and in sectors with serious adjustment problems (naval construction, textiles, and such).

The German government's view of the role of European industrial policy has been very different from that held by several partner governments and has shaped to a large extent the final form of the Action Program. The German government tended to support policies serving to reduce trade obstacles within the EC and to increase the degree of integration. Under this heading fall policies such as harmonization of technical and legal prescriptions, public orders, competition laws, and improved control of public subsidies.

As far as active policies are concerned, the German government objected to most of the initial proposals of the Spinelli plan. Examples are EC guidelines for investment projects to base structural change on a common strategy; declaration to the Commission of investment projects in critical sectors to allow elaboration of recommendations and increased financial engagement of the EC in priority or critical sectors; and creation of an European export-import bank. The basic reason for this attitude is the relatively stronger belief in market forces and the distrust of bureaucratic interventions by the EC prevailing in Germany, compared to some other European countries.

Turning now to specific issues, the choice of high-technology sectors for action on the level of the EC parallels national programs. This is one reason for the lack of commitment by partner countries and the failure of European industrial policy. Neither has the Commission been able to make precise proposals, nor have existing frameworks (for example, the European Atomic Energy Community, called Euratom) been adequate. Moreover, government-assisted private plans for cooperation failed as well (for example, the use of computers). Those projects which have been realized are intergovernmental arrangements, independent of the Community. Whether these ventures (Airbus, Concorde, MRCA, and others) will be success stories is still doubtful. Nevertheless, one can defend the viewpoint that it is necessary in Europe to socialize the short-run losses of these projects to remain in markets for advanced technology. A common European policy would certainly be preferable, in this respect, to bilateral arrangements, but agreement on such projects is very difficult to reach. The German government has, in general, a positive attitude toward bilateral or multilateral projects but not to the extent that it would ignore costs.

An implication of the Servan-Schreiber thesis is that within the Community, firms from different countries should merge to approach American sizes. Such a viewpoint is also expressed in the memorandum on industrial policy. Few transnational mergers have occurred, however. Nor has there been a wave of important takeovers. The major examples of mergers that involve European and German firms are Agfa-Gevaert, Hoesch-Hoogovens, and VFW-Fokker (at present, settling their divorce). German industry has invested in the rest of the Community but less than overseas. This is easily understandable since the major reasons for foreign investment seem to be lower factor costs and overcoming tariff and transport barriers. On both accounts, there is little reason to invest in the Community. The major foreign investors in Germany are the United States and Switzerland. No noticeable increase of investment by partner countries can be discerned.

Transnational mergers are still formidably difficult. A European company law certainly would help but would not make all difficulties disappear (resistance of national governments, organizational differences, and so on).

Recently, the Commission, represented by Étienne Davignon, has been very active in suggesting solutions for industries that are particularly affected by the current recession.[19] The basic idea here is not progress through concentration as previously discussed, but orderly retreat and adjustment through cartelization.[20] The German government agreed to the measures taken for steel and textiles with severe reservations. It strongly objects to using these cases as examples for others. The government accepts the idea of a truly temporary emergency measure but believes that industrial restructuring should not be prevented and that the most important motor for industrial adaptation is still competition.[21]

Germany's Attitude and Influence on Community Policy

Unlike several other European countries, Germany has emerged from World War II as a relatively market-oriented economy.[22] Perhaps surprising to those who look at a market economy skeptically, economic performance has been satisfactory and relations among social partners are better than in many other countries. This success has led German governments of different party compositions to adopt a fairly liberal attitude.[23] They have been persistently in favor of increased market integration and improved competition but equally persistent in their skepticism toward EC dirigisme and protectionism.

The basically liberal attitude has been influenced by two other factors that are at least as important. One is the distrust of the Community bureaucracy and the fear that Germany will lose control over its own economic environment and its own financial resources. Indeed, the original Spinelli program with investment priorities elaborated by the EC and financed out of a centralized fund would have had these implications. Germany so far has resisted domestic investment control proposals, and for even better reasons European proposals along that line.

A second reason relates to the policy horizon (atlantic or world) that induces German governments sometimes to give greater weight to Third World countries. The skeptical attitude toward "orderly marketing agreements" is founded not only on welfare considerations for German consumers but also on the negative impacts of Germany's relationships with the United States and the less developed countries, and on world trade in general. In this respect, it may also be worth pointing out that the importance of the Community as a trading partner has diminished over the last few years, as has trade with the United States (see table 7-7).

Although German governments have been opposed to economic dirigisme and specific controls, they have recognized that the differences in economic development and regional problems in Europe require action. To prevent rising protectionism and disintegration of the customs union, support has been given to a more comprehensive regional policy. Recent proposals for monetary integration are motivated by similar considerations.

Table 7-7
Foreign Trade of West Germany: 1970 and 1977
(percentages of total)

	Imports		Exports	
	1970	1977	1970	1977
European Community	49.6	48.2	46.3	44.9
United States	11.0	7.2	9.1	6.7
Japan	1.9	2.8	1.6	1.1
East Bloc	4.0	4.8	4.3	6.1
Oil-producing countries	7.7	9.9	2.8	9.1
Less developed countries	8.4	10.5	9.1	8.0

I consider Germany's generally liberal, pro-market attitude its most important positive contribution to, and influence on, the Community. Without this attitude, the evolution of the EC would have been substantially different, and in my opinion, erroneous.

This attitude of course, gives rise frequently to confrontation. Germany is often made responsible for the lack of a European industrial policy. Recently, the minister for economic affairs, Count Lambsdorff, was seriously attacked by his British and Belgian colleagues, Owen and Simonet, when he opposed higher protection for shoe producers in the EC. Owen felt that since Germany has fewer structural problems than partner countries, its liberal viewpoint cannot be a reference to them, while Simonet was of the opinion that liberalism belongs to the nineteenth century.[24]

Let me now summarize the results of this section. A favorable initial structure of German industry and an undervalued currency may explain why the EC provoked a lesser need for interindustry resource shifts than elsewhere. But within industries, substantial specialization occurred. The cost of this type of resource reallocation is, however, much smaller.

A reduced need and a market-oriented attitude of successive governments resulted in low-key intervention. Those interventions which we can observe are mostly caused by factors lying outside the EC. The Community's industrial policy, to the extent that it exists, has had no perceptible impact on German industry.

With respect to transnational cooperation within the Community, German firms seldom showed strong interest. Government provided support in a few cases that were judged important for Germany's industrial future. It is, however, uncertain whether these projects will be successes.

I consider Germany's major contribution its relatively liberal attitude, which prevented bureaucratic solutions of doubtful economic efficiency. This attitude does not imply, of course, any superior economic understanding or institutional set-up but can be entirely rationalized with a more competitive starting point. Nor does it prevent possible attitudinal reversals in the future.

Labor Policy

Creation of a common market requires unified markets for factors of production; that is, capital and labor. For both factors integration is not complete but, at least for labor (with the exception of some professions), an approximately unified market exists.[25]

Why is the integration of factor markets desirable? The factor-price-equalization theorem in international trade demonstrates that (under certain conditions) factor prices tend to converge through commodity trade alone. Hence, one might be tempted to conclude that if equal real incomes of factors of production in the Community is an objective, a common market for goods would be sufficient.

I do not share this view entirely. First, there is a value to be attached to the freedom of establishment and to nondiscriminatory work conditions. Second, to the extent that the integration of commodity markets is slow and remains imperfect, factor market integration speeds up factor-price equalization. Third, if some of the conditions upon which the factor-price-equalization theorem rests are not satisfied (such as perfect competition everywhere), then factor mobility again helps in bringing about factor-price equalization.

However, no substantial migrations have taken place within the Community. Germany has seen an important inflow of Italian workers. Immigration from other Community countries, and emigration from Germany, have been insignificant (although the experience of the present author is exemplary in this respect!). The high share of non-Community labor among foreign workers in Germany suggests that labor migration has little to do with the Community. I believe that Germany would have had the same number of foreign workers without an integrated labor market in the EC, with perhaps some Italian workers substituted by Turks or Yugoslavs.

In view of a possible enlargement of the Community, it may still be interesting to ask whether the foreign labor inflow has been beneficial to Germany and how high those gains might have been. It is often argued that labor-receiving countries exploit emigration countries ruthlessly by taking their best labor force away, not paying for the cost of their formation, not providing them with the same social wage as domestic labor, and sending them home when business conditions deteriorate. I shall not discuss these issues, which seems to be rather emotion-loaded and void of strong empirical support. Instead, I will try to answer whether massive immigration has been a good policy for Germany. I think not. In another study, we have shown that through international trade in 1972 there was less unskilled labor imported, less human capital exported, and more physical capital imported in Germany than in 1962.[26] This is contrary to what neoclassical trade theory would predict for a capital-rich country (both physical and human capital) like Germany. One of the main reasons for this evolution has been the immigration of unskilled foreign workers. Thus, direct labor imports have been substituted for indirect labor imports via commodities. This has allowed Germany to maintain activity in relatively labor-intensive sectors instead of forcing reallocations toward more capital and technology-intensive ones. It would undoubtedly have been advantageous to have accepted this restructuring during the sixties rather than having to face the problem with considerable delay now. Also, Germany would now be in a much better position with less developed countries: more labor-intensive products would be imported and less direct competition with German export products would exist. The undervaluation of the Deutsche mark would have been reduced through more rapidly rising real wages in Germany.[27]

Clearly, immigration led to greater profits at least before the recession (since real wages rose less than they would have otherwise). Whether it has been beneficial to the whole economy is doubtful; current problems certainly are enhanced by the lack of structural change (made possible through immigration) and the presence of a sizable foreign labor force in Germany. The fact that interindustry resource reallocations have been much less important in Germany than in other Community countries, and that Germany has become a slow-growth country, are certainly related to the policy of labor immigration as was pointed out before.

Conclusions

I have tried to give a tentative answer to the quite difficult question: how has the Community and its different policies affected German industrial policy and German industrial structure?

I tended to argue that neither the formation of the Community nor its policies have had substantial effects on Germany. If the EC had not been created, welfare in Germany would be slightly lower in the status quo; but the possibility of more general trade liberalization would have been available to Germany.

Moreover, I have tried to show that industry in Germany benefits from a number of factors; some allocative, others distributive. Although it is generally believed that Germany benefited more from market integration than others, this may not be the case. Germany's initial structural efficiency and its large domestic market reduce potential integration gains compared to initially highly protected and distorted economies (France, Italy) or economies with a small domestic market (Belgium, the Netherlands).

Nevertheless, there are economic justifications for Germany's entry into the Community. Even if the welfare gain for German society is negligible, some interest groups (capital owners in agriculture and industry) gain substantially. Moreover, if the present state of integration is viewed as intermediary to an economic union, then the latter *may* provide an additional motivation. It is indeed often argued (without convincing everybody) that policy harmonization and control of the business cycle provides substantial gains.[28]

What impact has Germany exercised on the Community? I argued that the most important contribution may have been the liberal economic philosophy prevailing in postwar Germany. This was instrumental for the Rome treaty and for rapid progress toward the customs union. Interventionism, attempts at giving economic planning a more important role, and protectionism in trade with non-Community countries have been constantly resisted by German governments. This is particularly important in present times. Community legislation, such as competition laws or the participatory structures for the European company law, also strongly reflects the liberal German viewpoint.

Notes

1. Industrial policy is generally defined as a set of policies that deal with market imperfections, usually in a specific and discriminatory manner, in contrast to macroeconomic policy. The goal of industrial policy is to assist industries in various ways. The motivation behind this goal may reflect concern with welfare of the country (full employment, rapid growth) or with welfare of some interest groups (capital owners, workers in a particular area, and so on). By this definition, regional, social, and labor market policies are examples of industrial policy.

2. A discussion of this issue, and the relevant references, can be found in Krauss (1972). One might, however, argue against this view that trade liberalization does not give as much assurance against reversals to protectionism as does the EC, so that the two alternatives are not directly comparable. Furthermore, the objective has not been to create a customs union, but a common market with all other discriminatory measures eliminated.

3. Ludwig Erhard defended as welfare superior, in particular, the idea of a European Free Trade Association comprising the EC and the EFTA countries. See, for example, "Was wird aus Europe?" *Handelsblatt*, Dec. 23-24, 1960.

4. Balassa (1975, p. 115) arrives at 0.15 percent of the GNP. Miller and Spencer (1977), using a general equilibrium approach, arrive at 0.16 percent for the United Kingdom.

5. In another paper (Morel and Steinherr, 1978) we show that German export industries indeed have been able to act as price leaders.

6. Muller and Hochreiter (1975) show that in all industries in their sample, total sales exceed several times minimum optimal plant scale.

7. Gains could be somewhat larger if increased international competition also reduces monopoly in domestic markets. In view of the probably minor effect of the EC on competition in Germany and the well-known insignificance of those welfare gains, our previous results would not be much affected. Moreover, optimal firm size adjusts to larger market size, so that it is not clear whether market power has really been reduced in the EC.

8. See Cairnes (1874).

9. Duren (1974) tends to argue the opposite. He points out that during the 1960s, whenever internal demand in Germany slackened, demand in partner countries increased and thus production in Germany was stabilized through increased exports. He sees, therefore, an advantage in differently phased business cycles. This can, however, hardly be attributed to the formation of the EC. If anything, the Common Market and policy cooperation should tend to harmonize the business cycle.

10. Reallocation is then less pronounced because of complementary factors in the production process and the subsidization of low-profit products from high-profit products, which is sometimes advantageous for keeping customers.

11. The undervaluation of the deutsche mark and, as will be argued in the next section of this chapter, the inflow of foreign workers, made it possible to retard restructuring until the mid-seventies. This provides perhaps the major explanation of the surprisingly small interindustry shifts.

12. Rapport du groupe d'experts d'analyses sectorielles (1978).

13. The competitiveness of the German economy during the sixties and early seventies certainly is, to a large extent, a result of the undervaluation of the deutsche mark, reinforced by low wage growth to which the inflow of foreign workers contributed. Whether German governments would have been equally liberal without such a competitive advantage and whether they will remain liberal in the future, remains, of course, an open question. In this regard, the implications of the future European monetary system (EMS) are noteworthy. If, in the absence of effective policy coordination, inflation rates in the rest of the EC continue to exceed the German rate, while exchange rates are relatively fixed, the deutsche mark will again be undervalued, and we will return to the situation that prevailed in the sixties.

14. An example of how size and efficiency are being married provides the following quotation from Mahotiere (1970) p. 73: "The Common Market's best performance is in motor cars, where Fiat, Volkswagen, and Renault/Peugeot come immediately behind the three American giants."

15. Recently, the Kartellamt has been overridden several times by the government, however.

16. The formula for computing the total effective protection rate can be found in Donges et al. (1973), p. 81.

17. The effective protection rates in table 7-6 tend to be underestimates since they do not comprise all subsidies and distortions resulting from the tax structure. Industrial standards, discrimination in public orders, and the effects of an undervalued currency are also neglected. As was pointed out to me by F. Wolters, effective rates have increased recently.

18. Bundesforschungsbericht V, p. 81.

19. Germany is less affected by the current recession (*given* the very low inflation rate that has certainly reduced employment in the short run) for a variety of reasons, among which can be found the greater flexibility of labor supply provided by an adjustable amount of foreign workers, a more cooperative attitude of labor unions (and of business), and, finally, less government intervention. For example, the oil crisis has been handled in Germany virtually without intervention. The increase in the price of oil has hardly perturbed the German economy (it has, of course, lowered welfare), which has been able to obtain a substantial market share in oil-exporting countries. Another example is the steel industry. The German steel industry considers itself as the most efficient in Europe and is violently opposed to European solutions preserving current market shares. Without government support, the size of the steel industry in Belgium, France, Italy, and the United Kingdom would have been reduced long ago and therefore also the present problem multiplied (but not created) by the current recession. Increased government support is certainly no solution.

20. The necessity of such measures is usually defended on the grounds that the market cannot cope with structural decline. Whether this is so, depends, however, on the rigidities existing in the economy, for example, the professional and regional mobility of workers. Even if government assistance were necessary, it would make better sense to provide investment incentives, regional transfers, and such, rather than to cartelize an industry.

21. Memorandum of the German Delegation on EC structural policy in the industrial economy R/1068/78, May 3, 1978. "Die wichtigste Triebfeder zur Anpassung uberholter Strukturen ist der Wettbewerb auf dem Markt" (p. 3). "Keinesfalls aber darf eine Branche nach der anderen erfasst und reglementiert werden. Die Regelungen im Stahlbereich dürfen nicht zum Muster für Eingriffe in andere Branchen werden" (p. 6).

22. "Relatively" since the public sector is as important in Germany as, on average, in other EC countries. Protective measures as well as intervention policies please their beneficiaries as much as elsewhere.

23. This success, of course, has made it also easier to be liberal, so that causality goes both ways: liberalism made economic expansion possible which, in turn, made a market-oriented approach more palatable.

24. "German Attacks on EEC Protectionism Widens Split over Handling Crisis," *The Times*, May 3, 1978.

25. The integration of the labor market is, however, more formal than real. Language, culture, and lack of information are still formidable barriers. The low rate of actual migration and the substantial differences in the ideological backgrounds of labor unions contribute to an explanation of maintained differences in labor and industrial relations, in spite of integration.

26. Steinherr and Runge (1978).

27. These conclusions require qualification in one respect. The foreign labor force has given increased flexibility to the German labor market. Since 1973, the labor force has been reduced by sending home half a million foreign workers.

28. See Cooper (1969).

References

Balassa, Bela "Trade Creation and Diversion in the European Common Market." In *European Economic Integration*, edited by B. Balassa, pp. 79-120. Amsterdam: North-Holland, 1975.

Cairnes, J.E. *Some Leading Principles of Political Economy*. London: Macmillan, 1974.

Commission des Communantés Européennes, Rapport du groupe d'experts d'analyses sectorielles. *Les Mutations Sectorielles des Economies Europeennes de 1960 à la Récession*. Brussels, 1978.

Cooper, Richard N. "Macroeconomic Policy Adjustment in Interdependent Economies." *The Quarterly Journal of Economics* 83 (February 1969):1-24.

Donges Jurgen et al. *Protektion und Branchenstruktur der Westdeutschen Wirtschaft*. Tubingen: J.C.B. Mohr, 1973.

Duren, A. "The Adjustment to Free Trade in the Common Market." In *Toward a New World Trade Policy: the Maidenhead Papers*, edited by C.F. Bergsten. Lexington, Mass.: Lexington Books, D.C. Heath and Co., 1974.

Jacquemin, Alex, and Cardon, M. "Size, Structure, Stability and Performance of the Largest British and EEC firms." *European Economic Review* 4 (1973).

Krauss, Melvyn "Recent Developments in Customs Union Theory: An Interpretive Survey." *Journal of Economic Literature* (June 1972):413-36.

Mahotière, Stuart de la. *Towards One Europe*. London: Penguin Books, 1970.

Miller, Merton H., and Spencer, John. "The Static Effects of the U.K. Joining the EEC and Their Welfare Significance." *Review of Economic Studies* (February, 1977):71-94.

Morel, C., and Steinherr, Alfred. "An Empirical Study of World Market Influences on Price Formation in West Germany." *Journal of Empirical Economics* 3 (1978):183-201.

Müller, Jürgen, and Hochreiter, Rolf. *Stand und Entwicklungstendenzen der Konzentration in der Bundesrepublik Deutschland.* Göttingen: Schwartz, 1975.

Petith, Howard. "European Integration and the Terms of Trade." *The Economics Journal* 87 (June 1977):262-72.

Prewo, Wilfried. "Integration Effects in the EEC, an Attempt at Quantification in a General Equilibrium Framework." *European Economic Review* 4 (December, 1974):379-406.

Steinherr, Alfred, and Runge, Jurgen. "The Evolution of West Germany's Structure of Foreign Trade from 1962 to 1972." *Zeitschrift für die Gesamte Staatswissenschaft* 2 (1978):301-26.

German Agricultural Policy and the European Community

Hermann Priebe

Introduction

1. The discussion in this chapter will be based upon the following theses: In the Federal Republic of Germany, agriculture has only slight economic significance—its contribution to the gross domestic product is less than 3 percent—but it has tremendous political weight. From the very beginning, as a result, Germany has had considerable influence on the formulation of the Common Agricultural Policy and has contributed accordingly in no small manner to the resultant imbalances and burdens.

2. The true interests of the Federal Republic lie in the realm of industry, in the export of high-value industrial commodities, which could be increased substantially within the European Community. The reason why, despite all this, Germany considers the Common Agricultural Policy to be of great value lies in the tradition of its agricultural protection which began a century ago. It was then strengthened under the Third Reich and had a revival even in the Federal Republic. On the other hand, Germany was in a position, and was even prepared, to assume the increasing financial burden of the agricultural policy because of the advantages it drew from the Common Market for its industrial and total economic growth. On the basis of these advantages for general economic growth, the Federal Republic was ready and able to accept the increasing financial burdens of the agricultural policy. In practice, a form of financial adjustment has developed among the member states to cover the common financing of expenditures for the agricultural policy, a system in which the Federal Republic is the largest net contributor.

3. The widely held opinion of the pacemaker role of agriculture in European integration is based on misconceptions that arise from the particular situation of the agricultural sector: This dirigiste agrarian system created an exceptional sphere which, with its administered prices, interventions, and managed investments, has become a foreign body in the democratic, market-oriented Community. Economic integration has not progressed further in the agricultural sector than in other realms; in recent times, one can even ascertain a certain retrogression.

4. Because of the resultant imbalances, the agricultural realm is becoming more and more an impediment to European integration. Structural

139

surpluses, high financial charges, rising consumer prices, misplaced investments, and foreign political burdens are causing numerous difficulties.

5. The causes of these false developments lie less in the diverse economic and financial evolution in the member states than in the system of the Common Agricultural Policy and its management. On the one side, the special interests of the member states led to the overestimation of the importance of farming to economic growth and to excessive demands on agricultural policy. On the other, traditional conceptions of the farm economy led to an underestimation of the consequences that governmental intervention and subsidies would have on agricultural production.

6. For the scholar, the Common Agricultural Policy is a model of the bankruptcy of governmental dirigisme in the economy. The European people have to pay dearly for this experience.

Concerning the Diversity of Interests

Difficulties in agricultural policy existed everywhere even before the beginning of the European Economic Community. Most industrial countries had not succeeded in finding a harmonious structural adaptation of agriculture to overall development. Ever since the end of the nineteenth century these incipient imbalances had led to political intervention in such a way that agricultural policy moved increasingly further away from the principles of a market economy. Step by step a form of competition for subsidies arose among countries: each strove to unload its surpluses on its neighbor's doorstep, as well as to shift to other countries the consequences of misplaced interventions in the market by means of further interventions. Thus, when the European Economic Community began, these problems of agricultural policy were brought in as dowry by all the member states.

The state of general economic development, however, was diverse in each country, and accordingly a variety of approaches had been taken in agricultural policy. Particular differences exist in agricultural policy among Germany, the Netherlands, and Denmark. German agricultural policy was directed toward a policy of high prices for basic commodities, to the advantage of the larger agricultural enterprises. This worsened the competitiveness of animal production and brought with it a general protectionist mentality. In contrast to this, the Netherlands and Denmark were able to achieve an exemplary modernization of their farm economy through a nonrestrictive agricultural policy and the pursuit of an expansive export policy.

Conflicts of interest between France and Germany arose from the diverse economic structures—at the beginning of the EEC, the earning population in France stood at 39 percent in industry and 20 percent in farming; in Germany at 49 percent in industry and 10 percent in farming. France's particular interest in the development of the agricultural sector was intensified by the geographic concentration of its economy. In broad regions far removed from industry a rapid improvement of the conditions of life seemed achievable only through increases in agricultural production. The safety valve for sales was to be opened by the Common Market and by common financing of agriculture. In this sense, the Common Agricultural Policy served for France as a sort of basic business condition for entry into the EEC.

In Italy, as well, the agricultural sector, with 35 percent of the earning population, had a significant weight. To favor its particular products, the country pursued special interests. At the same time, the problems of the underdeveloped areas in southern Italy gave great hope for stronger sales of agricultural products in the Common Market.

False Points of Departure

This shift of focus in the Community's policy to the agricultural sector, which was strengthened by specific conditions in Italy and France, was a false point of departure from the very beginning of the European Economic Community. Its impact was rendered even more unfortunate when momentous errors were made in the management of the existing agricultural political system.

For the general development of the European Community, it proved to be a particular disadvantage that the Treaty of Rome provided for no common regional policy. The European Community might well have had a better economic position today if the unproductive billions spent for agricultural surpluses had been used to open up rural regions to industrial enterprises. From the point of view of the long-term developmental trends in the economy and in society, the strengthening of the agricultural sector was in a certain measure a retrogression into obsolete economic structures.

By now the situation has become completely absurd. Agricultural pricing policy and structural assistance favor expansive production in the face of stagnating demand. Indeed, even storage costs for butter surpluses exceed the entire expenditure of the Community for the economic development of rural regions: In regional funds, barely 7 percent of earmarked expenditures for the agricultural market are available.

Misperceptions of Reality

At first, the system of market regulation, which developed after 1960 for the most important agricultural products, appeared to be a step forward when measured against the national agricultural systems of the member states. Through the elimination of all subsidies, quota regulations, special bilateral agreements and similar limits on trade, and on the basis of price levels secured against the outside world, free movement and competition were to follow in the common agricultural market.

The system is neutral in terms of economic policy, but dependent in its function on prices, which are related to the volume of sales. Here lies the vulnerable point of the whole system—in the fixing of prices by political commissions. Experience has shown that politicians are overtaxed by the task of finding the correct choice between the easily recognizable income effect of prices and their long-term influence on the market's equilibrium.

Even the controversy over common grain prices at the beginning of the 1960s showed this. The differences in the level of agricultural prices could only be bridged as the result of a compromise of "the middle way." On the German side, no readiness for the requisite lowering of traditionally high grain prices emerged. As a result of the stubborn stance of the German government, the powers were deadlocked for a long time and valuable years of integration were wasted. When the decision in favor of common grain prices finally came, in December 1964, things were already out of tune. The German demands led in the final analysis to price increases for grain in the EEC of 118 percent. In France, the country with the largest reserve of production, these increases reached 130 percent.

Moreover, in the span of the several years of negotiations in the search for a compromise among national interests, many a compensation was secured, thus introducing the unhealthy developments of the further extension of market controls and intervention, and of the unlimited responsibility for all the financial burdens that arose from it. The much extolled "pragmatic" process of integration led, in this instance, by small steps, to a falsification of the original conception. A summation of national wishes and the transfer of measures of protection to the Community level were the consequences.

Thus, the system of market regulation moved increasingly further away from the liberal principles of the early proposals and arrived at a well-nigh phantom perfectionism. In many thousands of agricultural regulations—comprising over 95 percent of all EEC regulations issued to the present—the most picayune details were regulated to several points beyond the comma, without the slightest regard for the economic and political importance of the basic information that preceded the comma. Those in charge were prisoners of a system in which the suggestions of technical experts at the European Commission set an ingeniously devised organization in gear. This process finally reached decisions that were nonsensical in terms of economic and agricultural policy, but were justified by the single concern that their rejection endangered the process of integration.

Obviously present from the beginning was the traditional assumption of predominantly static agricultural production. Thus productive reserves, the impact of technological progress in agriculture, and the economic thought processes of farmers were vastly underestimated, and the incentive to intensify production increased even more.

An added factor is the one-sided structural policy for agriculture. It led, through subsidies and investments, to the expansion of productive capacity, and to an intensification of the creation of surpluses. In addition, it had unpredictable consequences on the environment, the configuration of the countryside, and living conditions in rural regions.

Credits and Debits

In spite of the existing difficulties, one ought not to lose sight of the positive results of the Common Agricultural Policy: (1) The provisioning of the 260 million inhabitants of the European Community was secured through the abundant selection of high-quality foodstuffs, and (2) the independent European farm economy showed great capacities for adaptability and achievement and proved itself far superior to the large agricultural combines of the planned economies of the East.

On the other hand, precisely this great economic dynamism of the European farm economy led, in combination with the European Community's ordered market system and its investment subsidies, to substantial imbalances and general economic stresses. The Community learned to live with these to a certain degree. That fact can be even less a charter for the future in light of the pending expansion of the European Community, which will bring additional problems to the agricultural sector. In order to avoid additional injury to integration, the stresses and burdens that arise for the Community as a result of the agricultural policy must be clearly understood.

1. Structural surpluses lead to misallocation of capital and labor, and to growing financial burdens. The expenditures of member states and of the Community for the agricultural policy reached about 62 million DM in 1976 (17 million units of account).[1] That corresponds to about 24 percent of the overall value of EC agricultural production and represents accordingly the lion's share of its value added. Expenditures for the support of agricultural markets and prices in 1978 have already risen to more than 30 million DM.

2. Foreign political stresses as a result of the European Community's agricultural policy are to be reckoned with also. Contrary to the aims of the Treaty of Rome, the EEC is not an open market in the agricultural sector. It has become, rather, a substantially restricted preference zone, which results in increasing difficulties for the export possibilities of many countries of the Third World, and in stresses for the world market as a result of export dumping.

3. The increase in agricultural prices takes too little account of the

substantial development of productivity in the farm economy. It burdens the consumer and works counter to a policy of stabilization. Prices received by farmers rose between 1970 and mid-1976 by about 150 percent. Thus they rose more sharply than prices for industrial products and more sharply than the cost of living, up by about 140 percent.

4. The backwardness of the rural poor regions in Europe could not be reduced. Only a fraction of the funds that are actually being squandered unproductively on agricultural surpluses is available for the regional policy of the European Community.

5. The highly subsidized structural development of the farm economy increases concentration of land ownership and endangers the social structure of large rural zones. It leads to an intensification of production in the most fertile areas of cultivation and, as a result of increased application of chemical products, to the endangering of the ecological balance.

6. The aim of ensuring foodstuffs within the EC recedes ever further from realization, since the farm economy increases its dependence on the importation of fodder and foreign sources of energy. It uses today considerably more energy than it returns in the production of foodstuffs, so that the dependence of the food sector is shifted to the energy sector, to the neglect of natural resources, and is thereby intensified.

7. Given this situation, the assertion that the financial burden is the price for safeguarding the food supply does not stand up. Completely absurd, however, is the objection that only a relatively small share of the GNP would be required to cover the financial burden and that it would therefore be tolerable. Agriculture is a sector of the economy; as a result, its task is to produce a part of the GNP and not to consume it.

No Recognizable Change of Course

One could raise the question at this point of whether there are any changes to be seen in developing tendencies or in the general parameters of the situation which would encourage the hope that the agricultural problem would resolve itself.

With regard to developing production, no limits are evident in the foreseeable future. The rate of increase of production lies in the long run at 2 to 3 percent; in addition, the average yield for grains as well as for animal products is increasing, especially the milk production of cows. New biological developments and synthetic products could enhance production in other segments as well.

In contrast, the stagnation of demand is intensified by the decline in population. Moreover, per capita consumption is approaching the limits of physical satiety. Thus, one faces a trend toward a chronic accumulation of surpluses.

Nor can one reckon with any relief from the worldwide market. After a transitory change of trend around 1973-1974, world market prices for agricultural products have normalized at their lowest levels. Thus, there is no commercial demand for agricultural products at the EEC's high price levels that could justify an expansion of European agricultural production.

Hence, the Community faces the obligation of finding solutions through changes in its agricultural policy, in order to avoid additional economic and social waste, and to reduce an area of tension in the process of European integration.

Development of a New Approach

New solutions can only be sketched at this point. Their points of departure lie both in price and market policy, and in structural policy.

Based on recent experience, income policy more than price is the main cause of imbalances. The dual function of prices in securing the income of producers and regulating supply and demand must lead to conflicts in the event prices are derived not from market forces but from political decisions, and in addition, if they are bound to guaranteed sales.

One must try, through the supplementary elements of a new income policy, to divorce prices from their income function, and to facilitate their orientation to market balance. Practically, one ought to construct a combined system of income policy in which income derives: (1) so far as possible from prices in conformity with the market, and (2) so far as necessary from assistance that is neutral in its effect on production.

On the basis of discussions up to this point concerning the criteria for the distribution of income assistance, cultivated areas ought to be given preference. Acreage assistance has a neutral effect on production, without narrowing the entrepreneurial disposition and initiative. Practically, it lessens the input cost of the factor land, and favors an extensive form of cultivation. Whereas, in order to realize an increase in income the farmer must raise prices on matching quantities of production, acreage assistance comes to him directly, without any effect on the quantities produced.

Whether a turn away from the traditional commitment to intensive cultivation succeeds will also depend upon changes in structural policy. Up to now, aid has strengthened increases in production and ought to be shifted to goals commensurate with the times. Through the development of extensive methods of production, more acreage should be used for the same level of production, and the formation of fallow land, as well as the increasing environmental problems arising from intensive farming, will be counteracted.

The exploitation of natural sources of energy gains special meaning as a goal. The farm economy must realize that it has the obligation above all to create more energy and to use it less. In this sense, the natural bases of energy must not be set aside as waste but must be exploited to reclaim energy. Another question also bears examination: whether or not subsidies set false price signals for the application of foreign sources of energy.

In contrast to the subsidy of individual agricultural enterprises, the whole of the rural zone must become the main focus of structural assistance. In this sense, a shift of aid from a structural policy in agriculture to a regional policy ought to be pursued. Both have significance: a regional policy in the improvement of the economic strength of the region, a structural agrarian policy with the aim of retaining rural life's attraction through cultivation and care of the land. The leading role must be given in the future, however, to a regional policy; in this sense, a shift of capital from agricultural funds to regional funds ought to be sought. In this way, the objections to changes in this policy from those countries which have become net gainers as a result of the common agricultural financing could be met.

For in each change, one must consider that with the agricultural policy a certain form of balance of payments compromise has developed within the European Community, so that from the outset compensation must be taken into account. Thus, a strengthening of a regional policy would be an even more appropriate means, since it would allow expectations of more favorable ramifications for economic growth than the agricultural financing pursued up to now.

As in the initial years of the EEC, the possibility of constructive changes of this nature will once again depend on the political stance of the Federal Republic of Germany. Germany's farm economy will oppose them; it has a double advantage in the present situation because of monetary compensation amounts: it has the highest producer prices with relatively stable currency, and in addition, was able to raise its yearly export in short order to 15 billion DM. The expansion of its volume of production derives, however, less from the comparative cost advantages of German agriculture than from the monetary compensation paid out of the common agricultural fund, which has the effect of an export subsidy.

The costs of this are borne, however, by the general German economy, as a result of high consumer prices as well as by virtue of losses in the balance of payments caused by the increased expense of agricultural imports. This is so because the monetary compensation for agricultural imports is booked to the credit of the common agricultural fund and not to the German balance of payments. Moreover, large contributions to the agricultural fund must be supplied for the monetary compensation of other countries, since the system of currency adjustment in the agricultural sector is not entirely self-supporting.

Changes in agricultural policy lie accordingly in the interests of the German economy in general and, to the extent they contribute to the reduction of unproductive agricultural surpluses and financial burdens, they lie in the interests of the general economic growth of the entire European Community.

The Outlook for the Enlargement of the European Community

The prospective enlargement of the European Community to include Greece, Portugal and Spain also makes changes in the Common Agricultural Policy appear urgent.

The differences in the economic structures of the Mediterranean countries are so great when compared to the original countries of the EEC that the continuation of the present agricultural system must lead to new imbalances and further tensions. The admission of these countries ought to become the occasion to consider these problems anew and to ask, in view of the economic and social differences among member states: (1) whether a unified agricultural market with the same prices still makes sense or is even still possible; (2) whether a unified agricultural structural policy with the same goals might not lead to social tensions in the diverse countries which would endanger the further development of Europe.

Up to now, an effort has been made to hold fast to the common policy on prices, even though it has become a fiction in view of the differences in prices which exist in fact. The European Community's Commission takes pains to decrease the currency compensation in order to reconstruct a common pricing base and thus to incorporate the agricultural sector in a common monetary policy. One ought, however, to examine alternatives and to ask whether the system originally conceived for an EEC of six states can really be maintained as a community of twelve, given the diversity among the economic structures and comparative incomes.

It is possible to consider retaining external protection, while leaving agricultural prices within the Community to market forces, as in the rest of the economy, which would then bring about an adjustment in the various currency developments. This would only be possible, however, if the system of intervention and the unlimited possibility for sale at fixed minimum prices were abandoned, for without this, the risk arises that too many investment funds would flow to the points of intervention in countries with strong currencies. The monetary compensation amounts of our day are designed to prevent just this.

Solutions for the continuing development of the system might be sought in a variety of directions:

1. Dismantling of the system of monetary compensation and the reduction of common standard prices to the level of the member state with the lowest average income. In practice, this would lead to a reduction of the

intervention price in the majority of the member countries. Consequently, one might examine whether beyond this low, common base price, supplementary measures of income policy at the national level would be allowed. Perhaps one could consider leaving their surplus to the individual country, which could then make a decision based on its level of income and its overall economic possibilities. Such supplementary income assistance would obviously have to be neutral in its impact on production.

2. Retention of the monetary compensation system, at least during a transition period—until an extensive adjustment of income differentials among the member states had taken place. In the same process, the standard price system could be maintained for protection from without. Agricultural prices would thus be diverse from country to country, just as they were earlier with the help of the monetary compensation amounts, and would correspond to the economic conditions and currency parities in the individual countries. In practice, this would mean that intervention would take place at the national, differentiated level, which would be reinforced through monetary compensation amounts. Here, however, one cannot ignore the fact that this system becomes ever more problematic as differences among member states become greater. It leads to displacement of production, and has ramifications for other economic groups—among other factors.

In whichever direction the development in the sphere of market and price policy may take its course, it appears urgently necessary to abandon the common agricultural structural assistance with its consequences of increased production. In doing so, one must consider compensation for the financial adjustment among member states which is related to this situation. As a substitute, one ought to seek a strengthening of the common financing of regional economic assistance.

No one today can lay out complete proposals for the future development of the agricultural policy. It is valid, however, to give timely consideration to new points of departure in order to guard against increasing imbalances in an enlarged European Community, and to become adaptable in agricultural policy and open to the tasks of the future integration of Europe.

Note

1. Report of the European Community's Commission on the state of farming in the Community, 1976.

References

Bericht der vom Eidgenössischen Volkswirtschaftsdepartementes eingesetzten Expertenkommission (Kommission Popp) *Ausgleichszahlungen an die schweizerische Landwirtschaft.* Bern, 1973.

von der Groeben, Hans, and Mestmacker, Ernst-Joachim, eds., *Ziele und Methoden der Europäischen Integration*. Frankfurt, Atheneum Verlag, 1972.

Koester, Ulrich. *EG-Agrarpolitik in der Sackgasse*. Baden-Baden, Nomos Verlag, 1977.

Koester, Ulrich, and Tangermann, Stefan. "Alternativen der Agrarpolitik." *Landwirtschaft-Angewandte Wissenschaft* 182 Landwirtschafts Verlag, 1976.

Kommission der Europäischen Gemeinschaften. Bilanz der Gemeinsamen Agrarpolitik (Mitteilung der Kommission an das Parlament und den Rat), KOM (75) 100. Brussels, February 26, 1975.

Kommission der Europäischen Gemeinschaften. "Die Lage der Landwirtschaft in der Gemeinschaft," Berichte 1976 und 1977. Brussels-Luxembourg 1977 and 1978.

Organization for Economic Cooperation and Development. *Weltagrarmärkte 1975-1985,* edited by Bundesministerium für Ernährung, Landwirtschaft und Forsten. Hamburg, Verlag Weltarchiv, 1977.

Priebe, Hermann. "Fields of Conflict in European Farm Policy." In *Agricultural Trade Papers*, Number 3, edited by Trade Research Centre. London, July, 1972.

Priebe, Hermann. "The Changing Role of Agriculture 1920-1970." In *The Fontana Economic History of Europe*. London, Collins Publishers, 1976.

Priebe, Hermann. "Twenty Years of Agricultural Policy—Review and Forecast." *Intereconomics* Number 3-4 (1977).

Priebe, Hermann. "Zur Lösung der Konflikte swischen Einkommens und Marktpolitik." In *Die europäische Agrarpolitik vor neuen Alternativen*, edited by Binswanger. Bern and Stuttgart, Verlag Paul Hampt, 1977.

Priebe, Hermann. "Spannungsfeld Agrarpolitik." In *ORDO-Jahrbuch für die Ordnung von Wirtschaft und Gesellschaft*. Stuttgart, Gustav Fischer Verlag, 1977.

Statistisches Amt der Europäischen Gemeinschaften (eurostat). *Statische Grundzahlen der Gemeinschaft*, 16th ed. Luxembourg, 1978.

Statistisches Amt der Europäischen Gemeinschaften (eurostat). *Agrarstatistisches Jahrbuch* 1977. Luxembourg, 1978.

Wille, Martin. "Formen, Möglichkeiten und Wirkungen Direkter Einkommensübertragungen an die Landwirtschaft." *Landwirtschaft-Angewandte Wissenschaft* 184 Landwirtschafts Verlag, (1976).

Willer, Horst, and Haase, Fritz, F. "Der landwirtschaftliche Anpassungsprozeb unter veränderten Rahmenbedingungen." *Landwirtschaft-Angewandte Wissenschaft* 209 Landwirtschafts Verlag, (1978).

Wissenschaftlicher Beirat beim Bundesministerium für Ernährung, Landwirtschaft und Forsten. "Zur Reform der Agrarpolitik der EWG (Gutachten)." *Landwirtschaft—Angewandte Wissenschaft* 166 Landwirtschafts Verlag, (1973).

Wissenschaftlicher Beirat beim Bundesministerium für Ernährung, Landwirtschaft und Forsten *Analyse der EWG-Agrarmarktpolitik und Vorschläge zu ihrer künftigen Gestaltung (Gutachten)*. Landwirtschafts Verlag, (1975).

9

Germany and the Enlargement of the European Community

Beate Kohler

The Decision to Agree

A recent study has claimed that German foreign relations are determined by bureaucratic administrative bodies.[1] One of the examples to the contrary was the German government's response to the applications of Greece, Spain, and Portugal for entry into the Community. In this instance, Chancellor Helmut Schmidt committed himself publicly in favor of Greek membership before the German bureaucratic machinery had had a chance to ponder the pros and cons of such an enlargement.[2] It was only afterward that the advice of experts[3] was sought and the opinions of interest groups were solicited.[4] The German Parliament stuck to its usual role: it was the very last to take up the question of enlargement.[5]

The German government's commitment, even before a thorough cost-benefit analysis had been carried out, was not the result of any systematic foreign policymaking; rather, it was decisionmaking by reaction. The Greek application had taken the German government by surprise; hard pressed by Greek diplomacy, it had to be persuaded of the political necessity of Greek accession into the Community.[6] From a German perspective, the consolidation of the Community would have been more in its interest; and from the very beginning, it was pointed out that enlargement could weaken rather than strengthen the Community.[7] Internal changes within the three countries—Greece, Spain, and Portugal—are really responsible for a further enlargement and the shifting of focus to the South.

After the first round of enlargement, it soon became clear that the number of member countries would further increase. The Community had acquired such economic and political weight that its European neighbors could hardly continue to escape its influence. Greece in particular, which already in its Association Treaty had sought to establish a special relationship with the Community, was forced to face the fact that the Community does not readily take into account the vital interests of its smaller partner.[8] Thus, it became ever more interested in gaining full membership in order at least to have some control over the fundamental conditions of its own economic development. As international competition became more fierce and the Community's policy more internally oriented, Greece's desire grew more fervent.

A shortened version of this chapter was previously published in *The World Economy* 2, no. 2, May, 1979. Reprinted with permission.

The efforts of the three applicant countries to associate themselves more closely with the Community are by no means new. Until recently, however, realization of these efforts was impossible because of their dictatorial governments. With the takeover of the colonels, Greece's association status was frozen.[9] Spain was repeatedly reminded that even preferential agreements depended upon internal democratization,[10] and the Community intensified its relations with Portugal only after the coup.[11] Negotiations for entry having been made dependent on democratic government, it was only to be expected that after the fall of the dictatorships politicians in the three countries should press for membership. They looked upon membership not only as a way of obtaining economic advantages; but also as a means of strengthening democracy in their own countries.[12] It was this argument—that membership would reinforce political stability—which convinced German politicians to support the applications.[13]

Common Points of View

A consensus for such enlargement now extends through all the political parties and organized interest groups.[14] As a Community, one feels called upon to demonstrate to the three countries the superiority of one's own economic and political system. The strengthening of democracy is for all concerned not only only a good in itself, but also a guarantee of political stability in one's own country. Political stability is itself seen as the absolute prerequisite for economic and military security. European security is today regarded less as a matter of defense against external aggression than as a maintenance of a functioning social and political order. This security would be threatened should it prove impossible to meet the expectations for social progress in the three applicant countries.

Because this feeling is so widely shared, there has been hardly any public discussion of the entry question. This lack of public interest can easily be explained by the fact that there are no differences of opinion between the governing coalition and the opposition on European policy.

The lack of willingness to discuss has historical reasons: As the ruling party of the 1950s, the Christian Democratic Union (CDU) was the architect of today's Community. The Social Democratic party (SPD), the opposition party of that time, renounced its resistance to the integration of the Federal Republic into the West only after its change from a class party to a people's party, demonstrated by its acceptance of the Godesberg program of 1959. Ever since then, it has been trying to shake the odium of being inimical to Europe; this charge was made with renewed emphasis in connection with its initiatives for the Ostpolitik. This state of competition, in which the leading parties try to outdo each other in the manifestation of their joy over integration, cannot lead to a rational discussion of European political alternatives. In this way, traditional models and ideas of integration, whose relation to reality is questionable, are perpetuated. Moreover, an apparent consensus is maintained which must not be endangered by the critical discussion of even such a basic decision as the enlargement toward the South.

This is one of the reasons the German parliament took up the question of enlargement only at a very late stage. The hearings before the Foreign Relations Committee indeed showed how few members of parliament have any interest in the question.[15]

Differing Concepts of Integration

Nevertheless, the hearings before the Foreign Relations Committee, and observations expressed by individual parliamentarians, have revealed that there are significant conceptual differences in spite of apparent unanimity.[16]

Christian Democrats[17] and German industrialists[18] still adhere to the original concept of the Community. Their "Yes to Europe" has a political foundation. Political cooperation among the West European countries is seen as a guarantee to independence from the superpowers, and as preferable to each country trying to go it alone. By the same token, the opportunity for greater European unity should not be wasted. Furthermore, only if strong and healthy can Europe discharge its responsibilities toward the Third World.

According to the integration concepts spelled out in the Treaty of Rome, political unification is best to be achieved through economic cooperation. The merging of the individual economies will lead to political interdependence; an enlarged market will promote growth and prosperity and will forge common interests. Therefore, the determination as to whether an enlargement of the Community would be desirable hinges upon a positive answer to the following question: Can the economic structures of the three new member states—after a not too protracted period of transition—be integrated into the Common Market, that is, can they be exposed to the unrestricted competition existing in the highly industrialized Community countries? There are many who consider the first round of enlargement a violation of this principle. The accession of such industrial threshold powers as Spain, Greece, and Portugal would exacerbate the discrepancies in the levels of economic development of the individual Community countries to such an extent as to make a common domestic and foreign economic policy virtually impossible. A Community which, however, is no longer in a position "to speak with one voice," for Conservatives loses attractiveness. The European policy of the Christian Democrats has traditionally had in view a prosperous and politically consolidated Europe, which would attract

Third World countries and thus conceivably bring about an undermining of East European solidarity. Hence the unpopularity, among the Christian Democrats, of new members who evince neutralistic or anti-American tendencies.[19]

For Social Democrats and for trade union spokesmen, on the other hand, enlargement raises the question of whether the old integration concept is still valid.[20] They have always been critical of limiting European cooperation to the economic sphere and of overemphasizing the role of the market as an integrating factor.[21] Market mechanisms have indeed proved to be an inadequate instrument for achieving the general improvement and equalization of living conditions as postulated in the treaties. The necessary changes concomitant with the accession of partly industrialized countries into the Community are therefore considered most desirable. They welcome more state interference in economic matters which would facilitate the necessary processes of adaptation, through, for instance, regional and industrial policies. There are also domestic political reasons for their interest in making economic planning more respectable: even in the economically stable Federal Republic there is the danger of increasing employment problems through the implementation of new technologies and the international redistribution of labor. By the same token, the German trade unions (DGB) have been fighting for the adoption of an "employment-oriented economic policy" and they would welcome a watering down of the market economy dogma in the Federal Republic through European policies. The difficulties of a structural adaptation of the three South European countries are consequently considered a quantitative rather than a qualitative problem, which should be solved through a South Development Program.

Every group concerned wants to avoid a public discussion involving which integration concept would be adequate in the case of enlargement. Relying on market mechanisms as an integrating factor or hoping for the possible benefits of a South Development Program is really what the controversy, if it can be called a controversy, is all about. And of course the various interested parties have their own specific views on this issue.

Fears and Hopes

Above all, it has been the representatives of German industry, whose position has been largely supported by the Ministry of Economics, who have emphasized interest in the continuation and deepening of the Common Market in the debate on expansion.[22] For them, the Common Market's capability of functioning is the prerequisite for the successful adjustment of the entrepreneurs to changed world economic conditions. They are concerned with the assimilation of production conditions through the harmonization of technical norms; an adequate right of competition excluding, above all, competitive distortions through varying subsidies and other administrative interventions; and a higher mobility of the labor force. They vigorously support the goal of a European economic and monetary union, which they see as a prerequisite for a common "growth and stability-oriented policy."[23] Accordingly, they demand that the enlargement of the Community should be accompanied by forced efforts for a deepening of the European Economic Community. Without such targeted efforts, they see the danger of a loosening of the Community.

They fear that an enlargement of the Community might result in: (1) a restriction of competition in the enlarged market; (2) a supplanting of the market economy principle by planification; (3) an increased propensity toward inflation within the European Economic Community; and (4) an intensification of external protectionism.

Policies Governing Competition

It is generally understood that the applicant countries' low level of economic development and their regional and sectoral difficulties will necessitate extended transition periods. There is no agreement on exactly how long these periods should be, depending as they do not only on the degree of competitiveness of the applicant countries' industries but also on the Community countries' own short-term export expectations. It is generally felt that the transition period—until the applicants should fully discharge their responsibilities as laid down in the EEC treaty—should not be too long. This is the only way of ensuring a strong enough pressure to adapt to the competition standards of the Community. All three countries have a complicated system of veiled import restrictions and in various ways promote their own industrial goods exports. This, of course, is incompatible with full membership status, and therefore the court of the European Community is expected to play an important role in the integration of the new members.

At the same time, there is a strong suspicion that the elimination of tariff barriers might result in more nontariff barriers (NTBs). The EEC Commission and the old member countries are expected, for political reasons, to make concessions to the South Europeans against the principle of reciprocity, which would lead to an imbalance of competition for individual branches of industry and business sectors within the Community. After all, such things have happened before, as in the case of Italy where import restrictions were tolerated as inevitable and the lesser evil. In the past, such subsidized exports, especially as applied to metal-processing industries, have resulted in significant market upsets in the Federal Republic.

Within the Community there is no defense, in the shape of anti-dumping measures, against such low-priced imports, and the EC Commission was, for the reasons stated, not prepared to intervene according to Articles 91 and 92 of the EEC treaty. German industry has been upset by such leniency toward the applicant countries because it is afraid it might become the general rule. German industrialists are convinced that the propensity to increase competitiveness with state help has been more of a factor in countries other than the Federal Republic. They feel faced with a dumping competition that they oppose on national economic grounds as well as individual profit-making. A watering down of the competition concept laid down in the EEC treaty would run counter to the interests of German industry because it would undermine the competitiveness of German products in the market.[24]

Industrial Policy

For the same reason, German industrialists and the Ministry of Economics are not prepared, as they have firmly and repeatedly stressed, to accept a greater degree of state intervention. They are concerned about the possibility of the Community's further extending the most recent sectoral regulations under the pretext of helping the applicants—Greece, Portugal, and Spain—to adapt the structures of their economies to Community standards.[25] The Confederation of Germany Industry (BDI) has declared forcefully that the necessary structural changes in the applicant countries should be brought about only by market mechanisms and that one should facilitate investments by improving general economic conditions.[26] The Community is expected to provide the means for this from its various funds. Such monies are supposed to be tied to specific projects, and support should be restricted to businesses which, at least from a medium-range point of view, can be expected to become competitive.[27] The idea of a Marshall Plan for financing infrastructural development or budget deficits is regarded skeptically.[28] Subsidies should be kept to a minimum, not only to limit the Federal Republic's financial burden but also to avoid inflationary impulses within the Community. In this context, one especially deplores the fact that an enlargement might make more difficult the creation of an economic and monetary union.

Trade

Because of its dependence on exports, German industry is opposed to all protectionism and is worried about the idea that new members could use their entry in such a way as to further expand protectionism within the Community. In addition, some industries within the EEC will only be inclined to demand for themselves those same protective measures being permitted to the new members. There is "a danger that the justified protective needs of the industries in the applicant countries will be taken up by those branches of industry within the Community which are already demanding protectionistic measures today. This could lead to an unholy alliance between applicant and old-Community industries if they should find themselves under the same protective mantle. . . . a situation in which the representatives of industrial interests in the actual Community cheat their way into a kind of Trojan horse in order thus to lend emphasis to their own protectionist interests."[29]

German industrialists are nevertheless quite confident that the Federal Republic's political and eocnomic weight within the EEC is sufficient to maintain the principles of the Treaty of Rome. Should propensities toward protectionism, state planning, and inflation markedly increase, German industrialists would be determined to block any further integration. Certainly, the Germany economy does not only associate fears but also opportunities with southern expansion. Under present conditions, Germans expect: (1) enlargement of export markets; (2) better investment opportunities; and (3) improvements in the job market. Businesses in several branches expect to increase their exports in the near future.

In contrast to the first round of expansion, the advantages of tariff reductions coupled with admission are one-sided. The applicant countries already largely have the right to unimpeded access to the markets within the Community on the basis of existing Association or Free Trade agreements. They themselves, however, have been able to protect their home industry to a great degree from the competition of the EEC suppliers. The expected tariff reductions as a result of entry will affect, after all, 30 percent of present exports to Greece, 60 percent to Spain, and 15 percent to Portugal.[30]

More significant than traditional tariff barriers will be the NTBs such as import licenses, drawn-out procedures for permission to import, fixed price minimums, a lack of or diversions in standard specifications and quality controls, and cash deposits.[31] German industrialists are determined, if necessary, to apply sanctions in case NTBs should increase with the elimination of traditional tariffs. For instance, any protectionist measures not agreed upon with the EEC partners should automatically lead to the forfeiting of any protective measures specified in the treaties.

In general, German industrialists are confident that low-wage competition will not be a serious threat to high-quality German products. To be sure, industry points out that all other EEC countries will obtain the same advantages, and that their own chances for future sales will accordingly depend on how successfully they can assert themselves against this competition.[32] The reduction of tariffs will be especially favorable when the major competitors are outside the EEC.[33] Given the demand structure in the applicant countries, it is hoped that they may be won as potential markets for exchange goods from trade with eastern countries. As for access to Third World markets, the advantages derived from the special historical relationships of Greece, Spain, and Portugal to Third World countries are not considered to be all that beneficial.[34] On the other hand, it must be remembered that with admission, the three new member countries will receive access to orders in the entire EEC as well as in the area of the Association agreements; for the construction industry, this results in a much keener competition in Third World markets, especially in those of the African, Pacific, and Caribbean (APC) area.[35]

In the realm of agricultural trade, the Federal Republic expects more advantages than disadvantages because of the availability of a complementary palette of products. The food industry is only partially optimistic; it assumes that the inhibiting competition will hit the Italian and the French products more severely, but it fears that its own conditions will deteriorate. Especially those medium-sized businesses which are salary intensive fear that they will not be equal to the pressure of competition and that an increased movement of production to other EEC countries will result.[36] Large businesses in the food industry are more interested in being able to import raw materials freely from Third World countries, even after enlargement, in order to strengthen their competitive position compared to these.[37]

As a result of stronger imports from the new member states, difficulties in sales are expected in salary-intensive products and in mass goods; Spain, especially, and Greece and Portugal to a lesser degree, have already developed efficient industries in certain productive sectors. This competition will hit partly those branches which in the EEC are now facing a structural crisis.[38] Nevertheless, these fears of competition are generally of a short-term nature. On the whole, it is expected that the enlargement will lead to increased demand as a result of the economic impulses of an expanded market.

In the three new member countries, there is a considerable backlog of demand, specifically for consumer goods, whereas the highly industrialized countries are thought to have reached saturation levels in this sector. Furthermore, one expects growth and, consequently, an expansion of markets by virtue of the Community's financial assistance.

Investment

It is impossible to make more generalized comments on the investment expectations of German industry. All three applicant countries have, since the sixties, attracted foreign investment capital—the Federal Republic's share being considerable in each of the three countries. Investors have been more cautious ever since the fall of the dictatorships and in the face of the political and social uncertainties connected with the transition to democracy. The absorption of these states within the Community is general-ly considered the best guarantee for making future investments secure. Moreover, investments will be dependent on long-range profit expectations and on the particular government's ability to find an acceptable com-promise between the concept of free enterprise and the requirements for na-tional economic planning.

Projections of possible investment efforts by German firms in the three applicant countries reflect certain conceptions of an inner European divi-sion of labor. It is assumed that the Federal Republic will increasingly specialize in the production of high-grade industrial goods; whereas in the applicant countries, salary-intensive industry will be established for a cer-tain time. In addition, the production that is already highly technological will be expanded, and in these cases, cooperation between German and local firms is envisioned.[39] As a result of rising labor cost levels in the three coun-tries—and this applies even to Portugal—pure reallocation investments have not been attractive for years.[40] Aside from political considerations, in-vestment behavior will depend above all on whether expansion of the domestic market in these three countries will be sufficient to compensate for that investment stimulus lost through the removal of protection of the domestic market as a result of membership.[41]

Labor Market

The guaranteeing of completely free labor mobility in the event of accession is welcomed by employers but is a cause of anxiety for trade unions. Employers are hoping for a new increase in labor mobility and for relief in job sectors where the employment stoppage of guest workers has caused tightening in the labor market.[42] On the other hand, the DGB is afraid that an instant liberalization in migration will increase existing employment prob-lems. The problem is not that German workers will be competing against workers from the three new member countries for scarce jobs, but that there will be a battle for jobs between the guest workers and those from the three countries. For these reasons, the DGB has suggested guided free movement (*assistierte Freizügigkeit*); that is, at least for a transition period a worker from any of the three countries would have to give proof of a job offer in hand before being allowed to move to another Community country.[43] Such suggestions are directed toward Turkey, in particular. If Greek workers were to have complete freedom of movement, Turkey would certainly force the Community countries to stick to their treaties with Turkey.[44] This would cause problems for the Federal Republic, which is a favorite labor market with the Turks[45]—potentially explosive problems not only regarding numbers but even more regarding the social assimilation of Turkish workers.

Trade Unions

For the DGB, enlargement is, first of all, of political significance—that is, absorbing these three countries into the Community and thereby stabilizing democracy and improving workers' social conditions.[46] The DGB has been more active than other West European trade unions in its efforts to strengthen the trade union movement in these three countries, albeit with varying degrees of success. European integration is, for the DGB, above all a sociopolitical task. It hopes that the trade unions would work for a strengthening of the labor movement in the three countries, being mainly interested in the establishment of a powerful, unified trade union that would exert political influence by virtue of its size and organized power. Such a trade union would be in a good position to enforce, within the realm of practical economic possibilities, labor's demands in negotiations with labor and management.

South Development Program

The DGB is especially interested in speedy economic development of the new member countries, not least because the success of trade union policy guided by a spirit of cooperation is dependent upon the productivity of the economy.[47] It therefore supports the SPD proposal of a South Development Program and is convinced that there is nothing to hinder multilateral financing of such a program. What one has in mind is a reform and an increase of existing Community funds, as well as a Marshall Plan for southern Europe. There is some thinking that even some non-Community members should contribute to the financing of such a fund, and therefore this fund could be administered outside EC channels, if necessary. Nothing much, however, has come of it so far, just as nothing has been decided yet about the suggestion to use Germany's central bank currency reserves if necessary for such a project. Unlike the German industrial confederations, the DGB is rather more prepared to accept higher inflation in the Community if it were in the interest of economic development within the three new member countries. It is afraid that the envisaged common economic and monetary policy and concomitant stabilization measures in the three new countries might lead to a decrease in their GNPs, and that it would be the workers who would suffer through the redistribution process. Thus, the DGB links entry with a renewed demand for a greater emphasis on employment-oriented policymaking.

Agriculture

In contrast to French and Italian farmers, German farmers have no particular worries about enlargement in the South.[49] The new member countries are not potential competitors, but possible markets, and will presumably help alleviate the problem of overproduction in those branches which are of particular interest to German farmers. On the basis of this analysis, the Farmers' Confederation as well as the federal Ministry of Agriculture are in favor of the expansion and of the inclusion of the southern European countries into the existing system of European agricultural policy. Although even from a static viewpoint the inclusion of the applicant countries in the agricultural market will be tied to growing financial burdens, a reform of the European agricultural policy is not considered to be necessary; this is a position held by the Ministry of Agriculture, but not by any other economic group.[48] After the experiences of the first round of expansion, the German Farmers' Confederation is quite confident and has little worry that the entrance of new members may motivate a basic reform of the European agricultural policy, or that an alliance of the Mediterranean countries could end the preferential treatment of the moderate products.

All the same, it is evident that the German Farmers' Confederation would have preferred a consolidation (*approfondissement*) to an enlargement of the Community. Since the decision was made on a higher political level, the Confederation has resigned itself to the facts but is hoping that the efforts to establish a European monetary system will be successful. The Confederation is well aware of the difficulty of achieving political integration in a Community of Twelve: after enlargement, the number of Farmers' Confederations within the Committee of Agricultural Organizations in the European Community (COPA) would climb to more than twenty-five.[49] Diverse interests and a multitude of languages will hamper COPA's successful functioning, depending as it does on the work of honorary top-level appointees.

Enlargement and Foreign Relations

Enlargement will no doubt enhance the Community's importance in world economic terms, but at the same time, it will narrow its field of operation in economic and political policymaking. For the rest of the Mediterranean countries and the APC countries, enlargement will mean a loss of preferential treatment arrangements. This will have an effect not only on the Federal Republic's commercial policy interests, but also on its foreign policy priorities. The elimination of trade policy preferences and economic aid for Third World countries can only be justified if the development of countries on the European periphery is to be understood as a principal EC responsibility, and only if one expects them to recognize their own successful growth as proof of the success of its development.

In the discussions of development policy in the EEC, the Federal Republic has repeatedly resisted a regional limitation in the development of special relationships to countries of the Third World. There was a conflict of interests with those member countries which, on the basis of their colonial past, had developed special relationships with individual countries and then wished to continue them even as members of the EEC. But the philosophy of a globally planned development policy was supplanted during the seventies by considerations that are more strongly along the lines of a regionalization of spheres of interest. Both the changed role and the evolving self-consciousness of the United States as the leading western power play a major role in this. The efforts for the development of a regional monetary system in the form of a European economic and monetary union, or later of a European currency system, the special commitment of European political cooperation in conflicts on the African continent are, in this contest, as meaningful as the further expansion of the European Community in the Mediterranean, both in the sense of a global Mediterranean policy or an EEC expansion to the South.

European Political Cooperation

The integration of Greece, Spain, and Portugal into the European Political Cooperation (EPC) will result not only in an expansion of the subjects of interest of European foreign policy but also in a change of positions taken. The Nine are endeavoring to integrate the new members as soon as possible into the EPC system and are hoping that they will fully accept the *acquis communautaire*. This is not at all what the entering countries themselves would prefer. For their part, they are hoping to gain the Community's support for their interests. The Federal Republic in particular is concerned about the possible deterioration, as a result of Greek membership, of its traditionally excellent relations with Turkey.[50] The three new member countries' foreign policy conflicts will not only result in tensions in bilateral relationships with other countries, but also might affect the solidarity of the Twelve as such. As became apparent after the United Nations resolution on racism, Greece, for instance, will not necessarily take into account Community interests when canvassing for Third World votes.

The three new countries' rather pro-Arab attitude may even mar the Federal Republic's relationship with Israel. After the change in position of the United States and the Begin government, however, the German position is quite a bit closer to that of the other EC countries. On the whole, European foreign relations will be more concerned with the Mediterranean and South American countries.

European Security

Another consequence of the accession of the three southern European countries will be that the Community will have to become more concerned with security questions. This does not mean, however, that the Community would be able to assume the responsibilities of a European defense community. Obstacles of a strategic nature apart, such a redistribution of power in European-American relations would be neither feasible nor, at least for the Federal Republic, desirable. Membership in the Community can only contribute to a closer relationship of these states with the NATO. But it must not be overlooked that each applicant country has its own specific security problems and that defense against a military threat by the Warsaw Pact countries is not at all viewed as a major priority. Greece feels rather more threatened by Turkey, and its security anxieties are more focused on Cyprus and the Aegean. Spain and Portugal are preoccupied chiefly with cementing their own domestic security. Furthermore, Spain's possible joining of the NATO is controversial within Spain; and Portugal, although a NATO partner, has left open the alliance question in its constitution. The security interests of the Community and therefore of the Federal Republic are not so much dependent upon the contributions of these three countries toward the military alliance as on the maintenance of a conflict-free zone in the Mediterranean.[51]

Security in Europe today is limited less than ever to military defense against outside aggression. The East-West conflict for which the NATO alliance was created is increasingly being supplanted by the discussions between the developed countries and the Third World concerning the fashioning of the international economic system. The success of European interests becomes more difficult because of the increased international competition among the industrial countries. But the countries of the EEC are more dependent than others on a functioning world economy: an interruption in the delivery of their raw materials, the loss of international markets, and the convulsion of the international monetary system hits them much harder than it does a large economic power such as the United States. Furthermore, they—again in contrast to the United States—are not in a position to repel threats to their economic interests in connection with regional conflicts. The EEC has neither the possibilities of economic sanctions nor the means of military coercion to intervene in international conflicts and to resolve them to its advantage. The Cyprus crisis as well as the Middle East conflict have clearly demonstrated how little the EEC countries can influence the course of crises even on their own periphery, in spite of common efforts. Accordingly, they are necessarily interested in a long-term stability of this area, because only in this way can the marginal conditions for their own economic development be guaranteed. They see the best assurance for this in the security of a well-functioning social and political order in southern Europe.

Conclusions

Considering the already intense and prospering economic relations with the applicant countries, enlargement is a promising but not urgent prospect. German industrialists expect further export and investment opportunities, and even German farmers can hope to reap the benefits of an enlarged market without being troubled by increased competition. Apart from the somewhat touchy issue of free movement of labor, budgetary implications and above all the preservation of the principles of a market-oriented European economy are of major concern. Though there are different concepts of integration, they are hardly reflected in the negotiation position of the German government. When it comes to framing Germany's European policy, those critical of the traditional Common Market concept are in a minority position; in spite of all verbal support for a Marshall Plan for southern Europe, they did not manage to get a single dime for such a program.

In the broader political context, there is, however, a basic consensus as to the fundamental desirability of enlargement. The willingness to accept Greece, Portugal, and Spain into the Community has its roots in an ideologically determined concept of Europe to which the political elite still adheres and which motivates them to seize the opportunity of creating a greater Europe.

On the other hand, all political forces have been interested in using the opportunity of the dictatorships being overthrown in these countries to enforce their own sociopolitical concepts and to establish an isomorphic system. The participation of the leading German parties and the German trade unions in the buildup of a democratic party sytem and trade union movement—as they see it—in Portugal (and to a lesser degree in Spain and Greece) has been most spectacular. These efforts in transnational policymaking are considered to be supported by including these countries in the European Community. Establishing and maintaining political and economic stability in the countries of southern Europe are understood to be prerequisites for their own future well-being. These rather altruistic considerations, nevertheless, are not the main reason for Germany's interest in this area; its chief concern is the preservation of its own long-term economic and military security.

It is precisely because the countries of Western Europe cannot exercise a coercive influence to resolve conflicts on their periphery in a manner satisfactory to themselves that they are interested in long-range stabilization in this area. And more and more it is the Federal Republic which as a dominant power in Western Europe feels obliged to work for long-term stability in this part of the world.

Notes

1. See Helga Haftendorn, Wolf-Dieter Karl, Joachim Krause, and Lothar Wilker, ed., *Verwaltete Aussenpolitik. Sicherheits- und entspannungs- politische Entscheidungsprozesse in Bonn* (Cologne, 1978). Verlag Wissenschaft und Politik. In this work, the authors reach the following conclusion: "The political leadership—Chancellor, Cabinet, and Ministers—now deals only with a selection of political decisions, while the ministerial bureaucracy in Bonn and its counterparts in international staffs and secretariats are becoming the real foreign political actors" (p. 7). In the light of recent Euro-political decisions, this thesis is very questionable. The decision to introduce the direct vote for the European Parliament was already at that time not a "pliable reaction to changing international and domestic challenges," nor a "crisis decision" or the fulfillment of decisions preshaped by bureaucrats. In the same way, the pre-history of the European monetary system seems to confirm the opinion of those authors who attribute a leading role to the federal government "in the sense of a setting of goals and of influencing people, so that they will work towards these goals." See Karl Carstens, *Politische Führung* (Stuttgart, 1971), p. 11.

2. The representatives of those departments dealing with EEC questions felt that they had been bypassed, and they voiced heavy criticism of the procedure. (In this connection, it is interesting to note that the interministerial "EEC enlargement" task force, which had been set up in connection with the first round of enlargement, was reactivated only in 1976.) At the same time, the political soundness, or at least the economic value, of the decision was called into question by the representatives of various staffs. (Such a criticism was, to be sure, mostly oral and voiced in private conversations, but it is also reflected in some written positions.) As an example, see the critical remarks of the director of the European section of the federal

Ministry for Economics, Ulrich Everling, in "Zehn Thesen zur Erweiterung," *EG Magazin* 5 (1977):11-14. (These theses also found wise dissemination in other European countries and were much noted because of their critical content.) Everling's theses represent the synopsis of a talk in April 1977, published under the title "Integrations politische Probleme der Erweiterung der EG," in *Die Süd-Erweiterung der Europäischen Gemeinschaft. Wende oder Ende der Integration*? eds. Hajo Hasenpflug and Beate Kohler (Hamburg, Verlag Weltarchiv GMBH 1977), pp. 61-87. See further the contribution of another leading official in the federal Ministry of Economics: Rudolf Morowitz, "Die wirtschaftlichen Probleme eines Beitritts Griechenlands zur Europäischen Gemeinschaft,"*Europa-Archiv* 8 (1977):249-58. A reserved or negative attitude was shown not only by officials of the Bonn ministerial bureaucracy, but also was largely shared by representatives of the related ministries in other EEC capitals and members of the Commission. Even the official position of the Commission for the application of Greece let it be known that there were greater doubts than in the circle of the Council of Ministers, and this led to serious reactions from the Greek public. See Karl H. Buck, *Griechenland und die Europäische Gemeinschaft. Erwartungen und Probleme des Beitritts* (Bonn, 1978), pp. 89-92.

3. In 1976, after the fundamental decision in favor of membership had already been reached, the German Institute for Development Policy (DIE) suggested a closer examination of the related implications in a confidential statement for the Foreign Office. A further opinion was drawn up for the interministerial task force for "EEC Enlargement." See DIE, *Vorschläge zur Anpassung und zum Ausbau gemeinschaftlicher Politiken und Instrumente im Zusammenhang mit der Erweiterung der EG um Griechenland, Portugal und Spanien* (Berlin, 1978). Among other publications are: Stefan A. Musto, *Spaniens Beitritt zur Europäischen Gemeinschaft: Folgen und Probleme* (Berlin, 1977); Wilhelm Hummen, *Greek Industry in the European Community. Prospects and Problems* (Berlin, 1977)—in German: *Griechenland und die Europäische Gemeinschaft. Probleme und Lösungsansätze im Bereich der Industrie, Berlin, 1977*; Klaus Esser et al., *Portugal. Industrie und Industriepolitik vor dem Beitritt Zur Europäischen Gemeinschaft* (Berlin, 1977); Burghard Claus et al., *Zur Erweiterung der Europäischen Gemeinschaft in Südeuropa* (Berlin, 1977, 2nd ed. 1978); Klaus Esser et al., *Europäische Gemeinschaft und südeuropäische Beitrittsländer. Anforderungen an die Integrationsfähigkeit* (Berlin, 1978).

The Stiftung Wissenschaft und Politik, whose major task lies in advising the government in security and foreign political questions, presented a paper to the planning staff of the Foreign Office in November 1976. One of the topics was the enlargement of the EEC toward the South, about which a paper from the foundation was presented. Further advice was not given, nor was the foundation included in the work of the interministerial "EEC Enlargement" task force. To be sure, it worked on enlargement questions on its own initiative, and it was also asked to give its opinion before the Foreign Affairs Committee. (See Deutscher Bundestag, 8th Wahlperiode, Auswärtiger Ausschuss, Stenographisches Protokoll der 32nd und 33rd Sitzung, Offentliche Anhörung zum Thema "Erweiterung der EG nach Süden," May 29-31, 1978, [hereafter cited as the hearing before the Foreign Affairs Committee] pp. 705-47, as well as the oral presentations, p. 54.) The written position was published in a slightly revised form. See Christian Deubner, Heinz Kramer, and Götz Roth, "Die Erweiterung der Europäischen Gemeinschaft nach Süden, *Aus Politik und Zeitgeschichte, Beilage zum Parlament*, B 38/78, pp. 3-20. See also Heinz Kraimer, "Probleme und Folgn der Süderweiterung der Europaischen Gemeinschaft für die aussenpolitische Zusammenarbeit ihrer Mitgliedstaaten," SWP-AZ 2166, Ebenhausen, May 1978.

4. The fact that the Federation of German Industry (BDI), like the German Industrial and Trade Conference (DIHT), only asked for the opinion of the individual sectoral organizations in April 1978, in order to prepare its opinion before the Foreign Affairs Committee in Parliament, must not be allowed to obscure the fact that the economic and the farmers' associations as well as the trade unions had helped to influence the climate of opinion also on the question of enlargement through their regular and frequent contacts with the government—administration and Parliament. Insofar as interviews can establish a reliable impression of the formation of such a climate of opinion. (1) general political considerations and assessments played a greater role than specific groups or other concrete individual interests; (2) the position of the government acted markedly on the attitude of several associations; (3) all German associations are prejudiced in their attitude toward concrete Euro-political decisions through their repeated demonstration of a pro-European stance.

5. Even in the parliamentary debates on Europe, the enlargement question was touched on with few words until 1978. To be sure, individual parties or groups within the parties concerned themselves more intensely with the enlargement to the South of the EEC. On May 29 and 31, 1978, the Bundestag Foreign Affairs Committee organized a hearing (see note 3).

6. I have tried to sustain this thesis in another publication. See Beate Kohler, "Die Suderweitung der Gemeinschaft—Hintergründe, Motive und Konsequenzen—," in *Die Suderweiterung der Europäischen Gemeinschaft. Wende oder Ende der Integration?* ed. Hajo Hasenpflug and Beate Kohler (Hamburg, 1977) pp. 14-48.

7. According to the words of Chancellor Schmidt: "Now no one will maintain that an enlargement of the Community by three more members will promote the process of inner harmonization from today to tomorrow,

that it will work itself out quickly in an integration. The European Union is, as before, still in the far distance, the path to it will certainly not be shorter through an enlargement of the Community." Helmut Schmidt, "Solidarität der Partner festigen," in *Europäische Zeitung*, Number 12, December 1977, p. 1.

8. This became clear above all in connection with the agricultural negotiations between Greece and the Community after the reestablishment of the associate relationship. But it is also evident in the EEC's protectionist attitude toward sensitive products such as textiles in the case of Greece, or bulk steel in the case of Spain.

9. After the military coup, the treaty relationship was reduced to the "winding-up of the current administration (*géstion courante*)." See George N. Yannopoulos, *Greece and the European Economic Community: The First Decade of a Troubled Association*, Sage Research Papers in the Social Sciences, vol. 3, series no. 90-021 (Beverly Hills and London, 1975), p. 21. The resumption of all treaty obligations on the part of the EEC, including the freeing of a blocked loan from the European Investment Bank, followed relatively quickly after the fall of the military, namely, on the decision of the Commission on August 30, 1974 in reply to a memorandum from the Greek government of August 22, 1974. See Commission of the European Communities "Achter Gesamtbericht über die Tätigkeit der Europäischen Gemeinschaften 1974," Brussels, 1975, p. 281.

10. Spanish efforts to create special relations to the Community in the early sixties, induced by the British application for membership, were delayed for years. Within the circles of the Commission and the European Parliament it was clear from the beginning that a Spanish associate membership was out of the question on political grounds. In later years the shaping of Spain's relations with the EEC was also dependent on the judgment of its domestic political situation. Thus, the negotiations for a revision of the preferential agreement in 1975 were unilaterally interrupted by the EEC for political reasons. In this way, the Community showed its displeasure at the executions in Madrid and Burgos. For the prehistory of the Spanish application for membership, see Stefan A. Musto, *Spanien und die Europaische Gemeinschaft. Der schwierige Weg zur Mitgliedschaft* (Bonn, 1977), Europa Union Verlag pp. 47-71.

11. Relations between Portugal and the Community were visibly intensified after the fall of the dictatorship in April 1974. To that point there had been simply a free trade agreement which, after the membership of Great Britain, Denmark, and Ireland, was made with Portugal as the remaining EFTA country in mid-1972. Already at the time of the first visit of Soares to Brussels, the Commission assured him that the Community and its member countries would support a contribution "for the democratic and economic reconstruction of Portugal" especially in the economic, financial, and

technical areas, and it advanced the view that "a democratic Portugal naturally has its place in a Europe that is being built." See EEC Commission, Information IP (74) No. 77. In the following years, an additional agreement to the Free Trade Agreement of 1972 was negotiated, as well as an additional financial protocol. In addition to this, Portugal received immediate financial aid in October 1975, in order to be able to work against the acute economic crisis without having to wait for the financial protocol to come into force. For the development of relations between the EEC and Portugal see: EEC Commission, Information Aussenbeziehungen, "Die Beziehungen der EWG und Portugal," no. 133/76.

12. This connection was established on the occasion of the opening of membership negotiations with Greece by the Greek coordination minister Panayotis Papaligouras in his official position: "This passage from an authoritarian regime to democracy, effectuated without any trouble, is both, I think, a proof of the political maturity of our people and a title legitimizing our request to join a democratic Europe on the way to reinforcing its political and economic cohesion." Délégation permanente Hellenique auprès des Communautés Européennes, Déclaration du Ministre de la Coordination, M. Panayotis Papaligouras, à la Séance d'overture des Négociations d'adhesion, p. 1. The expectation that membership would strengthen democratic forces was later also emphasized by other leading Greek politicians—and later, by Spanish and Portuguese as well. See John Pesmazoglu, "Greece. A "special case" for EC membership," *European Community* Number 203 (September-October 1977):7.

13. "If the enlargement of the Community with Greece, Portugal and Spain, despite expected difficulties, is to be seen as a happy development . . . hailed by the Federal Republic of Germany, . . . the reasons are primarily of a political nature. . . . Besides, for them membership means a substantial element for the securing of democracy at home." See (note 7) Schmidt, "Solidarität der Partner festigen." "This decision [by the Council of Ministers on February 9, 1976, to recommend Greek membership without any conditions] was politically motivated. It is the expression of the will to support the Greek democracy after the fall of the colonels, and it is a contribution towards the stabilization of relations in the eastern Mediterranean." The chairman of the Euro-policy commission of the SPD. Bruno Friedrich, "Griechenland beabsichtigt Beitritt zur Europäischen Gemeinschaft," *Europa Union*, April 1976, p. 2.

14. This is documented in the hearing before the Foreign Affairs Committee (See note 3).

15. On both days together, only 18 of 66 committee members took part in the discussion. The participation of SPD deputies was somewhat stronger than that of the CDU and FDP. Eight out of 32 CDU committee members spoke; 9 out of 28 SPD committee members, as well as 2 additional SPD

deputies who were nonmembers; and 1 FDP member out of 6. This image is reinforced through a comparison of the frequency and intensity of requests to take the floor. Ibid.

16. Statements are based on numerous interviews with representatives of the parties and associations in the summer of 1978.

17. Compare, for instance, the section dealing with Euro-policy in the CDU basic program which was adopted at the party meeting of October 23-25, 1978. CDU, *Grundsatzprogramm der Christlich Demokratischen Union Deutschlands* (Bonn, 1978), p. 53.

18. See the written statements and the oral presentations of the Confederation of German Industry and the DIHI in the hearing before the Foreign Afairs Committee, pp. 161, 174, 840-47, 855-70.

19. The CDU states its goal of a European political union in the following three arguments of its basic program: (1) Only together can we Europeans make our interests carry weight in worldwide tasks, and can we be equal to our coresponsibility for the Third World; (2) Only if it is united can free Europe effectively realize its duties in the defense alliance and assure for itself the indispensable partnership of North America; (3) Only if it is united can free Europe encounter the increasing weight of the eastern Bloc and contribute to the unification of Europe and thereby also of Germany.

20. "A European Community which stubbornly retains its present tools for the strengthening of integration in the agricultural, capital and labor markets, and which would not be disposed to re-examine them critically towards the goal of opening the EEC to democratic countries of Europe, would sacrifice considerable impulses." Karsten D. Voigt, "Solidaritäts-programm für Südeuropa," *Die Neue Gesellschaft* 4 (1978): p. 321. See also the statements of some SPD deputies in the course of the hearings before the Foreign Affairs Committee, as well as the written and oral statements of the DGB, pp. 152, and 820-39.

21. The growing criticism of the market economic performance of the EEC is manifested in party meetings, as shown recently in the decisions at the Hamburg party meeting from November 15-19, 1977, on the question of European policy: "The European Community has led to an increase in economic growth and thus to a higher standard of living in the member countries. But the regional, sectoral and social imbalances between the member countries and within them have not been diminished." See *SPD Deokumente zur Europapolitik* (Bonn, 1978), p. 9. This view is also reflected in the SPD platform for the European Parliament elections. See SPD, *Soziale Demokratie für Europa. Programm der Sozialdemokrat-ischen Partei Deuteschlands für die erste europäische Direktwahl 1979* (Bonn, no date) adopted at the European Party meeting on December 10, 1978. On this question there is broad agreement with the DGB, which in its Euro-political position stresses above all the necessity for a regional and

structural policy that would foster jobs. See, for instance, Antrag zur Europapolitik DGB Bundeskongress Hamburg from May 21-26, 1978, Protokoll, Düsseldorf, 1978, p. 59.

22. The previously cited position of the BDI and the DIHT before the Foreign Affairs Committee should be mentioned here. The DIHT presented a brochure publishing the results of a questionnaire distributed to sixty-nine chambers of commerce domestically, and abroad in Greece, Spain, and Portugal. See DIHT, ed., *"Zwölf statt Neun. Chancen der EG-Erweiterung,"* DIHT 172, Bonn, 1978. See also the announcements in the DIHT Nachrichten 73/78 of November 15, 1978 and 54/78 of December 4, 1978 as well as the publications of the president of the DIHT, Otto Wolff von Amerongen, "Die Alt-EG und das Trojanische Pferd des Protektionismnus. Probleme einer zweiten EG-Erweiterung," *Europäische Zeitung*, December 1977, p. 4; see also von Amerongen, "Chancen und Risiken der EG-Erweiterung," *Wirtschaftsdienst*, December 1978, pp. 594-96. Other than its testimony before the Foreign Affairs Committee, the BDI had not presented any further publications up to the beginning of 1979. Its deliberations, however, were accepted in the position of Unice; on the occasion of the annual meeting of the BDI in Berlin, in May 1978, a work group concerned itself with the questions of enlargement in connection with a general assessment of Europe. There are also references in the annual report of the BDI. On the position of the Ministry of Economics, see note 2, Everling, "Integrationspolitische," and Morawitz, "Wirtschaftlichen Probleme."

23. Stability-oriented growth policy is a key concept in the discussion of economic policy in the Federal Republic. It expresses the economic policy creed of the BDI and DIHT, according to which total economic balance at high employment can be reached only through higher growth. Since, according to them, this depends on the expected earnings of entrepreneurs, these two associations foster control of inflation, above all a reduction of labor costs, tax burdens, and other federal taxes. See BDI, "Arbeitsplätze durch Wirtschaftswachstum," BDI Drucksache Number 112, Cologne, 1977. The BDI maintains that it is in accordance with current thinking, as can be proven by referring to the annual report of the Council of Economic Advisers for 1977-1978 which calls emphatically for a strategy of "total employment through economic growth." In the DGB demands for an economic policy oriented toward employment, or for a regional and structural policy oriented toward employment, the opposite conception of the trade unions is evident, according to which current unemployment is primarily a structural problem that can be removed only through a targeted structural policy of the government.

24. See, for instance, the statements of the representatives from the BDI, in the hearing before the Foreign Affairs Committee, p. 163.

25. ''The applicant countries, as developing countries, will naturally add to those opinions in the Community which see considerable government intervention and steering as indispensable. Whether this is the correct economic order for the highly developed member states as well, will be called into question at least on the part of Germany.'' See note 2, Everling, ''Integrationspolitische,'' p. 75. The BDI has formulated its opposition to a broadening of the European or also of the national industrial policy in several statements: ''An industrial policy which includes as many sectors as possible can never be an 'engine of European industrial policy.' '' BDI, *Jahresbericht des Bundesverbandes der Deutschen Industrie,* Cologne, May 1978, p. 35. See also ''Memorandum of the German Delegation on EEC Structural Policy in the Industrial Economy,'' R/1068/78, May 3, 1978; and BDI, ''Position Paper on the SPD Concept of a Forward-Looking Structural Policy,'' September 19, 1977.

26. See the position of the BDI in the hearing before the Foreign Affairs Committee.

27. Behind this—apparently—so clear claim lie market political interests and a disagreement about basic order policy questions, as the case of Portugal clearly showed. Portuguese government authorities and entrepreneurial circles were interested in the maintenance and partial increase of the state capitalistic structures, whereas the International Monetary Fund (IMF) urged a wider privatization; this is a position that is supported by German industrialists.

28. In this connection, reference is often made to the experiences with southern Italy. The continuing underdevelopment of the Mezzogiorno confirms the belief that even with a large supply of means, improvements can hardly be made in the short run.

29. See (note 22) von Amerongen, ''Die Alt-EG,'' p. 4.

30. See (note 22) DIHT, ''Zwolf statt Neun,'' p. 13.

31. Such measures work particularly to hamper trade because they are not calculable and elude effective control. To be sure, German enterprises even in the original EC countries (such as Italy) are repeatedly confronted with related measures. In these cases, the long established cooperation of the national as well as regional chambers of industry and commerce see to it that such offenses against the EEC treaty are relatively quickly revealed and either informally handled or brought to the attention of the Commission, which then handles the problem.

32. Reference was made to this by the German mechanical industry; on the estimates for future export possibilities and sales difficulties, see the list of products in (see note 22) DIHT, ''Zwölf statt Heun,'' pp. 9-13.

33. Included are special products of the chemical and mechanical industries.

34. In some cases, to be sure, it is assumed that the ''easier market

access of the applicant countries to those third countries . . . will offer beginnings for new ways of co-operation both in commercial trade and services as well as in the investment field." (See note 22) DIHT, "Zwölf statt Neun," p. 10. In the case of Portugal, one refers to the traditional relations with Angola, Mozambique, and Guinea; of Greece, to the relations with Egypt and other Arab countries; of Spain, to the relations with Morocco, Algeria, and Tunisia, but also to Spanish-speaking Latin America.

35. Spain, especially, is considered a powerful rival in the construction industry.

36. See the position of the German Federation of Food Industries in the hearing before the Foreign Affairs Committee, pp. 167 and 848-54.

37. This appears, for instance, in the studies by the Unilever Company. See Unilever, Common Market Survey Number 168, March 10, 1978.

38. Difficulties are expected above all in certain areas of the textile and clothing industry, in numerous products of the iron and steel industry, and in shipbuilding. See the exact listing of the sectors in (note 22) DIHT, "Zwölf statt Neun," p. 12.

39. The German Development Association (DEG) judges the opportunities for investment in the three applicant countries and also the willingness to invest in this region on the part of German enterprises much more optimistically than the BDI and the DIHT. See the business report for 1978 as well as the statement of the DEG representative in the hearing before the Foreign Affairs Committee, p. 284.

40. See (note 3) Esser et al., *Portugal.*

41. See DIHT, "Zwölf statt Neun," p. 16.

42. This applies to services, the construction industry, and in general, for relief work and simple technical occupations. Industry representatives voice a certain preference, especially for Spanish workers, with whom they have had good experiences: they are very willing to integrate, are industrious, and present no "disruptive factor."

43. See DGB in the hearing before the Foreign Affairs Committee, pp. 152 and 820-39. During the hearing, this suggestion was sharply criticized, which moved the DGB to substantiate its position again in a more detailed form through a member of the executive committee: Karl Schwab, "Wanderarbeiter ohne Identität und ohne Lebensperspektive?" *Welt der Arbeit,* Number 30, July 27, 1978, p. 5. Reference is made therein to the fact that the DGB had already promoted the introduction of a "limited mobility" in February 1977. That the government largely appropriated this position is documented on the one hand in its negotiations with Greece, and on the other in an article by the Minister of Labor and Social Order, Herbert Ehrenberg, "Warum es in einer Zwölfer-Gemeinschaft keine Freizügigkeit für Arbeitskrafte geben darf!" *EG-Magazin* (1978):7.

44. Article 36 of the Association Treaty with Turkey provides that the workers' mobility between the EEC and Turkey be established step by step from the end of 1976 to the end of 1978. In face of the growing number of unemployed in Turkey and the limited ability to absorb them in the German labor market, the government had already considered forms of a "controlled mobility" before the decision on enlargement. Morawitz also raises this question in his article, (see note 2) "Wirtschaftlichen Probleme," p. 255.

45. Almost 90 percent of the Turks who worked in the EEC in 1976 were employed in the Federal Republic. Their share of foreign employment was 27 percent; that of workers from Greece, Spain, and Portugal together was barely 18 percent. The greatest share of this went to the Greeks, with about 170,000 employed. See "Arbeitsmarkt Probleme durch EG-Erweiterung," *DIW-Wochenbericht* Number 51-52/78, December 21, 1978.

46. "The democratic conditions in these three countries can develop in the interest of the worker only when Portugal, Spain and Greece belong to the European Community." Position of the DGB, in the hearing before the Foreign Affairs Committee, p. 822.

47. The first suggestions were developed in the Deutschen Institut für Entwicklungspolitik. See Christian Heimpel, "Motive, Folgen und Verpflichtungen des Beitritts Spaniens und Portugals zur Europäischen Gemeinschaft," in (see note 2), *Sud-Erweiterung*, Hasenpflug and Kohler, eds., p. 175.

48. A correspondingly comprehensive analysis had been prepared already in March 1976 in the Ministry of Agriculture. It shows clearly that German agriculture will be affected only indirectly; that is, that inhibiting competition will affect primarily other EEC countries and that, accordingly, it would be in the interest of the government to decline compensatory demands in the course of membership negotiations. Furthermore, it is urged that the costs of the those products for which a surplus can be calculated—wine, durum wheat, and olive oil—should be reduced in such a way that the adjustment of these market orders be promoted before the membership of Greece.

49. See the Position of the German Farmers' Confederation at the hearing before the Foreign Affairs Committee, p. 181, 871-82. In contrast, the BDI and DIHT emphatically propose a reform of the European agricultural policy.

50. Leading members of Parliament have voiced great concern about Greek membership in the EEC in face of the tense relations between Turkey and Greece. See, for instance, the remarks of Kurt Mattick, *Frankfurter Rundschau*, Number 169, August 3, 1976, p. 2.

51. "The European Mediterranean countries are developing more and more a certain resemblance to the Third World; this fact represents an important element in the instability of the European security order, since the

cold war has receded into the background. Strong tensions exist in the countries of southern Europe, deep clefts gape between society and the state, between the hopes for economic development for a new distribution of values within the society and the political measures of the concerned regimes.'' Johan Holst, "Verteidigungsplanung und europäische Sicherheitspolitik. Das Spektrum potentieller Konflikte," *Europa-Archiv*, 10 (1978):285. See also the position of the Director of the Research Institute of the German Society for Foreign Policy, Karl Kaiser, at the hearing before the Foreign Affairs Committee, p. 92, as well as the position of Lothar Ruehl, Zweites Deutsches Fersehen (ZDF) correspondent, before the Foreign Affairs Committee, pp. 1028-57.

10 Germany's Monetary and Financial Policy and the European Community

Norbert Kloten

At its meeting in Bremen on July 6-7, 1978, the European Council agreed on the broad outlines of a new European monetary system (EMS). The originators of the plan were the French President Giscard d'Estaing and the German Chancellor Helmut Schmidt. The French interest in a new monetary initiative was not unexpected, but the German attitude did come as a surprise. Was it the result of political considerations, or did it signal a turnaround in German monetary thinking? So far, no answer has been forthcoming to this question; by pointing this out I do not wish to evade the issue, but I should like to postpone discussion of the question and the answer; that is to broach the subject without regard to the decisions taken at Bremen, for the German role in the Bremen summit does not fit in with the widely accepted picture of German interests and behavior as seen in European initiatives in recent years.

Criticism by the European Partners and the German Standpoint

Only a short time after the EEC was established, the Germans were being reproached for being insufficiently European-minded, for being too strongly oriented toward the Atlantic. More recently, the partner countries have stepped up their criticism, claiming that the Germans' tiredness of Europe is becoming increasingly noticeable. The Germans, it is asserted, not only give the cold shoulder to programmatic initiatives of the Commission and to constructive proposals by European committees, but also criticize the European authorities wholesale for alleged bureaucracy and unwarranted lavish expenditure. Inwardly, it is maintained, they long ago dissociated themselves from solutions they had originally supported (for example, the European agricultural market organization), but without being able to suggest acceptable alternatives. Their lack of interest in Europe, their lack of any desire for integration, is reflected in their reluctance to make concessions in questions of monetary policy. Germany is not prepared to accept the role of a key currency for the Deutsche mark, and its monetary assistance for its European partners is not so far-reaching as the situation

177

demands. The Germans are selfishly pursuing their own stabilization objectives and are failing to discharge their duties as an *économie dominante* Europe. Germany's partners are in effect compelled to submit to German priorities. The underlying cause of all this, it is claimed, is a dogmatic German attitude to the question of monetary stability and a no less marked regulatory dogmatism in favor of what the Germans call a "market system."

The German reaction to these criticisms by its European partners has always been one of astonishment, even consternation. What has surprised the Germans is not the reference to the specifically German manner of thinking, but the accusation of lack of interest in European integration. The Germans have declared that they have always regarded European union as a historical necessity and as an act of vital interest to Germany. The few people who think differently can be disregarded. The Germans play the Atlantic card only for the sake of achieving a proper balance, which is in everybody's interest. And there can be no question of Germany being tired of Europe. What is discernible in Germany—and not only in Germany—is a certain disenchantment about the prospects of making further headway in the field of European integration. But disenchantment is quite different from being tired of Europe. Exasperation at the bureaucracy in Brussels is another matter; after all, there is no mistaking the fact that a costly organization has been built up their which does not even make use of the powers it has been given, and which—as Germans can hardly help noticing—is for the most part financed by Germany (the paymaster of Europe). The EC agricultural market organization is no longer a market system nowadays, but rather a perversion of such a system. And if the Germans frequently speak out against dirigisme and government planning, in the last analysis they do so in the interests of the Community at large, which in the long run has nothing to gain from a system of internal and external dirigiste interventions. This also applies to the Germans' cool attitude toward the use of monetary initiatives as a means of bringing a European economic and monetary system closer. After all, the German misgivings are borne out by experience. But despite all previous bad experiences, the Germans have always been among the first to advocate the enlargement of the Community and the intensification of cooperation.

Thus, there is indeed no lack of claims and counterclaims. However, such differences are typical not only of the relations between Germany and its partners; there are also disagreements between the partners themselves. I am not interested in the polemics as such; what matters is actual behavior—on the one hand, at international conferences, at the levels of target formulation among the European authorities and opinion formation among the committees; and on the other hand, when shaping actual economic and monetary policy decisions. This chapter is concerned almost entirely with the role of monetary policy; I shall deal with financial policy only in so far as it constitutes short-term economic policy at the same time. Questions of tax harmonization, the coordination of the European financial system as a whole, and the financing of European organizations will not be discussed.

European Implications of German Economic Policy

The Sources: Basic Positions and Priorities

It must be conceded right away that the specific German attitude toward the question of approaches to an economic and monetary union reflects conceptual judgments; however, the roots of these judgments are evident only to those who are prepared to put themselves in the position of the German nation following World War II. Besides the military and political disaster, the Germans experienced the near total erosion of the purchasing power of their currency. This time, in contrast to 1923, it was caused not by open inflation but by pent-up inflation—pent up by price fixing and quantitative controls (the coupon system)—but, like the first hyperinflation, it led in the end to the destruction of almost all financial assets. This experience made people determined not to let such things happen again. Monetary stability became a national issue of very high priority (in terms of monetary policy, since the currency reform of June 20, 1948). This was reflected in the decision of principle, taken when establishing the Bank deutscher Länder in 1948, to grant the central bank independence. This autonomy was admittedly a gift of the allies, particularly the Americans, but it was entirely consistent with the German bias. The counterpart was the belief that a dependent central bank (or a central bank forming a department of the Ministry of Finance) would sooner or later be bound to become an agent of the government in the unsound financing of its budget.

Moreover, the years during and immediately after the war, with their systems of coupons and controls of every kind, had discredited official dirigisme so lastingly that confidence in government quantitative controls was largely destroyed. Direct personal experience therefore backed the votes of the supporters of the Freiburg School and other neoliberals in favor of a market coordination system, which though hardly known at the time, rapidly proved to be highly efficient from mid-1948 onward. An effective conceptual foundation for the new system—a foundation that was quickly accepted by a large proportion of the population—was provided in the political sphere mainly by the model of the social market economy of the Christian Democratic Union-Christian Social Union (CDU-CSU). Needless to say, it also met with opposition; rival solutions were put forward, especially by the Social Democratic Party (SPD) and the trade unions. None of them, however, achieved general acceptance. At the latest in its Godesberg program of 1959, the SPD too opted for the market economy model.

The basis of the German market philosophy was the practice of thinking in terms of compatible regulatory forms. As a consequence, regulatory policy was in the forefront of economic policy; interventionist policy was considered to be suspect, although this did not prevent great importance being attached to monetary policy, whose task it was to determine monetary conditions. The contrast of the full employment doctrine in the United Kingdom or the philosophy of "planifcation" in France or the "new way" in the Netherlands, with the development of econometric forecasting models and the transformation of their results into economic policy decisions, was unmistakable. Of course, Keynes was discovered in Germany too, albeit with a considerable time lag; at first for the textbooks and then—mainly in the variant of fiscal policy—for financial policy. The result was the 1967 Stability and Growth Act. This act regulated the forms of anticyclical financial policy within a framework of stabilization policy; it also contained provisions on a compatible incomes policy (concerted action) as an ancillary policy area. In this act, Schiller believed he had achieved the optimum synthesis between modern regulatory thinking and modern economic management. It was no accident that beside the picture of John Meynard Keynes in his office hung the portrait of Walter Eucken.

The Stability and Growth Act—like the 1963 act concerning the creation of a council of economic experts (for assessing overall economic trends)—embodied a catalog of economic policy objectives. According to this act, the task of stabilization policy is to ensure, in the context of a free market system, stable purchasing power, a high level of employment, and external equilibrium, accompanied by steady and appropriate economic growth. This "magic quadrangle" of economic policy targets is still adhered to today even though the targets have so often been at risk or violated—indeed, even though doubts about the catalog of targets itself are growing. Here, as everywhere else, the setting of standards is not synonymous with their achievement. Actions detrimental to stabilization are committed by every policy area, by monetary policy less often than by other areas. But monetary policy did create the monetary conditions for an upsurge in prices that accelerated from the beginning of the sixties throughout the economic cycles till about the middle of 1974—not because the Bundesbank failed to advocate monetary stability on every possible occasion, but because it saw its efforts repeatedly undermined on the "external flank.

Although external equilibrium was an element in the German market philosophy, it was rarely achieved. Particularly in the sixties, the German authorities were for a long time quite content to have an undervalued currency; the state of running a permanent surplus on current account was convenient and supported by the social groups. But a price had to be paid for this mistaken attitude: the German economy acquired a growing export bias, and almost imperceptibly an enormous need for structural change built up. In addition, prices were pushed up by international price relationships and the effects of the trade surpluses on incomes and liquidity (imported inflation). It thus became clear that any attempt at stabilization under a system of fixed exchange rates is self-defeating because of the open external flank. After the monetary crisis in the autumn of 1968, and even more so after the renewed crisis at the beginning of May 1969, the exchange rate question was the dominant topic of economic policy discussions in Germany. In 1969, revaluing the Deutsche mark even became the main issue in an election campaign—"a unique case of a debate on a change in the exchange rate of a major currency continuing for many months 'in the market place.'"[1] Forms of imported inflation cropped up intermittently until March 1973. But by then the lesson had been learned; the objections to any monetary solution that facilitated the transmission of inflation from abroad had gathered strength.

*The German Attitude at Conferences
and in Negotiations*

Even before the actual negotiations on the creation of an economic and monetary union began at the end of the sixties, Germany was viewing plans to form a European monetary arrangement with some reserve.[2] On the one hand, it argued that the establishment of a regional European monetary arrangement might adversely affect transatlantic monetary cooperation; such cooperation should, however, be given priority for political and economic reasons. On the other hand, it feared that the reciprocal monetary assistance regularly envisaged in such plans might exacerbate inflationary tendencies by increasing international liquidity.[3]

But by 1964-1965 at the latest, it was recognized that the degree of integration achieved within the Community necessitated a coordination of the short-term economic policies of Community countries. The fact that Germany then accepted forms of medium-term programming that owed a great deal to French models amounted to a much greater concession than foreigners are probably able to appreciate; as late as 1963, Ludwig Erhard was flatly rejecting any kind of economic planning. From about 1968 onward, there were seen to be reasons for creating a monetary union:[4] (1) doubts about the viability of the Bretton Woods system were increasing; (2) uncertainty about the willingness of the United States to fulfill the obligations of a key currency country was growing; (3) the Common Market, especially the agricultural market organization, was increasingly exposed to disturbances on the monetary side (as in 1968 and 1969);[5] and (4) the time seemed ripe to underpin the envisaged transition from a mere customs union to a comprehensive economic union by measures of monetary policy.

The proposals of the then Chancellor Willy Brandt at the summit conference at The Hague in December 1969 reflected the change in the German attitude and its constants. He advocated the establishment of an economic and monetary union, but suggested that in an initial phase quantitative medium-term objectives should be formulated at Community level and short-term economic policy harmonized at the same time. Only in a second phase should the monetary union be realized. Germany would then be prepared to transfer a fixed percentage of its monetary reserves to a common reserve fund.[6] The French proposals at the summit conference, by contrast, provided for the immediate creation of a system of balance of payments assistance at Community level and the formation of a uniform monetary bloc in relation to Third World countries. This foreshadowed what later became known as the controversy between the economists and monetarists.[7]

The monetarists wanted to initiate the integration process—indeed, to force it upon the Community countries—by means of monetary ties; these included the "gradual narrowing of the margin of exchange rate fluctuation, the establishment of a European reserve fund with a gradual pooling of monetary reserves, the introduction of a European unit of account."[8] In particular, they asserted, fixed rates of exchange accompanied by narrow margins of fluctuation oblige the participating countries to coordinate their economic policies. The result is a convergence of economic developments. The economists, on the other hand, questioned the suitability of monetary constraints as a means of fostering integration; they maintained that prematurely fixed exchange rates are disintegrative since, under a system of fixed rates, divergent economic trends cause structural distortion, reduce the efficiency of monetary and fiscal policy, and necessitate restrictions on capital movements that are in principle inimical to integration. Coordination of the basic economic factors (economic policy priorities, the behavior of economic agents, regional differences, and so on) in partner countries and above all a successful concerted stabilization policy are essential first, in order to pave the way for the establishment of a monetary union. Hence the system of fixed parities must come not at the beginning, but at the end of the integration process, as the crowning achievement, so to speak.

This controversy, which on the surface appears to be a theoretical dispute about methods of integration, in reality masks deep-seated political differences regarding objectives and conflicting interests. The monetarist approach ties the partners to each other to a much greater extent than does action along the lines proposed by the economists. In the first case, the stability-oriented surplus countries can hardly help granting large-scale financial assistance as a result of the solidarity imperative. If there are no means of inducing the deficit countries to take corrective action, the surplus countries feel obliged to tolerate a parallel inflation. In the economists' approach, the arrangement is much looser; during the process of harmonization it is in principle possible at any time to detach oneself from the "inflation convoy" by revaluation. This is admittedly inconsistent with the idea of convergence, but it is the lesser evil.

The conference at the Hague decided on a compromise. The heads of state and government requested the Council of Ministers to work out a phased plan for the establishment of an economic and monetary union.[9] The development of cooperation in monetary matters was to be based on the harmonization of economic policies; this clearly reflects the German standpoint. On the other hand, the question of creating a European reserve fund was also to be examined; this was an issue of importance to the French.

The group of experts set up by the Council put forward a phased plan for the establishment of an economic and monetary union (Werner plan) in October 1970.[10] This plan was likewise based on the principle of parallelism between economic and monetary policy measures. In the final phase, a joint economic decision-making body answerable to the European Parliament and an independent European central bank system were envisaged. All of this seemed to be not too inconsistent with the German views. Even so, the resolution of the Council of Ministers in March 1971 on the phased realization of the economic and monetary union[11] had something of a monetarist bias: in the very first phase, the mutual margins of fluctuation of the exchange rates of Community currencies were to be reduced and a monetary cooperation fund was perhaps to be set up, while the obligations to coordinate monetary policy were mostly of a noncommittal kind; in the second and third phases they were not mentioned at all. These monetary concessions seemed acceptable to Germany only because their period of validity—like that of the medium-term monetary assistance scheme, which was likewise approved in March 1971—was limited, at German request, initially to five years. This period was, however, to be extended automatically if the Community had in the meantime entered the second phase of development toward an economic and monetary union.

But before any concrete measures had been taken, the monetary crisis of spring 1971 erupted. From May 9 onward the Deutsche mark floated, and on August 15 the gold convertibility of dollars held by central banks was suspended. Under the Smithsonian Monetary Agreement of December 1971, a new system of central rates came into being, and a new Council resolution of March 1972[12] created the European "snake" by narrowing the margins of fluctuation between currencies. The system of intervention agreed upon at the same time by the EC central banks was based on the following principles: (1) unlimited obligations to intervene in the currencies of participating countries once the published upper and lower limit rates have been reached; intervention within these limits only after prior consultation (concertation) among the central banks; (2) financing of the balances arising from such intervention in Community currencies in unlimited amounts, but for rather strictly limited periods; (3) settlement of the balances in accordance with the composition of the official gross monetary reserves of the respective "debtor central bank."

These intervention rules also represent a compromise, but it would probably not have been reached without strong German pressure. The rules produced a system of constraints which, if they are complied with, lead to the desired convergence of economic policy; if they are not complied with, they discredit the entire approach, and in the process confirm the preconceptions of the economists.[13] The intervention system results in an inflationary deficit country continuously losing monetary reserves; it can counteract this by recourse to the common monetary assistance scheme,[14] but very short-term assistance, while unlimited in amount, is quite unsuitable for financing a balance of payments deficit because of its brief period to maturity (averaging six weeks). Short-term assistance, with its maturity of not more than six months, can also be used to only a very limited extent for this purpose. Recourse to medium-term assistance, with a maturity of up to five years, is likewise not intended for financing inflation-induced balance of payments deficits as its granting is subject to economic policy conditions. The same applies to borrowing under the system of Community loans. Thus, in the last analysis only two possibilities are open to a deficit country: it must either adopt stabilizing measures and possibly devalue its currency, or it must leave the narrower margins arrrangement. However, this does largely avert the danger of a country being obliged to "adjust through inflation" as a result of the EC intervention system coupled with the EC monetary assistance scheme.

The establishment of the European monetary cooperation fund by a Council ordinance in April 1973, after the system of fixed exchange rates had been replaced by a system of floating rates, made no fundamental difference to the situation; in its present form the fund is not much more than an institutional combination of existing mechanisms of the Community exchange rate system and monetary assistance scheme.[15] In 1973, the Commission put forward a plan for pooling Community monetary reserves. The plan came to nothing, mainly owing to technical objections; but on the German side the real reason for rejecting it was the fear that the reserve pool might become a kind of "self-service store."

At the turn of 1973-1974, the transition to the second phase was due according to the resolution of March 1971; during this phase, the transfer of economic and monetary powers to supranational bodies was to begin. But as the objectives of the first phase—in particular, the coordination of economic policy—had not yet been achieved, the first phase was in effect extended. Even today, however, the coordination of economic policy has not progressed beyond the customary manifestations of goodwill, in spite of the principle—which is still valid—of permanent consultations on general economic policy measures planned by member states and on the compatibility of such measures with the Council's economic policy guidelines (convergence guidelines of February 18, 1974).[16] Partly, no doubt, for this reason, nearly all plans and proposals concerning the further development of the EC into an economic and monetary union met with little interest in Germany. But plans that explicitly or implicitly envisaged the Deutsche mark assuming the function of a key and reserve currency (most recently the plan of de Strycker)[17] were also rejected. On the one hand, it was feared that any attempt to establish the Deutsche mark as a key currency would subject it to even greater exchange rate fluctuations than in the past; on the other, it is probable that such efforts would seriously disrupt domestic monetary and credit policy as the absorptive capacity of the German money and capital market is far too small for a key currency country.

As we see, the German negotiating position has regularly been determined by a clear preference for a coordination of general economic policies. Germany felt able to agree to a joint system of intervention and monetary assistance, but not to a monetary assistance scheme of lavish proportions that was largely free from conditions or to a pooling of monetary reserves.

*The Effects of German Monetary
and Financial Policy Measures*

When the Deutsche mark was revalued by 5 percent in March 1961—both too little and too late—[18] this monetary policy measure had not been preceded by consultations with the partner countries (apart from the Netherlands, which also revalued by 5 percent. This measure led, at least indirectly, to the proposals made by the Commission in its 1962 action program, in which it recommended among other things the establishment of a monetary union by 1970.[19]

The "substitute revaluation" of the Deutsche mark in November 1968, the devaluation of the franc in August 1969, and the final revaluation of the Deutsche mark in October of the latter year after a short period of floating were likewise not the outcome of concerted action at Community level, although both countries were under an obligation to take such action;[20] but as a consequence, they fostered the efforts to create a European monetary union.

The German answer to the severe dollar-Deutsche mark crisis in the spring of 1971 was the floating of the exchange rate of the Deutsche mark on May 9, 1971. This step, which was intended to curb the high rate of price rises at that time (and did, in fact, accomplish it), nullified the initial moves toward a monetary union hardly a month after the agreements had been concluded. Criticism from the Community countries was correspondingly sharp. The Germans were accused of "going it alone" without having been authorized to do so. This accusation was rejected by the German authorities. After all, the German decision to float had been preceded by a meeting of Community ministers of finance at which Schiller, the German minister of economics, had proposed to the partner countries that the Community currencies should float jointly against the dollar. This proposal was turned down by France and Italy; both countries were reluctant to attach their currencies to the Deutsche mark, which was strong and apt to appreciate, even though a corresponding safety margin through the Deutsche mark was explicitly offered to them.[21]

On the other hand, the Commission's proposal to deal with the monetary crisis by introducing controls on capital movements was rejected by the Germans. For one thing, such controls were wholly at variance with the German philosophy of a market economy; for another, neither the psychological nor the administrative conditions for the introduction of controls on capital movements existed in Germany.

But the fact that the Community countries' criticism was not without effect became evident in July 1972, when the federal government responded to new inflows of foreign exchange not by floating the Deutsch mark—which would have undermined the package of measures adopted in March 1972 and thus the second attempt at a European economic and monetary union—but by introducing controls on capital movements after all. It was not easy for the Germans to commit this sin against the market economy, and it was at least the ostensible cause of the resignation of Schiller. The introduction of the controls showed that in Germany, too, views on the advantages and drawbacks of floating diverged; but no less important was the desire to be a good partner, at least on this occasion, and not to endanger the "snake," which had just been established. The extent to which the German authorities were prepared to display a spirit of partnership became clear in the first few months of 1973. Within five weeks—from the beginning of February to the beginning of March—the Bundesbank purchased foreign exchange amounting to 24 billion DM (net), thus accepting an immense inflation of the domestic money circulation. But the system of fixed exchange rates was doomed.

However, a move that had failed in 1971 was successful in mid-March 1973: after negotiations with the EC partner countries and the United States, the participants in the European narrower margins arrangement decided to float jointly against the dollar. To make this step easier for the Community partners, the Deutsche mark was revalued by 3 percent against the "snake currencies." With the transition to the joint float, the Bundesbank largely regained control over monetary developments. For the first time for many years, the German monetary authorities were able to regulate monetary expansion without the successes of monetary policy again becoming the source of its failures. However, protection against external constraints was not perfect: in the first place, the desire to avoid excessive jumps in the rate of the dollar repeatedly led to not inconsiderable interventions in the dollar market (this applies mainly to 1977 and 1978; see table 10-1). Second, interventions were often necessary within the snake as well, sometimes on a fairly large scale (particularly in 1973 and 1976).

Thus Germany can hardly be said to have neglected its responsibilities in the snake, even though it must be admitted that on the whole German faithfulness to the agreed principles has not been tested too severely. The interventions in the snake have not been nearly as large as were the dollar interventions in the days of fixed exchange rates. This is not least because of the present comparatively loose form of the European narrower margins arrangement. Countries with higher rates of inflation can decide between stabilizing measures, possibly coupled with devaluation, and withdrawing from the snake. Countries with relatively stable currencies can, if necessary, revalue. Frequent use has been made of all these possibilities, as table 10-2, which outlines the history of the narrower margins arrangement, shows. The possibility of withdrawing from the snake has not been open to all countries in the same way. What the larger countries—France, Italy, and the United Kingdom—could afford to do was not feasible to the same extent for the smaller countries, whose economic situations are largely determined by conditions in Germany. For them, Germany is an *économie dominante* in the literal sense of the term. If the Germans pursue an anti-inflationary policy, as they have been doing since mid-1974, the smaller partners have to adjust first in one direction and then in another. While this may on occasion fit in with their own plans, it is nevertheless a form of dependence that is painful, and it has no doubt fostered the wish to involve the major partner in a scheme for formulating objectives jointly.

Table 10-1
Changes in the Net External Position of the Bundesbank since 1973
(in billion DM)

Period	Total	Interventions in the "Snake"	Other Foreign Exchange Movements
1973			
January-March	+ 19.9	− 0.6	+ 20.5
April-May	− 0.9	− 1.5	+ 0.6
June-July	+ 8.5	+ 5.8	+ 2.7
August-September	+ 3.4	+ 4.3	− 0.9
October-December	− 4.5	− 1.1	− 3.4
1974			
January-December	+ 26.4	+ 6.8	+ 19.6
January	− 2.5	+ 0.2	− 2.8
February-June	+ 5.4	+ 4.1	+ 1.3
July-September	− 6.4	− 3.5	− 2.9
October-December	+ 1.6	− 0.7	+ 2.3
1975			
January-December	− 1.9	+ 0.2	− 2.1
January-March	+ 5.0	—	+ 5.0
April-September	− 6.6	− 1.8	− 4.8
October-December	− 0.6	—	− 0.6
1976			
January-December	− 2.2	− 1.8	− 0.4
January	+ 0.1	—	+ 0.1
February-March	+ 9.7	+ 8.7	+ 1.0
April-July	− 4.6	− 1.4	− 3.2
August-mid-October	+ 7.7	+ 8.0	− 0.4
mid-October-December	− 4.1	− 3.5	− 0.6
1977			
January-December	+ 8.8	+ 11.9	− 3.1
January-June	− 0.8	− 1.5	+ 0.7
July	+ 2.0	+ 0.0	+ 2.0
August-September	− 2.0	− 0.3	− 1.7
October-December	+ 11.3	+ 3.1	+ 8.2
1978			
January-December	+ 10.5	+ 1.3	+ 9.1
January-March	+ 4.5	− 0.7	+ 5.2

Assessment of German Behavior

A Methodological Note

To assess something means to judge something. But to pass a judgment, one must have a standard of judgment, a yardstick, or at least a suitable basis for discrimination. Normally, however, there are no generally accepted

Table 10-2
History of the Narrower Margins Arrangement

1972	
April 24	Basol Agreement enters into force. Participants: Belgium, France, Germany, Italy, Luxembourg, the Netherlands
May 1	The United Kingdom and Denmark join
May 23	Norway becomes associated
June 23	The United Kingdom withdraws
June 27	Denmark withdraws
October 10	Denmark returns
1973	
February 13	Italy withdraws
March 19	Transition to the joint float; interventions to maintain fixed margins against the dollar (tunnel) are discontinued
March 19	Sweden becomes associated
March 19	The Deutschemark is revalued by 3 percent
April 3	The establishment of a European monetary cooperation fund is approved
June 29	The Deutschemark is revalued by 5.5 percent
September 17	The guilder is revalued by 5 percent
November 16	The Norwegian krone is revalued by 5 percent
1974	
January 19	France withdraws
1975	
July 10	France returns
1976	
March 15	France withdraws again
October 17	Agreement on exchange rate adjustment (Frankfurt realignment)
1977	
April 1	The Swedish krona is devalued by 6 percent and the Danish and Norwegian kroner are devalued by 3 percent each
August 28	Sweden withdraws temporarily; the Danish and Norwegian kroner are devalued by 5 percent each
1978	
February 13	The Norwegian krone is devalued by 8 percent

Source: Jennemann, Gorhard, "Der Europäische Wechseikarsverbund," in Giovanni Magnifico, *Eine Währung und Wirtschaft*, (Baden-Baden, 1977), p. 245. Supplemented by Kloten.

criteria for judgments of political behavior. As a rule, several criteria compete with each other; moreover, these criteria tend in the nature of things to be qualitative rather than quantitative.

We could base our attempt to assess German behavior on the generally accepted target of creating a European economic and monetary system; that is, we could ask whether the German negotiating position and German actions were conductive to the attainment of this target or not. This would be a question about the suitability of the instruments of the matter to be judged. As many roads lead to Rome, and as all of them have pros and cons, each of which can be valued differently, various alternative ways of achieving the union can be substantiated and highlighted more or less, depending on one's bias. For a valuation of the alternative routes to economic and monetary union, and thus for the actual design of such a union, the current overall economic objectives are important. It is no secret that in this respect—that is, among national target packages—there are considerable differences in the European camp. I have explained the German position. But how is one or other of the various competing targets to be assigned the priority that is due to it? Which counts more: the French, the British, or the German standpoint, or any other standpoint? The problem is simplified if the alternative national objectives (assuming they are clearly defined and generally accepted) are regarded as given, and an optimum compromise is aimed at on this basis. In the event of conflicting interests, joint action is in any case inconceivable without a willingness to compromise. For each of those concerned, however, a compromise on a joint course of action entails a loss of well-being because of concessions made and a gain of well-being because of the closer approximation to the superordinate common objective—an approximation that would not have been possible otherwise. Working out the balance between these two is hardly easier than in other comparisons of well-being; besides, the result may be affected by the way in which the various national interests are represented. Finally, the primarily economic considerations are accompanied by political considerations of equal weight; any decision in favor of a common solution such as the economic and monetary union has far-reaching political implications; indeed, it may be predominantly motivated by political factors. The same applies to any judgment on the preferable route toward such a union. One view can be set against another, each backed with plausible arguments; even if the problems are clearly recognized, any attempt at an assessment is tantamount to untying the Gordian knot.

In this situation, a fairly strict limitation is advisable: to begin with, we shall simply ask whether or not the respective national attitude—in our case that of the Germans—with regard to the setting of national priorities that were recognizable and known to the partners has been consistent; then we shall ask whether or not this attitude is justifiable in light of the underlying (as a rule, primarily economic) reasoning. Such an approach neither excludes other, equally plausible starting points, nor forms an impermissible barrier to more detailed assessments, particularly those covering the political implications.

The Essentials of the German Negotiating Position

The German negotiators at European conferences have supported either the pure economist variant—convergence of economic developments   only through the harmonization of economic (that is, stabilization) policies—or the compromise variant: monetary and stabilization measures must be taken in parallel; the monetary ties must be such as to make coordinated and stability-oriented economic policy measures advisable, if not compulsory. I do not hesitate to assert, in conformity with the great majority of German academic economists and many economic policymakers, that the German position is backed by strong theoretical arguments, and hardly less by past experience. The brief history of the European narrower margins arrangement has at any rate shown that ambitious monetary agreements between countries with different target priorities and economic structures have little chance of success, as shown in the following hypotheses.

1. If the monetary ties are effective and force the authorities to take action designed to promote internal and external stability, and if the initial conditions (inflation rate, balance of payments position, growth, and employment) are unfavorable, the consequences are very soon felt to be intolerable to domestic society. This results in substitutes such as restrictions on capital movements, temporary special regulations, a softening of the system of rules, or withdrawal from the exchange rate arrangement. Since March 1972, that is, since the last major effort (with German support) in the field of monetary policy, all of these expedients have been practiced.

2. If the monetary ties are not effective, if, for instance, the rules on intervention and assistance are very lenient from the outset, the constraints are missing; but then either individual countries try to "go it alone" in all kinds of fields so that the Community is left to "muddle through," or the preeminence of the requirement of monetary solidarity results in the adjustment of the more stability-minded partners to the conditions set by the weaker countries. In the former case, a new attempt at reform is soon imperative; in the latter, it likewise becomes clear sooner or later that joint inflation does not help the weak countries but harms the strong ones. In the long run, a solution of this kind is beneficial to none of the participants.

These are, of course, only hypotheses, and as such are not conclusive. But it is probably impossible to produce empirical evidence against them, while there is no lack of corroborative experience. Since the advent of worldwide anti-inflationary policy from about mid-1974 onward, it has been generally recognized that the Phillips curve, that is, the tradeoff between the growth rate of the price level and the unemployment rate, is fictitious in its generalized version. (That this anti-inflationary policy was leading to a kind of stabilization crisis is quite a different matter.) This is not to deny that the priority of the target of monetary stability is still disputed. It is generally understood as a target that competes with the objectives of full employment and economic growth, but monetary stability is in fact rather a prerequisite for the attainment of these other objectives. Appropriate growth and a satisfactory level of employment are not possible in the long run without a minimum of monetary stability, which ensures that the actions of economic agents are not determined by inflationary expectations. If they are, the upward movement of prices accelerates under the conditions prevailing in modern industrial society (anticipatory demand of the social groups, and also of the state); the concept of inflationary equilibrium is an illusion. A half-hearted anti-inflationary policy then soon produces a situation that has stagflationary features.

One may regard German concern about the dangers of inflationary processes as exaggerated, but one can hardly help considering these misgivings to be legitimate; hence the German reservations about solutions that appear inflation-prone are at least worthy of discussion.

German Political Action

Germany, too, has undoubtedly "gone it alone" in the monetary field, but hardly more often—indeed, probably less often—than comparable European partners. The most important example of such action was the May 1971 decision to float the exchange rate of the Deutsche mark, which delayed the establishment of the European narrower margins arrangement for about a year.

One should, I think, be prepared to concede even with hindsight that there were at the time good reasons for adopting the German proposal to start a joint float. The roundabout route via controls on capital movements and the almost disastrous monetary crisis of spring 1973 was in nobody's interest. As so often happens, this recognition was gained only at the cost of enormous economic burdens. After 1971, Germany took no measures of monetary policy in the strict sense that had not been agreed upon with its partners beforehand. In general, German actions—not least its interventions in the foreign exchange market—were fully in line with the national interests of its partner countries.

The general direction of German stabilization policy since the transition to floating in the spring of 1973 could be judged differently. By its second stabilization program of May 9, 1973, the German government cut short the sixth postwar upswing for fear of uncontrollable cyclical and (to an even greater extent) inflationary trends. This program, which was already showing signs off success, was torpedoed by the oil price hike and its repercussions. The rate of price rises accelerated again, albeit to a lesser degree than in most other western industrial nations; the answer was a systematic anti-inflationary policy by monetary means, even though the conditions created by incomes policy at the beginning of 1974 were wholly incompatible with this approach. The reproach that German policies are hampering the recovery of economic activity in western Europe has been with us since that time. Against this, it must be said that German monetary policy has been guided not only by the so-called unavoidable rate of inflation but also by the prevailing overall production potential and the current degree of capacity utilization. In each of the last three years, the quantitative monetary targets have been considerably exceeded. Moreover, in order to bolster economic activity and with a view to ensuring long-term growth, Germany has since the end of 1974 accepted higher budget deficits than any other country in the western world except Italy and the United Kingdom (whose deficits undoubtedly boosted inflation, at least in the short run). The consequence has been that German public debt and a "structural deficit" have increased so rapidly that a consolidation of government finance has generally been advocated. However, the measures taken in 1977 by the federal and Lánder governments, and even more by the local authorities, went further than was necessary; taken as a whole, financial policy did not conform to cyclical requirements. But the adverse effects should not be overrated, particularly in view of the situation of its European partners. Since 1975, German imports have risen much faster than German exports. Besides, it must be borne in mind that in Germany a fiscal federalism is practiced which, while it has many advantages, makes it extremely difficult to coordinate fiscal policies at the various levels of government (federal government, Lánder governments, and local authorities). Public discussion of the various alternatives for further government stabilization programs had an additional adverse impact. The programs themselves were far from being ideal; in particular, they were insufficiently medium term in scope. Once again it turned out that, taken as a whole, the public sector cannot make up for what the private sector is unable to provide. Government action can contribute much to private sector dynamism, but large government financial deficits are not in themselves a proof that this is happening.

The Decisions of the Bremen Summit Meeting

The Bremen decisions have undoubtedly opened up new perspectives in Europe. Through the European monetary system, the European Community is to become a zone of relatively stable exchange rates. The EMS is not simply a revival of the measures of March 1971 or March 1972. This time, monetarist views have been even more generally accepted. In the final sentence of the Bremen statement, the participating countries are admittedly called upon to "pursue policies conducive to greater stability at home and abroad," but "this applies to deficit and surplus countries alike." Thus, what is really meant by stability remains unclear. The only things that had been fixed in Bremen were the vanishing points of a European monetary system that hardly appears to be consistent with the traditional German negotiating position. Does Germany's vote reflect a turnaround in its thinking? So far, the public debate has not supported this view. And yet certain statements by persons close to the chancellor imply this. The chancellor himself has repeatedly spoken out against so-called courageous monetary policy measures:[22] "changes in existing mechanisms or the creation of new ones would not foster the economic and monetary union, any more than it would benefit Europe."[23] Even if, as some people now claim, Helmut Schmidt has at heart always been a supporter of the system of fixed exchange rates (although he used to present the decision in favor of floating in spring 1973 not least as a personal achievement), it can hardly have been monetary considerations alone that tipped the scales.

The opinion that flexible exchange rates did not accomplish what had been expected in theory became increasingly widespread. Of course, it must be admitted that this had its effect in the political camp. Loosely phrased, fixed exchange rates seem to be "in" again. And the justifications again come from deep inside the bag of old and well-known arguments. More important, though not necessarily convincing in a sphere of divergent inflationary trends, may have been the attitude of the United States. Indeed, in this specific case, the U.S. policy was affected less by the cherished virtues of a fixed exchange system, than by the experience matured in the last dollar crisis when it had remained deaf to the need for concerted negotiations and cooperation in monetary policy. At the same time, despite good arguments to the contrary, the United States did not cease to impose upon Germany the role of a (friendly overheated) locomotive. By contrast, according to Schmidt, a European monetary system could lead one to expect that "speculation could not allow the currency of a country, even of a very large country, to fluctuate so extremely in relation to an enlarged European currency area with a large volume, as in relation to small currency areas with a small volume."[24]

The use of such advantages of a synchronized monetary policy recommended itself also in the stronger position of the French President as a result of the elections of March 1978. With the support of his Premier, Raymond Barre, he wanted to steer the French economy on a course of stability. European solidarity was the need of the moment. This applies also to Italy, with its special socioeconomic and political burdens, and to Great Britain which, as a member of the Community, stays on the sidelines almost much too often. It applies also to the smaller partner countries which, although they had learned to live (not badly) with the Federal Republic as *économie dominante*, were nonetheless interested in increasing their right of participation. Further—as an aside—it was good for a new and well-planned Euro-political initiative to arise during the period of German chairmanship of the Council of Ministers.

This has nothing to do with the oft-mentioned conjecture that the true reason for the German attitude is another new variant of a traditional export-oriented policy. Ever since the experiences of the late sixties and early seventies, it is no longer opportune in Germany to secure competitive advantages through false exchange rates and thereby to increase exports. The lesson has been learned that temporary advantages can be gained only through structural distortions that are difficult to correct. As before, there is, of course, a general desire to work against distortions of competition resulting from false exchange rates, and against the uncertainty arising from even temporarily erratic fluctuations in the exchange rates. If the solution was seen to be a fixed exchange system, it also means that the risks to the stability policy in such a choice were considered to be lesser than the advantages derived from the new solution. Such a calculation can, of course, be quite deceptive; it is entirely possible that the monetary policy reactions are underestimated. In any case, that was the prevalent opinion in the Federal Republic for many years.

Of course, this question was tested constantly, even during the negotiations concerning the concrete shaping of the EMS, not least by the central bank council of the Bundesbank. The council was moved above all by the concern that the effectiveness of monetary policy in the EMS could be impaired by a Deutsche mark creation forced from outside. To be sure, the result would be a convergence in the cost and price trends of the member countries, but only in the form of a harmonization of inflation rates and not with the result of a greater purchasing power stability in the confederation. Ultimately, the question was whether the will toward greater stability in the Community has increased everywhere, so that it can be built upon, or whether the capability for it is still quite variously distributed.

Thus, as the EMS was passed by the European Council on December 5, 1978, it represents a monetary policy solidarity system whose essential elements are a common numéraire, coordinated foreign exchange rates, rules for interventions, forms of monetary assistance with a partial pooling of monetary reserves, and consultative agreements.[25]

The heart of the new solution is the European currency unit (ECU). Together with the common reserve fund, this central denominator represents the best chance for the development of the EMS into a true currency union over the years. The other elements of the system will probably be postponed after the two-year transitional phase, with the establishment of the European monetary fund and the definition of its competence and business. The breakthrough would occur if, at any time, a parallel currency would develop on the basis of the ECU. But that which is to happen after the transitional phase was outlined only in a very rough form at Bremen.

The intervention system of the EMS is a compromise solution. The obligatory interventions are oriented in a so-called parity grid system for which an early warning system was established. This alarm was set at the threshold of divergence from the basket, at the maximum rate of 75 percent, and whether or not it will, in fact, operate is not at all settled. Whether future interventions in the currency market will be determined de facto by one or another of currencies that make up the ECU system is disputed. Something can be said for the fact that the dominant role belongs to the divergence indicator; the essential consultation agreements, which in their turn are to lead to concerted monetary policy negotiations, are tied to the indicator. The very concept of "divergent country" implies the attribution of the burden of proof and therefore also the latent obligation to negotiate. On the other hand, an obligation to negotiate was not established. There remains only the presumption, as it is called in the decision of the European Council, that the relevant authorities "will correct with appropriate measures" the overstepping of the threshold. "In the event that such measures are not taken, due to special circumstances, then the reasons therefore must be given to the other authorities."[26]

For countries with a strong currency, this is unproblematic only if an implicit pressure does not result, causing them to negotiate with less insistence on stability. Still, the asymmetry of the system can hardly be missed.

The new regulations do, to be sure, foresee completely obligatory negotiations, but mostly in favor of an external stability of the currency. As far as the internal stability of money in the European Community is concerned, there is a decided lack of disciplining preventive measures and clauses. And because of the strong expansion of credit facilities and the longer terms for assistance, it is hardly likely that the monetary system will itself exert sustained pressure to further stability. Thus, whether and to what extent the EMS will become a strong currency bloc depends only on the political will, and the ability to implement it, of the participating countries. If this should not result, or if the strong currency countries should not see themselves forced to an inflation adjustment, then the leading exchange rates would have to be made prophylactic, that is to say, promptly adaptable. But the mandate to create mutual agreement, imminent in the system, should prove more difficult here.

It is therefore not at all certain that the EMS can fulfill the expectations placed in the system. Nor do the specific European experiences support the thesis that the already traditional European compromise pragmatism will work (or, if you will, be reestablished) in the management of compatible regulations. However that may be, the EMS, once initiated, should be given a fair chance to prove itself. But it will prove itself only if, in the management of regulations, the will for integration accomplishes stability. A failure of the EMS would burden thoughts of European integration with a heavy mortgage that would not be quickly redeemable.

Notes

1. Otmar Emminger, "Deutsche Geld- und Währungspolitik im Spannungsfeld zwischen innerem und außerem Gleichgewicht (1948-1975)," (The Deutsche mark in the Conflict between Internal and External Equilibrium, 1948-75) in *Wahrung und Wirtschaft in Deutschland 1876-1975* (Frankfurt on the Main: Deutsche Bundesbank, 1976, p. 519.

2. Loukas Tsoukalis, *The Politics and Economics of European Monetary Integration* (London, Allen & Unwin 1977), p. 57.

3. Memorandum der Kommission über das Aktionsprogramm der Gemeinschaft fur die zweite Stufe (vom Oktober 1962), (Memorandum of the Commission on the Community Action program for the Second Stage [of October 1962]), in *Monetäre Integration in der EWG, Dokumente und Bibliographie*, (Monetary Integration in the EEC, Documents and Bibliography), ed. D. Gehrmann and S. Harmsen (Hamburg, 1972), p. 36.

4. Leonhard Gleske, "Nationale Geldpolitik auf dem Wege zur europäischen Währungsunion," (National Monetary Policy on the Way to European Monetary Union) in W*ährung und Wirtschaft in Deutschland 1876-1975* (Frankfurt am Main: Deutsche Bundesbank, 1976), p. 745.

5, In 1968, any impairment of free trade and payments within the Community would have affected no less than 37.6 percent of German exports, compared with 27.3 percent in 1958.

6. Tsoukalis, *Politics and Economics*, p. 84.

7. Regarding this controversy, see Sachverstandigenrat (Council of Economic Experts) Jahresgutachten (Annual Report) 1971-72, Stuttgart and Mainz, 1971, p. 101; ibid., Jahresgutachten 1972-73, p. 1; Hubertus Adebahr, *Währungstheorie und Währungspolitik (Monetary Theory and Monetary Policy) Berlin, 1978, p. 445; Otmar Emminger, Bemerkungen zum Werner-Bericht* über die europäische Wirtschafts- und Wahrungsunion (Remarks on the Werner Report on European Economic and Monetary Union), in Bankbetrieb 1970/12, pp. 443-5.

8. Gleske, "Nationale Geldpolitik," p. 767.

9. See Kommuniqué der Konferenz der Staats- und Regierungschefs der EWG-Mitgliedstaaten in Den Haag am 1. und 2. Dezember 1969 (Communiqué of the Conference of the Heads of State and Government of the EEC Member States at the Hague on December 1 and 2, 1969), in *Monetäre Integration in der EWG, Dokumente und Bibliographie*, ed. D. Gehrmann and S. Harmsen (Hamburg 1972), pp. 82-84.

10. Council/Commission of the European Communities, Bericht an Rat und Kommission über die stufenweise Verwirklichung der Wirtschafts- und Währungsunion in der Gemeinschaft (Report to the Council and Com-

mission on the Phased Realization of Economic and Monetary Union in the Community) "Werner Report" (final version), Luxembourg, October 8, 1970.

11. EntschlieBung des Rates und der Vertreter der Regierungen der Mitgliedstaaten vom 22. März 1971 über die stufenweise Verwirklichung der Wirtschafts- und Währungsunion in der Gemeinschaft (Resolution of the Council and the Representatives of the Governments of Member States of March 22, 1971 on the Phased Realization of Economic and Monetary Union in the Community) in *Monetäre Integration in der EWG, Dokumente und Bibliographie*, ed. D. Gehrmann and S. Harmsen (Hamburg, 1972), pp. 176-81.

12. EntschlieBung des Rates und der Vertreter der Regierungen der Mitgliedstaaten vom 21. März 1971 betreffend die Anwendung der EntschlieBung vom 22. März 1971 über die stufenweise Verwirklichung der Wirtschafts- und Währungsunion in der Gemeinschaft (Resolution of the Council and the Representatives of the Governments of Member States of March 21, 1971 concerning the Application of the Resolution of March 22, 1971 on the Phased Realization of Economic and Monetary Union in the Community), in *Amtsblatt der Europäischen Gemeinschaften*, Number C 38, April 18, 1972, p. 3.

13. Gerhard Jennemann, "Der Europäische Wechselkursverbund" (The European Narrower Margins Arrangement) in *Eine Währung fur Europa* (A Currency for Europe), Giovanni Magnifico (Baden-Baden, 1977), p. 243.

14. Regarding the EC monetary assistance scheme, see Deutsche Bundesbank, "Internationale Organisationen und Abkommen im Bereich von Währung und Wirtschaft" (International Organizations and Agreements in the Monetary and Economic Field), Frankfurt, 1978, p. 201.

15. See Gleske, "Nationale Geldpolitik," p. 781.

16. See Deutsche Bundesbank, "Internationale Organisationen," p. 185.

17. de Strycker, *Towards a Greater Convergence of Foreign Exchange Policies within the Community (Reflections by the Belgian Presidency)* (Brussels, April 3, 1978).

18. Emminger, "Deutsche Geld," p. 508.

19. Tsoukalis, *Politics and Economics*, p. 56.

20. Ibid., p. 76.

21. Emminger, "Deutsche Geld," p. 525.

22. *Die Zeit*, May 17, 1974.

23. Chancellor Helmut Schmidt in the Bundestag on April 8, 1976.

24. Deutsche Bundesbank, *Auszüge aus Presseartikeln*, Number 87, 1978, pp. 8-9.

25. "Decision of the European Council, December 5, 1978, concerning the establishment of the European Monetary System and Related Questions," Bulletin des Presse-und Informationsamtes der Bundesrregierung, Bonn, December 8, 1978, and: "Agreement between the Central Banks of the Member States of the European Economic Community concerning the Functioning of the European Monetary System."

26. Bulletin des Presse- und Informationsamtes der Bundesregierung, Bonn, vom 8, Dezember 1978: "Decision of the European Council, December 5, 1978, concerning the establishment of the European Monetary System . . ." No. 3.6.

Part III
Commentary

Benjamin J. Cohen

I am going to try to present to you *an* American—not *the* but *an* American—view of Germany. Being an economist, I will focus primarily on economic issues. My starting point is that international economic relations require a degree of management. There must be some country, or group of countries, that assumes the responsibility for the management of macroeconomic relations and the balance of payments adjustment process. The reason for this is familiar; it has to do with the potential inconsistency in policies of governments if all governments simultaneously are pursuing independent targets.

International monetary relations have *never* been stable except when some country or countries, consciously or unconsciously, have taken the role of manager of the system. Management of international monetary and related issues necessarily imposes a certain kind of responsibility on the managers. The manager can pursue its own national interests only while at the same time paying attention to systemic interests. That is to say, the national interest must be perceived to include an interest in systemic stability. Such a responsibility is not imposed on smaller countries in the system. One of the few privileges that smaller countries have in the international hierarchy is the ability to be a free rider—that is to say, the ability to pursue its own self-interests without necessarily worrying about the effect on systemic stability. When some small country, or even a few small countries, pursue their interests self-centeredly, there is little threat to the stability of the system. But as you go up the hierarchy to larger and larger countries, the threat to stability in the system is correspondingly increased if these countries do not take account of the influences of their pursuit of national self-interest on the stability of the system.

Now, with that as background, let me suggest that, seen from the United States, Germany has in the past enjoyed the role of free rider and has tried to preserve the privileges of being a free rider in circumstances where this is no longer appropriate. To use Susan Strange's terms, Germany is trying to continue to be a Lone Ranger and refrain from exercising the responsibilities of management—to be a Switzerland if you will, or, to borrow a term used in another context of this book, to be a Finland and pursue self-Finlandization. In circumstances where it has become a "Gulliver" in international economic relations, Germany is still trying to play the role of "Lilliputian" and escape the responsibility of management which is thrust upon it by what is now a very large size and weight in international economic relations. Germany now accounts for approximately 15 percent of the collective GNP of the countries of the OECD area. This is a size, a weight in economic relations, which imposes on it responsibilities that until now, in the American perception, Germany has been trying to avoid. Karl Kaiser used the phrase "to internalize systemic needs." From the American point of view, it appears that Germany has tried to resist doing this—has tried to resist internalizing systemic needs.

Now, just let me add two caveats very quickly. The first caveat is the question of blame. There are those who say that if international economic relations have been mismanaged, it is not because of Germany's refusal to accept any responsibility. You have to look to the country that has traditionally exercised that responsibility—the United States. If these affairs have been mismanaged, it is the fault of the United States. Some Americans—in particular, certain scholars and commentators—seem to enjoy breast-beating (*la colpa nostra*), accepting the blame for mismanagement of affairs.

Now, I think this is a little overdone. I do not absolve the United States from blame. American policy has been mismanaged, in some respects very badly mismanaged, at least since 1965, with the decision to fight the Vietnam War without raising taxes. And it certainly was mismanaged in 1970-1971 when the Texan John Connally was riding the saddle of United States economic policy. I am not here to defend American economic policy since the Carter administration came to power. But I would like to point out two factors in American policy. One is that policymakers in Washington have traditionally accepted, and still do accept, that the national self-interest of the United States does include an interest in systemic stability. The only time this was not evident was during Connally's tenure as Secretary of the Treasury. The other factor is that United States policymakers now accept the realization that they can no longer operate on their own. If it was ever true that the United States could exercise hegemony in international economic affairs, the conditions necessary for that have long since passed. The United States understands that this responsibility must be shared. Granted, American policymakers would like it to be shared with minimum costs to the United States, but that, of course, is understandable.

From the American point of view, what is striking is the refusal of the obvious other candidates for collective management—Germany, and also Japan—to accept the role. This is viewed more in disappointment or sorrow than in anger, but it is viewed that way.

The other caveat is a question of perspective. It is clear that the view just described comes from a rather large continental power across the Atlantic. But closer up, Germany looms rather larger; its influence and dominance appear greater. Pierre Elliot Trudeau once said about living next to the United States, that it is like being in bed with an elephant. It does not necessarily mean you any harm, but you have to be very careful nonetheless. No doubt from the point of view of its immediate neighbors, Germany does look more like an elephant. But from the perspective of the United States,

Germany looks like an elephant trying to disguise itself as something rather smaller hiding behind a tree.

All of this was crystallized in the so-called locomotive debate, which was concerned with the problem of how to recover from the great recession of 1974-1975. The United States' position was that the world needed joint, selective expansion of demand to get out of the great recession. Germany resisted this advice—resisted on the grounds that (1) there were institutional obstacles to expansion of demand in Germany; (2) even if these could be overcome, expansion would simply result in inflation rather than growth; and (3) even if it resulted in growth, it would not produce growth elsewhere.

All three parts of that position were debatable, and in fact, the result of this debate was a stalemate. There were attempts without success to camouflage the issue by changing the locomotive to a convoy. Two years at least of economic growth in the OECD zone were lost as a result. The debate has faded out as circumstances have changed—as the United States starts to move toward recession, and the European economies have finally begun to show some signs of life. Talk now is of convergence of economic growth rates, which was the whole point of the exercise two years ago. But what I would like to point out, of course, is that the underlying conflict about who is to take responsibility for management remains as real as ever and is likely to reemerge in a not too distant future. From the American point of view—as I say, more in disappointment and sorrow than anger—we continue to see Germany resisting the responsibilities that its size in the world economy would thrust upon it.

Andrew Shonfield

The feature of our arguments about both politics and economic policy that remains with me is the extraordinary way in which decisions about long-term policy are being taken on the basis of short-term emotions. Beate Kohler told us about Chancellor Schmidt's visit to Greece and his subsequent decision on Greek accession to the European Community. There was only a small element of parody in this. The fact is that important and long-term decisions are frequently taken on the basis of short-term considerations.

If this is the style in which we are conducting our affairs, and the style in which Germany—with all that it has to lose, being the most vulnerable large country in the European system—is deciding policy, then I want to register the point that here is a problem in international relations that needs to be thought about. When I say short-term, I mean that the deeper business involved in Community enlargement was not considered. It raises profound questions which are in Beate Kohler's chapter, very difficult questions that were not considered until the decision was already made. We may also look at the Franco-German honeymoon over the creation of the European monetary system, and we see that this issue, too, is riddled with deep problems. And then we are told that it looks as if Chancellor Schmidt mistook Barre for Erhard, and so on. All this is psychological analysis, rather than international relations analysis. If this is the style in which Europe is being managed, why are the Germans so extraordinarily relaxed? They ought to be more worried. They are behaving in an impulsive fashion.

The second point that comes out of my experience in the conference I will precede with a remark from one of my Italian colleagues who said, "Are the Germans really behaving as well as this; are they as *good* as they are suggesting to us?" And my answer to him was, "Yes, I think they are. Of the big nations of Europe, their performance is a very remarkable one. Fairly consistently over a period, they have behaved with responsibility and with restraint, and they contribute to the system in a moderate way." That was my answer, but what I've been impressed by, especially when Germans become official, is the note of complacency in the words that they use. There is a sort of national self-complacency which is a feature of German official and quasi-official statements. For example, Hans-Herbert Weber, a man whom I have respected for years for his competence, has seriously ignored the most remarkable of all the achievements of the European economies of the last three years, which is that of Italy, and has talked as if nobody had managed to export anything to the OPEC except Germany and one or two other virtuous people like the Dutch and the Swiss. What has happened in this period is that Italy, with no North Sea oil, has turned its

206

balance of payments around so that it has a balance of payments surplus that is at least as big as Germany's, perhaps even bigger.

The Germans are apparently not acknowledging this sort of thing. They also don't recognize that the British, with all the various failures of the Labor party, did have a year in which they accepted a reduction in average real wages of 5 percent. That these developments at present on the periphery of German consciousness really ought to be recognized as more central is the point that I am making. I am left with an unchanged admiration for Germany as the most consistently well-behaved and, in an international sense, successful of the big European nations, but I am amazed at the continuing and indeed reinforced complacency that I notice coming out of official German statements.

Continuing from this observation, the one point of substance that I really want to make draws on the extremely informative chapters of Weber and of my old friend Norbert Kloten. Here is Germany launching something that looks like a great novelty. Yet, when you begin to take it apart, it has no novelty at all. By some extraordinary piece of diplomatic skill, they seem to have got the rest of the Europeans to agree once again to enter a German "snake," which has become more and more like a Deutsch mark zone, on the basis of a fixed parity grid. And what are they offering? They are offering, instead of a one-month credit, a one-year credit system. At the moment that is the only substantial difference between the "snake" and the new system when you strip it down. If the Germans are as skillful nowadays as they were in Bismarckian times, and manage to bamboozle the rest of Europe into this scheme, well that's their luck. But the more profound point is this: that scheme will fail in its *present form*. And I think, in fact, Kloten gave a fair indication that he had strong suspicions in this direction himself.

Now, what is it all about? It's about Germany wishing to avoid the unpleasantness of running an international currency. They have seen the British do it, and the Americans do it, and it's not fun. It is all right if you happen to have an empire to cope with, but even then, it is a doubtful game. Susan Strange gave us one or two excellent adjectives to describe it. So Germany resists having the Deutsche mark become an international currency and thinks it can use the European Community in some way in order to share the load, because some other pole than the dollar is plainly required. Any of us who are conversant with the international monetary system know that the era of the dollar as the sole international key currency is at an end. The Deutsche mark is the natural next candidate. Germany is resisting for perfectly good reasons. It even looked as if by using the European Community to resist, it was giving new substance to the EEC. However, it now has become clear that Germany simply is not prepared to adapt itself to the needs or desires of its partners in the European Community. This leads to one conclusion that relates to the various alternatives set out in Susan Strange's very useful chapter. She says Germany has now reached the stage where it must accept the logic of responsibility for some portion of the international monetary system. And she suggests that this is also a rather helpful situation in that it is useful to have an alternative to the main international money, the dollar. She then goes on to say that Germany should elect itself, with the acclamation of the other members of the European Community, to be the leader of the opposition to the dollar.

I go with her some distance, but I think the point she is making is so substantial that it's important for me just to express the doubts that I have because they have political consequences for her conclusion. Yes, we have come to the end of the epoch of dollar hegemony. Yes, the pressures on Germany to become an international economy grow daily. Kloten made the distinction between becoming a reserve currency and becoming a key currency. I don't want to go into this. I think you may find that the distinction, although it's there in logic, is less important in practice. My real point is that Germany could only use the European Community as an alternative pole if it were prepared to accept a system of a basket of currencies. The European Currency Unit (ECU) system really offers Germany a device that would take the heat off the Deutsche mark. But in order to take the heat off the Deutsche mark, Germany would have to adapt to its own external financial relations, which is, after all, normal for a country that is in the position of riding an international currency. It was what the British had to do for a while, and then they found it too inconvenient or too difficult to do it very well. But the idea that Germans are really engaged in a scheme for avoiding becoming an international currency and using the European Community as a surrogate is false. This is the conclusion that I reach.

Albert Bressand

It has been mentioned earlier that French and German relations were now in a love affair state. Speaking in my personal capacity only, I agree with this remark, with the caveat that we are not talking about a couple but about multiple partners in each of the countries. The love link is not exactly the same depending on what partner you have in mind. In fact, if you look at the different segments of French public opinion, you have to recognize that in some cases it is a love-hate relationship. Communist reactions on the extreme left are of course quite different from the government attitudes. Let us also remember that there are different types of love affairs: the French government might find itself in the same situation as a lover as Humphrey Bogart, which means in love, but keeping a certain distance.

In order to elaborate briefly on this spectrum, as far as the opposition is concerned, let me refer to a cartoon in *L'Humanité*, the French communist newspaper, by Wolinski, one of the most talented French cartoonists who recently joined the Communist party. It shows Giscard on the podium singing a tune obviously for Eurovision, and it says "I'm now going to interpret to you the song that obtained the European Community prize. The words are by Helmut Schmidt and the music is by Jimmy Carter and it is called 'How Could Inflation Matter Compared to Our Love.'" Obviously the special relationship between Giscard and Schmidt does not elict full-fledged support from the whole body of opinion. The communist position is a very peculiar one, stemming from communist opposition to European integration, the capitalist system, and the role of the United States. And this culminates in what I find to be a very worrisome anti-German trend, which should be recognized and dealt with properly.

In the Socialist party the situation has many more nuances. When one talks with some of its leaders in private, one gets the feeling that they are deeply fascinated by German successes, both on the economic front and in the political sphere. In fact, the violence of the French socialist rejection of the German social-democracy model stems as much from this fascination as from an intellectual position.

On the side of the majority, we find both an envy and an admiration for German performance, which has in fact been at the center of economic debate within the French bureaucracy for the last two or three years. But this envy is accompanied by what Andrew Shonfield called the self-complacency of too many German economists. French observers are aware of the weaknesses of the German economic model, and notably of its limitations when you try to apply it to the French case. After all, one should remember, when talking about the German model, that in terms of real growth rate and general economic performance, French achievements over the last twenty years are roughly equivalent to German ones.

As for the limitations of taking the German model as a model for French economy, they come from the special circumstances that have allowed the German model to work in Germany: the *tabula rasa* factor of the postwar period, the fact that the Deutsche mark was undervalued for a long period of time and had a lot of slack resources before the present overevaluation began to bite; and also the very popular "vicious and virtuous circle theory," which is even better applied to Switzerland or Japan than to Germany, and tends to suggest that there is something almost self-fulfilling above a certain threshold in the positive feedback cycle ("reevaluation-lower-inflation-external competitiveness-reevaluation"). The French reaction then is rather one of trying to jump on this virtuous cycle bandwagon by linking oneself to the Deutsche mark even at a slightly unrealistic level for a while.

Having sketched this broad perspective, let me add a personal comment on what I would choose to call the French puzzlement in front of the German domestic economic consensus. And I think our debates here have been quite characteristic, with a few noteworthy exceptions, of this consensus. It's not that each element of this consensus among German economists of the mainstream school are contrary to what is believed in France. When it comes to the role of wages and profits, exports, and all that, we can agree on the details. But the strength of this consensus and its tone sometimes strike us as almost unhealthy. Maybe the word "complacency" explains what I have in mind. Even the French liberal economists, and there are a great many of them, who share the same basic philosophy as their German counterparts, tend to devote more attention in their work to market failures, second theory, and other grey areas of liberal thinking. It is difficult for us to understand how the German institute system and the economic "wisemen" role in wage-setting process operate in Germany.

Several explanations could be advanced. One would be that vigorous German insistence on free trade theory simply stems from the fact that Germany, being one of the strongest economies, finds it in its interest to push these free trade theories. In fact, there has been a report by the French planning agency showing that German liberalization of trade toward the southern countries was very beneficial in terms of lowering the costs of German goods and conquering or maintaining export markets, and that France would have the same interest in imitating this attitude rather than in protecting ourselves. But I think this technical explanation does not go far enough, and that we may wonder whether the economic side of German thinking is not hypertrophied because the political one is "hypotrophied." That was the impression I got from our conference debates. I was wondering how different this debate would have been in a French setting on things like North-

South issues, trade with the East, or relations with the European Community. A discussion in France would have dealt much more with the political dimension. Why do you trade with the East? What are the long-term repercussions? What goals is the Soviet Union pursuing through trade with Western Europe? What are the Soviets trying to achieve in using France against Germany and vice versa, what should be our attitude with respect to American embargoes on computers or oil drilling equipment? This is a whole set of quite different issues.

If I may venture into an area where I am not specially qualified, I even have the feeling that the economic bias is more pronounced in the German academic community than in the German government, and that there is in fact a lag, a gap, developing here. If I think about the attitude of German representatives at the UN or IMF or in the EC, I see the beginning of a new strategy on the part of the government. Germany obviously enjoyed its role in the Namibia negotiations, being one of the five to intervene and pronounce themselves on the issue and seems to be considering whether this role could not become more permanent. Similarly at the IMF, very quietly, Germany seems to have dropped its opposition to debt cancellation, in opposition to the economic thinking at home. I would not be surprised if similar moves took place with the common fund, for instance. Similarly, also my analysis of what happened on the monetary front would have more nuances than the one we just heard, because I would think that here we have a clear dichotomy in the German attitude. There seems to have been a two-stage phenomenon: in the first stage, there was a broad political understanding between Schmidt and Giscard, agreed on in very broad terms, and then the pressure in Germany of the academic community and of the bureaucratic community, which shares broadly the same views and interests, has slowly eroded this line and may explain why, after all this, we end up with a kind of "super-snake."

I conclude by explaining that I am not trying to be normative at all in saying that too much economic emphasis is bad, but rather to ask whether this particular emphasis is going to be an asset or a liability when Germany tries to define its role in the world. In the past, as explained by Benjamin Cohen, the free rider theory used to be clearly an asset. I now have the feeling that at a time when the United States is less and less able and willing to insure the broad political framework in which Germany could pursue its objectives, defined in mostly economic terms, this emphasis may turn out to be a liability.

Luigi Spaventa

First, I must confess to a disturbing feeling which will be familiar to those of you who share, for instance, Kindleberger's views in his political economic explanation of the Great Depression in terms of a vacuum of power. By now we all recognize that Keynes's dream of cooperation and coordination has remained unfulfilled, and at the same time we no longer have hegemony, if by hegemony we mean power with responsibility. And that power by itself is not enough. I think it has been said several times, but no other solution has been found. Susan Strange's plea seems to have remained unanswered.

Underlying some of the things that have been said in this book, and in particular the opinions expressed by Weber in his very lucid chapter, there seems to emerge what looks to me like a very peculiar model. In international economics we are accustomed by now to dealing with models where there are tradable goods and nontradable goods. But the underlying and implicit model to which I am referring, and which is being applied in the case of Germany, appears to be far more complicated. There appears to be a sector that can be labeled "exportable." And internal demand for exportables is presumed to be income inelastic, so that domestic demand for this sector cannot be increased. Imports, on the other hand, seem to be income elastic and, as it was explicitly stated by both Weber and Steinherr, there appears to be little scope for import substitution at home. Further, internal demand appears not to be responsive to exogenous stimuli deriving from economic policy measures. In some formulations, such as in Weber's, the marginal propensity to save seems to be near unity, while the propensity to invest is lowered by the existence of excess capacity in the export sector.

Now the remarkable thing in this model is that it apparently resembles very much that of a less developed country, where exportables are primary products. The difference, of course, is obvious. Germany's exports depend upon Germany's income and demand. It is thus clear that this model which I have tried to sketch is a model of permanent stagnation. Germany cannot grow enough unless its exports do not grow fast, but its exports cannot grow fast unless its partners' incomes grow fast enough. But its partners' income, given the balance of payments constraint, cannot grow fast enough unless Germany grows. So, we are back in the circle. We thus get stuck in permanent depression. So, if these assumptions hold, Germany cannot import unless it exports. But it cannot export unless somebody else can import.

But are these assumptions true? Well, I personally do not believe they are, unless and until enough evidence is provided, and no such evidence was provided here. Is this good news, the fact that no evidence was provided? Well, not necessarily so, because these assumptions seem to gain growing acceptance in a kind of common sense of political economy with an increasing divorce, in my view, from the good sense of political economy.

We should then ask ourselves, why is this common sense spreading? And I think that it can hardly be denied that this is a peculiarly German doctrine, if not entirely in its origin, because its academic origin may lie elsewhere, at least in its official political applications at the international level. Now my surprise, if I may say so, arises from the fact that no alternative model, explanation, or interpretation was provided in this book. Why, we may ask, is this model so widespread? A conscious or unconscious craving for a balance of payments surplus is by itself no explanation. Craving for exports is one thing, but craving for a foreign surplus is an entirely different thing. Exports suit industrial interests, but surplus by itself does not. Because you can have a surplus with a depression. You can have surplus with depressed demand. You can have surplus with a squeeze on profits, as you had in Germany in the last few years.

So, this is my real unanswered question. It is an important question because this conflict of interests is often not sufficiently appreciated in some left wing views of German questions abroad. There is a very easy explanation that everything happens because of a grand design of German capital. But an economist's analysis detects here a contradiction between different interests. This poses the real question, to which I have found no answer in this book. What are the underlying reasons inspiring this kind of German view, which translates itself into German economic policy very often, and which affects other countries' economic policy? For this view, or model, is not necessarily in the general welfare interest of the international community at large. It is not even in the interest of internal sectors within Germany.

Niels Thygesen

My remarks about policies of the Federal Republic of Germany are made from the viewpoint of a small partner country; whatever indicator you use, the size of Denmark is something like a tenth to a twelfth of the German economy. It may be useful to distinguish between various groups of decision makers in my country: (1) the official view—which could be subsumed under the heading of the obedient ally, to use Susan Strange's term; and (2) the critical opinion, particularly at the present time, as a result of mounting criticism of Germany and possibly because of the election campaign for the European Parliament. I should say that this critical opinion is clearly a minority view. Let me first turn to the more official view of Germany.

When my country joined the European Community about six years ago, we did not think primarily in terms of cooperating with Germany inside the Community. We were looking more toward other partners as natural allies, the United Kingdom in many questions, political questions in particular, possibly France in connection with the agricultural policy. We did in fact tie our application to that of the United Kingdom, assuming that our political views were closer to those of the United Kingdom than to those of any other country in Europe.

As things have turned out, it would be fair to say that Germany has in fact become *the* main partner country in the Community for Denmark. Germany has turned out to be the least national in its view of normal Community proceedings. It has been the one least apt to use a veto in the Council of Ministers against normal decision making. And generally, it has been easier to openly discuss current policy issues in Bonn.

Denmark may have shied away from teaming up regularly with the other small countries in the Community—the Netherlands and Belgium—partly because they were in a somewhat stronger position economically than we were. We also felt them to be excessively enthusiastic about some aspects of the Community. Instead, we have found ourselves to be leaning considerably toward Germany. Let me outline briefly the aspects of economic policy and political cooperation in which this leaning toward Bonn has materialized.

Andrew Shonfield spoke about a certain German complacency concerning what goes on in other Community countries. I could supply an illustration of that in respect to Denmark. We are, I suppose, a clear case of a free rider in economic policy. We have had an external deficit on current account for the last fifteen years without interruption. Sometimes we feel that Germany does not even notice what is going on, and how large the deficit is. We have not been under any pressure to rapidly adjust our balance of payments; nor have we been under any pressure to adjust our exchange rate, even at times when substantial interventions by Germany were required. There was some mild and friendly advice in 1976 and 1977 when adjustments were undertaken inside the "snake."

The snake in this period has gradually developed some implicit limits to the kind of exchange rate change acceptable to Germany, both in terms of the size of individual changes and the frequency with which they can take place. The Norwegians are not a member of the Community, but of the snake; they certainly found that out when they came with a request for a large devaluation in February 1978. There may well have developed inside the Community a different standard for small and large countries. For small countries, it appears to be permissible to remain in substantial imbalance for a long time. This does not materially affect the stability of the system, to use the term of Benjamin Cohen. Germany has proved to be remarkably tolerant of this kind of performance, possibly because it may have suited Germany's interests to have small economies like Denmark running a substantial external deficit to keep up demand inside the Community. Luigi Spaventa referred to the preference in Germany for having demand generated from the export side. Obviously, the continued relatively high activity in my country has helped the German export industry to some extent, and has made this, let's say deviant, behavior more acceptable to the Germans.

There has been a lot of criticism in my own country, very much along the lines Luigi Spaventa suggested, of German economic policy. We are less than fully convinced about the constraints that the Germans claim to be operative on their growth performance. We think they have been too cautious, too adverse to risk. They have allowed us a second-best solution, that is, to finance our external deficits for a long time. But we would much have preferred a more actively expansionist line in economic policy in Germany.

As for political cooperation, it is important to note that the links between the political parties in Denmark and Germany are particularly close. They are developed by Chancellor Brandt during his tenure of office. A positive attitude in Denmark toward joining the European Community and cooperating with Germany was very much the result of the personal efforts of Brandt. Initially, there was a lot of skepticism, but in both our major parties—the Social Democratic party and the Liberal party, which followed in August 1978 the German pattern of joining the Social Democrats in government—links to their counterparts in Germany are close. There are no serious differences of opinion with respect to the enlargement of the Community, Ostpolitik, and other major matters of current European policy.

It is interesting to speculate to what extent this confidence at an official level in the German political system would survive a shift to a government of the Christian Democrats and the Christian Social Union in Germany. I think it would survive such a shift—after a period of adjustment. There is cause for worry that cooperation in political terms for Germany would become more difficult after a change in government.

Let me point very briefly to the role of public opinion in my country and the criticism that one hears of Germany. Having recently participated in the campaign for elections to the European Parliament, I have no doubt that the political leaders in my country have run somewhat ahead of public opinion in their attitude toward European cooperation and toward Germany. There is a growing interest in German affairs; in fact, it is covered extremely well in our press. But there are two main sorts of criticism, two main groups in our public opinion that remain critical of Germany. One is, not surprisingly, the political Left, to the left of our Social Democratic party, representing possibly 15 of opinion. The Left is worried about the narrowing of options in our society as we conform more or less to the German market system. This group is not all that influential, partly because the Danish Social Democrats have never been much in favor of planning on a substantial scale. We are a new industrial nation with generally small firms and new industries, which do not lend themselves easily to planning activities and nationalization of enterprises. There is among most of our labor unions and the government a strong belief in the benefits of a free market system. This certainly helps to check this kind of criticism. But the left-wing criticism is also of a more political nature; it worries about tendencies toward more regimentation of political life in Germany, for example, the *Beruftsverbot*. Several marginal cases surrounding the *Berufsverbot*, for example, have been reported in apparently excessive detail in our press.

On closer reflection, what contains this kind of criticism is the realization that the degree of social consensus is basically no weaker in Germany than it is in the Scandinavian countries; rather, the contrary. Performance in the labor market illustrates that point very clearly, and our labor unions and Social Democrats are well aware of it. What makes the discussion of German issues more complicated in my country is that it is not strictly a criticism from the political Left. It is also a criticism from an older liberal center in the political spectrum. It may be partly a generation problem. There are strong memories in this center of the political spectrum of that part of our history which has been an attempt to liberate ourselves from German cultural and political influences over the last one hundred years.

In our agriculture and in our public high schools a popular movement has also been developed with a tinge of anti-German feelings and a longing for belonging to a part of a Nordic community instead. Through much of our postwar history, we have had to confront a longing to have effective relations with the Nordic countries in defense and trade. It has never proved to be a viable alternative in any of these fields. But it is unavoidably a cause for reflection and some disappointment to Denmark that the European Community and cooperation with Germany seems to be more attractive to countries in southern Europe than to our traditional partners in Scandinavia. This has one consequence that should be appreciated. Along with the political cooperation inside the European Community—which is developing well, in our view—there is an attempt to perpetuate the fiction that we are also a part of a Nordic group in the United Nations and elsewhere. On development policy, in particular, we like to make clear that we are in a sense still as much aligned with Sweden and Norway as we are with the other Community countries. This makes us at times appear a bit disloyal to common Community concerns when they are discussed in the United Nations and the North-South dialogue.

To conclude, public opinion may explain the reluctance of the Danish government and political establishment to push opinion too far in the question of links with Germany. But the degree of cooperation that has actually developed with Germany over the last five or ten years is very close indeed.

Giorgio Basevi

I would like to indicate what seems to me a contradiction that has emerged from this conference, and particularly in the interventions by Luigi Spaventa and Andrew Shonfield. The contradiction is the following; On the one hand, throughout the conference and in those two comments, the idea has been expressed again and again that what Germany is not accepting is the role of leader in the European Community, and that her partners should convince themselves and Germany to accept that role. On the other hand, we have heard complaints about Germany's craving for exports, or rather, as explained by Professor Spaventa, for surpluses.

I shall try to explain why I think there is a contradiction here, and in so doing reply to Professor Spaventa's question: Why is Germany constantly craving surpluses? Imagine a country like Germany, which cannot rely on military or other political means to assert her leadership role, and yet, through the developments of the last decades is being brought by virtue of its economic strength to play that role. How could such a country assert itself as a leader? It seems to me that at least one way in the economic realm to play this role is to be a surplus country. Indeed, it is perhaps the main way. First, however, it is necessary to clarify the concept of a surplus country. What that country has to be is an overall balance of payments—surplus country, rather than simply a current account—or trade account-surplus country. In fact, what matters in monetary terms is an overall balance of payments surplus, and my point is that what matters in order to be a leader is to be a strong currency country.

If Germany is an overall-surplus country, then it can call the tune on a lot of affairs. As Albert Bressand has just suggested from the cartoon in *L'Humanité*, it may compel others to sing a song with words by Helmut Schmidt, that is, it can call the tune of the monetary unification policy. It might also call the tune on EC enlargement, on regional policy, on transfers to new members, and generally on any issue that involves financial assistance.

Thus, it seems to me that it would be contradictory for some of us to complain about an overall structural surplus position for Germany while others ask Germany to play an active leadership role. It would be more fruitful to take a constructive position and say, "All right, if we want Germany—and the question is *do we want Germany*—to be the leader, then Germany must have, at least for some years, an overall surplus." In fact, that was the experience of the United States after the war. Initially, the United States had a surplus and only during the fifties and sixties did it become a deficit country, as dollars were injected into international reserves. At the time of the Marshall Plan, dollars were scarce.

Thus, it seems to me that a consistent approach for those who want Germany to play the role of leader in the EC is to accept the fact that the leader country must have military power or economic power, expressed in terms of an overall surplus. But Germany's partners should then control the leader's position by sharing in the allocation of its surplus. In other words, personally I would accept such a role and such a structural surplus position for Germany, provided it is controlled within a European monetary system where the German monetary surplus is some how reallocated among other countries, checked through some kind of central bank of Europe. Such a system would also make possible the eventual conversion of the German surplus into an overall deficit, when the time comes for the leader's currency to become the reserve currency of the system.

About the Contributors

Albert Bressand, former chargé de mission at the Centre d'Analyse et de Prévision of the Ministère des Affairs Estrangères, is now deputy director of the Institute Français des Relations Internationales in Paris. He has consulted for the World Bank and is the author of a recent contribution to *Daedalus,* "The New European Economies."

Benjamin J. Cohen is William L. Clayton Professor of International Economic Relations at the Fletcher School of Law and Diplomacy, Tufts University. Among his publications are *Organizing the World's Money* (1977) and *The Question of Imperialism* (1973).

Ernst-Otto Czempiel is professor of international relations at the University of Frankfurt/Main, and codirector of the Hessische Stiftung Friedens-und Konfliktforschung, Frankfurt/Main. His recent publications are *Amerikanische Aussenpolitik—Gesellschaftliche Anforderungen und politische Entscheidungen* (1979); *Friedenspolitik im Südlichen Afrika* (1976); *Südafrika in der Politik Grossbritanniens und der USA* (with F. Ansprenger, 1977).

Wolfgang Hager is professorial research fellow at the European University Institute, Florence. He was for several years a senior fellow of the Deutsche Gesellschaft für Auswärtige Politik, Bonn. His publications include *Europe's Economic Security* (1975) and *Erdöl und Internationale Politik* (ed., 1976).

Wilhelm Hankel is guest professor of economics at the University of Frankfurt, and senior visiting professor at The Johns Hopkins University Bologna Center. Previously he served as an assistant secretary for international monetary affairs in the Ministry of Economics in Bonn. Among his publications are *Prosperität trotz Energiekrise* (1979); *Caesar: Goldene Zeiten führt ich ein* (1978); and *Weltwirtschaft,* (1977).

Norbert Kloten is president of the Landeszentralbank Baden-Württenberg, Stuttgart, and formerly professor of economics at the Universities of Bonn and Tübingen, and has also taught for one year at The Johns Hopkins University Bologna Center. He is a member of the Advisory Council of the Deutsche Gesellschaft für Auswärtige Politik, Bonn, and the Fritz Thyssen-Stiftung, Frankfurt/Main.

Beate Kohler is professor of political science at the University of Darmstadt and in 1977 was visiting professor at The Johns Hopkins University Bologna

Center. Her field of interest is European Community affairs. Among her recent publications is *Die Süd-Erweiterung der Europäischen Gemeinschaften* (with H. Hasenpflug, 1977).

Hermann Priebe is professor of agricultural policy and director of the Institut für Ländliche Strukturforschung of the University of Frankfurt. He was an advisor to the EEC Commission in Brussels from 1958 to 1970. His publications include *Landwirtschaft in der Welt von morgen* (1970); *Fields of Conflict in European Farm Policy* (1972); *Der ländliche Raum—eine Zukunftsaufgabe* (1973); and numerous articles in professional journals.

Reinhardt Rummel is lecturer in international relations at the Ludwig-Maximilian-Universität, Munich, and a research fellow at Stiftung für Wissenschaft und Politik at Ebenhausen, Munich. His publications include *Soziale Politik für Europa* (1975) and *Gemeinschaftsbildung Westeuropas in der Aussenpolitik* (1978).

Andrew Shonfield is chairman of the Department of Economics at the European University Institute, Florence, and formerly was director of the Royal Institute for International Affairs, London. His publications include *International Economic Relations of the Western World 1959-1971* (1971).

Luigi Spaventa is professor of economics at the University of Rome and a member of Parliament. He contributes articles on distribution theory and stabilization policy to numerous international professional journals.

Alfred Steinherr is associate professor of economics at the Catholic University of Louvain and is currently consultant at the International Monetary Fund in Washington. His numerous articles in professional journals are on international adjustment problems and incentive design in industry.

Susan Strange is Montague Burton Professor of International Relations at the London School of Economics and Political Science and was formerly senior research fellow at the Royal Institute of International Affairs, London, and a U.S. German Marshall Fund fellow. She has taught international relations at the University College, London, and her main field of interest is international political economy. Her publications are *Sterling and British Policy* (1971) and *International Monetary Relations* (1976).

Niels Thygesen is professor of economics at the University of Copenhagen. He was a consultant for the OECD on monetary policy and is presently advisor to the central bank of Denmark. He is the author of numerous articles in professional journals.

Hans-Herbert Weber is assistant secretary at the Ministry of Finance of the German Federal Republic, where he is in charge of the Department for External and Internal Monetary Affairs, Banking and the Federal Debt. Previously he held various positions with the Federal Ministry of Economics and also served as managing director of the Federal Association of German Banks.

About the Editors

Wilfrid L. Kohl is director and associate professor of international relations of The John Hopkins University Bologna Center. He has also taught at Columbia University and has served on the staffs of the Ford Foundation and the National Security Council. He is the author of *French Nuclear Diplomacy* (1971) and the editor of *Economic Foreign Policies of Industrial States* (1976).

Giorgio Basevi is professor of economics at the University of Bologna and visiting professor at The John Hopkins University Bologna Center. He was previously professor of economics at the Catholic University of Louvain and has been advisor to the Commission of the European Community in Brussels. He is a contributor of numerous articles to international professional journals.